Martha Washington

Martha Washington

AN AMERICAN LIFE

Patricia Brady

Viking

VIKING

Published by the Penguin Group

Penguin Group (USA) Inc., 375 Hudson Street, New York, New York 10014, U.S.A.
Penguin Group (Canada), 10 Alcorn Avenue, Toronto, Ontario, Canada M4V 3B2
(a division of Pearson Penguin Canada Inc.)
Penguin Books Ltd., 80 Strand, London WC2R 0RL, England
Penguin Ireland, 25 St. Stephen's Green, Dublin 2, Ireland (a division of Penguin Books Ltd)
Penguin Books Australia Ltd, 250 Camberwell Road, Camberwell, Victoria 3124, Australia
(a division of Pearson Australia Group Pty Ltd)
Penguin Books India Pvt Ltd, 11 Community Centre, Panchsheel Park,
New Delhi – 110 017, India
Penguin Group (NZ), Cnr Airborne and Rosedale Roads, Albany, Auckland 1310,
New Zealand (a division of Pearson New Zealand Ltd)
Penguin Books (South Africa) (Pty) Ltd, 24 Sturdee Avenue, Rosebank,
Johannesburg 2196, South Africa

Penguin Books Ltd, Registered Offices: 80 Strand, London WC2R 0RL, England

First published in 2005 by Viking Penguin, a member of Penguin Group (USA) Inc.

1   3   5   7   9   10   8   6   4   2

Copyright © Patricia Brady, 2005
All rights reserved

LIBRARY OF CONGRESS CATALOGING IN PUBLICATION DATA
Brady, Patricia, date.
Martha Washington : an American life / Patricia Brady.
p. cm.
Includes bibliographical references and index.
ISBN 0-670-03430-4
1. Washington, Martha, 1731–1802.   2. Presidents' spouses—United States—Biography.
I. Title.
E312.19.W34B73 2005
973.4'1'092—dc22
[B]   2004061242

This book is printed on acid-free paper. ∞

Printed in the United States of America
Designed by Nancy Resnick

For my sisters,
Jane Brady and Melissa Brady Cosenza,
and my children,
Colin and Elizabeth Schmit

The past is a foreign country. They do things differently there.

— L. P. HARTLEY

Contents

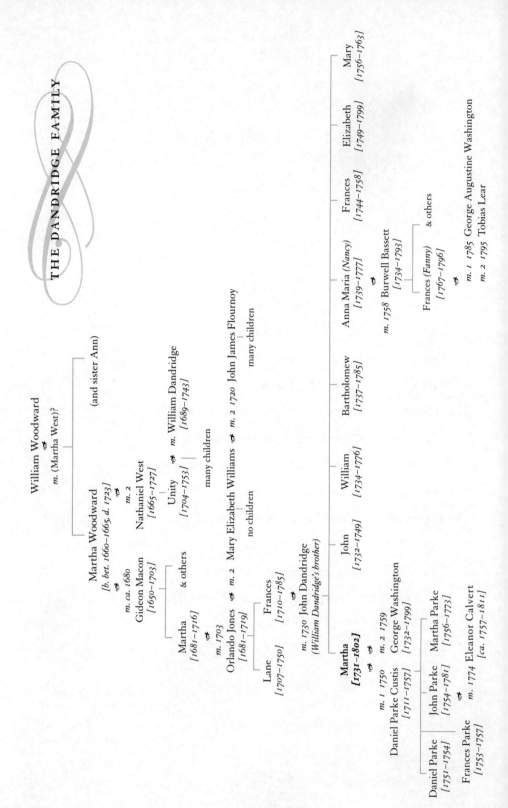

THE DANDRIDGE FAMILY

William Woodward
m. (Martha West)?

(and sister Ann)

Martha Woodward
[b. bet. 1660–1665, d. 1723]

m. ca. 1680   m. 2
Gideon Macon   Nathaniel West
[1650–1703]   [1665–1727]

Martha   & others   Unity   m. William Dandridge
[1681–1716]   [1704–1753]   [1689–1743]

m. 1703   many children
Orlando Jones   m. 2 Mary Elizabeth Williams   m. 2 1720 John James Flournoy
[1681–1719]   many children

Lane   Frances   no children
[1707–1750] [1710–1785]

                    John   William   Bartholomew   Anna Maria (Nancy)   Frances   Elizabeth   Mary
m. 1730 John Dandridge [1732–1749]   [1734–1776]   [1737–1785]   [1739–1777]   [1744–1758]   [1749–1799]   [1756–1763]
(William Dandridge's brother)
                                                                     m. 1758 Burwell Bassett
                                                                              [1734–1793]
Martha   m. 2 1759
[1731–1802] George Washington   Frances (Fanny)   & others
            [1732–1799]   [1767–1796]
m. 1 1750   m. 1 1785 George Augustine Washington
Daniel Parke Custis   m. 2 1795 Tobias Lear
[1711–1757]

Daniel Parke │ John Parke   Martha Parke
[1751–1754] │ [1754–1781]   [1756–1773]

Frances Parke   m. 1774 Eleanor Calvert
[1753–1757]   [ca. 1757–1811]

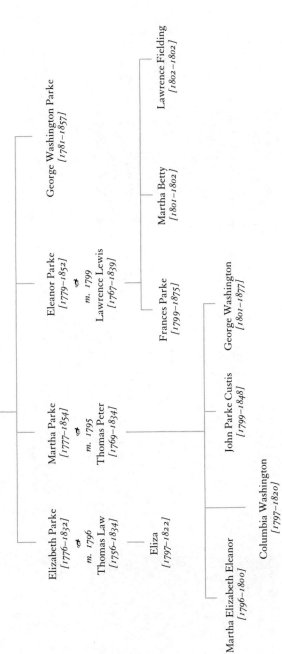

John Parke Custis
[1754–1781] ❧ m. 1774 Eleanor Calvert
[ca. 1757–1811]

Elizabeth Parke
[1776–1832]
❧
m. 1796
Thomas Law
[1756–1834]

Eliza
[1797–1822]

Martha Parke
[1777–1854]
❧
m. 1795
Thomas Peter
[1769–1834]

Eleanor Parke
[1779–1852]
❧
m. 1799
Lawrence Lewis
[1767–1839]

George Washington Parke
[1781–1857]

Frances Parke
[1799–1875]

Martha Betty
[1801–1802]

Lawrence Fielding
[1802–1802]

John Parke Custis
[1799–1848]

George Washington
[1801–1877]

Martha Elizabeth Eleanor
[1796–1800]

Columbia Washington
[1797–1820]

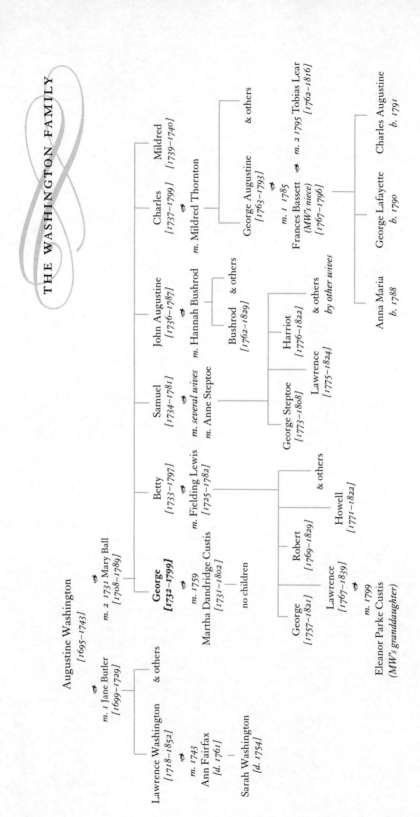

THE WASHINGTON FAMILY

Augustine Washington
[1695–1743]

m. 1 Jane Butler
[1699–1729]

m. 2 1731 Mary Ball
[1708–1789]

Lawrence Washington
[1718–1852]

& others

m. 1743
Ann Fairfax
[d. 1761]

Sarah Washington
[d. 1754]

George
[**1732–1799**]

m. 1759
Martha Dandridge Custis
[1731–1802]

no children

Betty
[1733–1797]

m. Fielding Lewis
[1725–1782]

George
[1757–1821]

Robert
[1769–1829]

Howell
[1771–1822]

& others

Lawrence
[1767–1839]

m. 1799

Eleanor Parke Custis
(MW's granddaughter)

Samuel
[1734–1781]

m. several wives
m. Anne Steptoe

George Steptoe
[1773–1808]

Lawrence
[1775–1824]

Harriot
[1776–1822]

John Augustine
[1736–1787]

m. Hannah Bushrod

Bushrod
[1762–1829]

& others

& others
by other wives

Charles
[1737–1799]

m. Mildred Thornton

George Augustine
[1763–1793]

m. 1 1785
Frances Bassett
(MW's niece)
[1767–1796]

m. 2 1795 Tobias Lear
[1762–1816]

Anna Maria
b. 1788

George Lafayette
b. 1790

Charles Augustine
b. 1791

Mildred
[1739–1740]

& others

PROLOGUE

On the Road to History

*I*t was a quiet love story, but a lasting one, not one of those tempestuous romances that blaze up suddenly and just as quickly turn to ashes. Both Martha and George Washington had been in love with others, but once they married in their late twenties, their relationship became a joyful duet that lasted more than four decades. Together, they created a life of tender companionship and, in his often repeated phrase, "domestic enjoyments." Politics, war, or business sometimes kept them apart—but always to their deep distress. They couldn't, or more truly didn't, want to live without each other.

For the last third of his life, George Washington was widely revered as the greatest man of the age, and contemporaries recognized his wife's critical role in that success. Today, he is still an overpowering figure in American history, while Martha Washington's image has nearly faded away. She is both famous as the first First Lady and completely unknown. After her husband's death, to keep their private life safe from inquisitive eyes, she destroyed all forty-one years of their correspondence. Scores, perhaps hundreds, of the letters they wrote to each other disappeared into the flames: only five letters are known to have survived destruction.

Martha Washington's desire for privacy means that her life story has been assembled from fleeting glimpses—her few remaining letters to relatives and friends, descriptions and anecdotes written by contemporaries, and an informed understanding of the eighteenth-century world she lived in. Painstaking research reveals a delight-ful, intelligent, and passionate woman who shared a life of mutual love and support with the country's foremost founding father.

In April 1789, George Washington, just turned fifty-seven, rum-bled off in Mount Vernon's best coach and four for New York City, the temporary capital of the United States. Elected unanimously under the brand-new Constitution, he would be the first president of the reorganized nation, charged with creating a federal govern-ment from scratch. Martha Washington stayed behind in Virginia to oversee the logistical nightmare of moving their household 250 miles away. Today this is not far, but then it meant a week of hard travel. All this for a sojourn of at least four years or (heaven forbid!) eight if her husband accepted a second term.

Martha was not happy to leave Mount Vernon and didn't hesi-tate to say so. She wrote to a nephew, "I am truly sorry to tell that the General is gone to New York . . . when, or wheather he will ever come home again god only knows. I think it was much too late for him to go in to publick life again, but it was not to be avoided, our family will be deranged as I must soon follow him." As far as she was concerned, their family upsets, icy wintertime journeys, and makeshift lodgings during the eight years of the American Revolu-tion had been enough sacrifice for a lifetime.

Many politicians' wives stayed back home while their husbands served in the capital, but Martha Washington wasn't like many wives. When *her* husband heard the call of duty, she sometimes ar-gued passionately against it, but in the end she always went along. Whether as planter, lawmaker, general, or president, George Wash-ington relied on Martha emotionally. He needed her with him, and that's where she wanted to be.

Dismayed as she was at this fresh upheaval, she forged ahead with her preparations while awaiting the return of the coach and horses from New York. Every day was filled with arrangements great and small. On May 3, Washington's secretary wrote to George

Augustine Washington, his favorite nephew, at Mount Vernon. He urged the younger Washington to hurry Mrs. Washington along, "for we are extremely desirous of seeing her here." She ignored the suggestion until she was ready to go. Whole wardrobes of clothing for herself, her husband, and the two grandchildren who would accompany her to New York, as well as a multitude of household items necessary for the family's comfort and pleasure in a rented house—a month hardly seemed long enough to organize such a move.

Decisions had to be mulled over with George Augustine and his wife, Martha's own favorite niece, Fanny Bassett Washington. The young couple would be in charge at Mount Vernon during the presidency. Long-term visitors had to be sorted out. A nephew was summoned from New Kent County to retrieve his teenage sister, who had been staying with the Washingtons for the past nine months. Another nephew and his new bride, making a round of extended family visits, were abandoned with kisses and regrets. An orphaned niece, unruly and troublesome, was left under Fanny Washington's kind supervision.

Travel was always uncomfortable and sometimes dangerous. What with coach breakdowns, runaway horses, overturned ferries, collapsing bridges, flooded fords, unmarked or even undetectable roads, and squalid inns (when there were any at all), ladies did not travel alone. Mundane arrangements and any and all disasters were the purview of their male escorts. At Washington's invitation, his nephew Robert Lewis arrived on May 14, 1789, to accompany Martha on the trip to the capital, where he would serve as one of the president's aides.

The next youngest of a large brood, son of George's widowed only sister, Bob Lewis was a fresh-faced young man of nineteen, something of a mama's boy who loved singing, dancing, and kissing "all the girls." Taking his first important responsibility very seriously, he was upset when he found that "everything appeared to be in confusion" at Mount Vernon. To his chagrin, his aunt refused to leave until the masses of boxes and trunks had been packed and repacked to her satisfaction, chests and closets ransacked one more time, lost items unearthed, and last minute matters talked over with George Augustine and Fanny.

Gentle, kind, and feminine as she genuinely was, Martha Washington was also strong-willed and determined; once Bob understood that his aunt would make the important decisions on their trip, he had an easier time of it. Like everyone, he succumbed to her matchless charm and passed a happy couple of days walking about and "viewing all the curiosities that was to be seen" while she completed her tasks.

Finally, after dinner in the early afternoon and a last round of family tears and farewells, they were ready to leave Mount Vernon on Monday, May 16. The house servants and a number of the field hands came up "to take leave of their mistress—numbers of these poor wretches seemed much affected—My aunt equally so." The slaves were also saying good-bye to their relatives and friends who accompanied Martha to New York.

At three that afternoon, she and the Washingtons' adopted children—her youngest grandchildren, Nelly and Wash Custis (ten and eight years old, respectively)—climbed into the family coach, rolled down the serpentine drive, turned right on the road to Alexandria, and almost immediately lost sight of Mount Vernon among the trees. Bob Lewis rode along on horseback, as did the male servants. Assorted friends and cousins also rode with the travelers as far as Maryland. A small chariot carried Martha's maids, Molly and Oney; a high-piled baggage wagon jolted along behind. It was quite a cavalcade.

The crane-necked coach was still impressive despite its age. Twelve years before, early in the Revolution, the state of Pennsylvania had presented the London-built carriage as a gift to Martha. Painted a pleasant stone color with scenes of the four seasons on its panels, the coach was lined with green superfine cloth and boasted green silk cushions; its gilt-and-green appointments appeared rather grand even when coated thickly with road dust. Best of all, highway travel was somewhat less bone jarring than in most vehicles, thanks to the finest German steel springs.

The first leg of the trip was very short—only twelve miles to Abingdon, a plantation on the Potomac north of Alexandria, where they would spend the next two nights with Nelly Calvert Custis Stuart and her second husband. Nelly was the children's mother: their father, Jack Custis, had been Martha's son by a youthful first marriage. Even after her son's death seven and a half years earlier and Nelly's remarriage, Martha continued to think of her as a daughter-in-law. Living through sixteen years of family joys and sorrows together, the two women loved each other dearly. Nelly Stuart had agreed to let little Nelly and Wash go to New York with their grandmother, while their two older sisters and three little half-sisters would remain with her at Abingdon.

"All was silent melancholy" on the second evening as the close-knit family anticipated the long parting to come. At five the following morning, after the horses were hitched up and baggage loaded, "the dreaded hour appeared—[a] pathetic and affecting . . . scene." As the tenderhearted Bob described their departure: "We at length got off by which I was greatly relieved—leaving the family in tears—the children a bawling—and everything in a most lamentable situation."

About nine that morning, they arrived at Mason's ferry, which crossed the Potomac between northern Virginia and Georgetown, Maryland, a bustling little tobacco port built on a river bluff. The men unhitched the Mount Vernon team and sent them home with the coachman; fresh horses waited on the opposite shore. Despite the popularity of boat trips among the Virginia gentry, Martha never cared for being on the water. But travelers couldn't be choosers: ferry crossings were a given on any journey in early America.

Now she was alarmed to see the broad river running very high with a strong spring current. Things went as badly as she feared. The current drove the boat a considerable distance downriver, no matter how hard the boatmen struggled. When they finally landed, the shaken travelers were met by Colonel Gabriel Van Horne and his hostlers with a new team. Relying as usual on Revolutionary comrades, George Washington had arranged with the former militia commander to provide horses and lodgings for Martha's journey through the "unimproved" country from Georgetown to Philadelphia. Van Horne ran a stagecoach line that carried passengers and mail between Philadelphia and Alexandria; he also rented horses and carriages. Upset by the rough crossing, Martha decided not to wait for the coach. Instead she took the children and walked straight uphill on Water Street to get their breakfast at Georgetown's best hostelry, Suter's Tavern. The story-and-a-half frame structure with its large inn yard for coaches, wagons, and horses was located at the corner of Water and Bridge, the town's main street. Meanwhile, down at the riverside, the new horses balked at the unfamiliar harness. The coachman lashed them severely, but they reared, bucked, and broke the harness; repairing it and fetching a better-trained team caused a two-hour delay.

When they pushed on, Van Horne rode along with them, as he had promised Washington, on what he called "the most dangerous and difficult part of the journey" through Maryland, Delaware, and southern Pennsylvania. Their crossing of the Anacostia was uneventful, as was a brief stop at the small port town of Bladensburg for wine and cold cuts. At four that afternoon, they reached the turnoff to Thomas and Anne Ridgely Snowden's plantation. Major Snowden was another Revolutionary soldier, a wealthy man whose Patuxent River ironworks had supplied munitions to the patriot forces.

The muddy road was narrow, hemmed in by the surrounding woods—so narrow, in fact, that the coach got wedged between two trees, shuddering to an abrupt halt before it could be shoved free. But a delightful sight awaited them: Montpelier was an elegant red-brick Georgian mansion with tall chimneys and side wings, set off by a formal boxwood garden. The Snowdens welcomed them with open arms and alarming volubility, chattering like parrots in their happiness at entertaining the famous Mrs. Washington.

Despite her hosts' pleas and a strong threat of rain the next morning, they set off again, accompanied by Snowden for ten or twelve miles to show them a shortcut and to make sure that they didn't stray from the road. According to their fond grandmama, "the children were very well and chearfull all the way." Poor Nelly complained only "a very little" of coach sickness as the coach bounded and jolted, lurched, shook, and shuddered on the terrible road.

From Bladensburg to Elk Ridge near Baltimore, much of their route passed through the wilderness—the native forest that eighteenth-century travelers found so monotonous and dispiriting, a desolate landscape crying for the touch of a human hand. Never mind the magnificent oaks, ashes, loblolly pines, flowering redbuds, white-blossomed dogwoods, blooming cascades of coral bells, tall columbines, and blue flag iris of springtime Maryland. Bob waxed lyrical when he finally spied a settlement with houses, plowed fields, fences, and orchards—*here* was beauty!

Twelve miles south of Baltimore, they stopped at Spurrier's Tavern. As the president's wife, Martha Washington would be under constant observation in these more heavily settled regions. Public spectacle was vital to the new nation's self-definition, and she instinctively understood the symbolic importance of her appearance— elegant but not opulent, simple in style, unadorned with ostrich plumes or gaudy jewels. Warned that she would be met by a group of Baltimore gentlemen outside the city, she "shifted herself"—that is, changed clothes—before continuing on.

Riding in a coach on unpaved roads was dirty work. Even with the curtains drawn, clouds of dust billowed in through the windows, settling on her traveling clothes until everything looked uniformly tan. Servants at Spurrier's would have rushed to bring hot water for the ewer and basin in the room set aside for her. She needed to wash and change out of her grimy dress, its every pleat clogged with dirt. Oney or Molly would have brushed the dust from her hair, combing it straight back from her forehead in her usual style, rebraiding the back, and tucking the tail in neatly. The maids would have opened a trunk, shaken out the wrinkles from a modish gown, and helped their mistress put it on. When Martha emerged looking considerably cleaner and more presentable, the coach and horses were ready and waiting at the door.

One more alarming ferry trip lay ahead. Although the branch of the Patapsco River they crossed was no more than forty yards wide at the landing, it was very deep. A swift tide was running in against the wind, cresting in steep waves. After they embarked, the wind rose almost to a gale, and the boat took on a great deal of water. Martha was frightened that the boat would sink, and Bob Lewis and Van Horne pitched in to help the ferrymen reach the opposite shore safely. On landing, she had to pull herself together to greet the waiting horsemen, but Martha never gave in to her fears for long. She was spared the windy speeches delivered at every stop on her husband's trips: ceremonial rhetoric was generally reserved for men. Dignified and erect at her full five feet tall, she enjoyed all the excitement and public acclamation, taking pleasure and pride in "the great parade that was made for us all the way we come." It was the honeymoon of her life in the limelight. *Everyone* wanted to entertain her and her party. An urgent messenger begged them to turn aside on the outskirts of Baltimore at the Mount Clare estate, where the men regaled themselves with iced punch (more than two gallons in a quarter of an hour!) and fresh fruit from the estate's greenhouse.

Martha finally reached the city later that afternoon. All Baltimore's visitors were amazed by its growth. The fifth largest city in the nation and the leading port of the vast Chesapeake Bay, Baltimore boasted a population of 13,500, double its size in 1776. Compare that to the 12,300 residents in all of Fairfax County, where Mount Vernon was located, or the 3,700 souls in Richmond, Virginia's capital and largest city.

Baltimore was all about business—from the busy wharves, the shipyards of Fell's Point, and the fifty flour mills lining its streams to the lively wholesale and retail stores, warehouses, long ropewalks, chandleries, and brickyards with clouds of smoke rising from their kilns. Some of the streets had even been paved and lighted, the money raised by private lottery. High on Calvert Street loomed the imposing, if wildly eccentric, brick courthouse, its two stories topped by a tall lookout and spire, finished off with a weather cock and compass points. Like a witch's house perched on a giant stool, the building stood twenty feet in the air on an arched base, a novel means of preserving the building when the ground under it had been excavated for a street extension. Brick mansions had gone up throughout the town since the war, interspersed among modest, brightly painted frame houses.

Her hosts for the night were James and Margaret Caldwell McHenry; Major McHenry was yet another Revolutionary officer, a steadfast aide to both Washington and Lafayette, who was now a state representative with a large Federal-style house near the public square. He had written in early March inviting both the president and "my dear Mrs. Washington" to treat his house as their own on their separate journeys north. Like all the headquarters staff from the war years, McHenry was devoted to Martha, who had spent every winter of the war with the army.

George had declined this offer on his own behalf, staying instead at the Fountain Inn in the heart of the port area. He pled the "scenes of bustle & trouble" that would be caused by the expected crowds of well-wishers, as well as the appearance of favoritism in his new position. But he was less of a stickler where his beloved wife was concerned. She chose to stay in comfort with the McHenrys rather than at a noisy tavern.

They invited a large group of friends to take tea and spend the evening with Mrs. Washington. McHenry apologized for "harass[ing] her with company," but as he frankly admitted, his neighbors "would never have forgiven me" if they had not been invited to meet her. Even at fifty-seven, with much of her youthful beauty faded, this middle-aged woman captivated them all. Now stout and gray-haired, she still drew people to her with her fair open face, lively hazel eyes, and bright smile. Her interest in everyone and everything made her a charming conversationalist.

Enlivened by fireworks before and after supper, the party didn't break up until eleven that night. Martha promptly went to bed, but some choice spirits among the citizenry serenaded the house until two in the morning. After only three hours of sleep, the travelers got up to leave town early, avoiding "any parade that might be intended." With misplaced civic pride, the *Maryland Journal and Baltimore Advertiser* described the intrusive late night serenade as "an excellent Band of Music, Conducted by Gentlemen of the Town."

Tailored riding dresses were often worn as traveling attire, and Martha seems to have followed that custom. From New England mills that spring, she had received both bottle green and dark brown wool fabric intended to make riding dresses. That she "was clothed in the manufacture of our country" was praised as a mark of "her native goodness and patriotism." They stayed two more nights on the road before reaching Philadelphia.

Beset by throngs of applicants for office and conflicting recommendations from his advisers, George missed his wife badly and followed reports of her progress. His friends dispatched information about her whereabouts via mail coaches or horsemen on their way to the capital. He sent her a letter in care of his Philadelphia factor to await her arrival there, suggesting that she might need to send him a letter by the Friday morning stagecoach to New York City.

But she missed that post, not coming near Philadelphia until the late morning of May 20, "without the least accident to distress us," according to Martha's own account. Rough ferry rides and rambunctious horses were already forgotten by a woman who never dwelled on mishaps. New celebrations lay ahead. Scouts, stationed on the highway to watch for her coach, galloped into the city to alert her escort.

After quickly saddling up, two companies of dragoons and the city's leading citizens and government officials rode out to greet the president's lady—a gesture of respect almost as great as the clouds of dust they raised. At Darby, she was met by her friend and Philadelphia hostess, Mary White Morris, the elegant wife of financier Robert Morris, as well as many other ladies in their coaches. The entire group stopped on the western bank of the Schuylkill River at Gray's pleasure garden, with its trees, flowers, walkways, and "artistic decorations" modeled after London's public gardens. There the Philadelphians—about a hundred men and women—welcomed her with a "cold collation." By the time they were finished, it was two in the afternoon. Back in the coach, they crossed the river at Gray's

Ferry; happily enough for Martha, the ferry had been replaced by a floating pontoon bridge in 1778.

Philadelphia! Grand, scandalous, elegant, dangerous, sinful, learned, commercial, pious, tumultuous, peaceful, rich, riotous, tolerant, rebellious, squalid—almost any adjective could be applied to the Queen City of the United States with some measure of truth. By American standards, Philadelphia was enormous—with 42,500 people, it dwarfed both New York City and Boston. William Penn's vision of a green country town, its elegant grid of streets softened by gardens and orchards, had not yet been completely supplanted. The city's two main streets, High (soon to be renamed Market) and Broad, were an impressive hundred feet wide, while the other streets were a respectable fifty feet in width. Most of the streets in the main part of town were paved with cobblestones or paving blocks and lit by whale-oil lamp fixtures. Red bricks, that mark of wealth and permanence, set the tone of the city from stately public buildings, schools, churches of every persuasion (religious toleration was one of Philadelphia's hallmarks), three public markets, and houses down to the sidewalks and even some street gutters. Foreign imports and the handiwork of the nation's most skilled craftsmen filled the tempting shops.

Streets, windows, and fences were jammed with applauding crowds eager to catch a glimpse of Mrs. Washington. Church bells pealed joyously, while the city's artillery company blasted away with a thirteen-gun salute—the new "federal salute"—in her honor. Down High Street, they clickety-clacked along briskly—horseshoes and metal-clad coach wheels ringing on the pavement, the very rhythm of urban life. They drew up at the Morrises' mansion at No. 190 High Street, near Sixth. Here they would all spend a restful weekend before the final leg of the trip. Expansive, fat, and sociable, the middle-aged Robert Morris had already joined the president in New York to consult on fiscal affairs. He was an immensely rich merchant and speculator, whose financial acuity, organizational expertise, and stalwart use of his personal credit had helped bankroll the Revolution and keep Washington's troops supplied and in the field.

Martha felt at home with Mary Morris, eighteen years younger than she but sharing much the same worldview. Fond of entertaining and being entertained by the elite of the Philadelphia social world, Mary was the sister of the American Episcopal bishop and the mother of five sons and two daughters. Ten-year-old Maria became Nelly's friend, her first ever besides her sisters and cousins in the intimate family world of Virginia plantations. "Dear little Washington," Nelly's little brother, was "lost in a mase" at all the excitement.

Here in the most cosmopolitan city of North America, shopping was a pleasure and a delight. Martha sent for a stay maker and a shoemaker, ordering custom-made luxuries—corsets and "new fashioned" shoes for Fanny Washington, Nelly Stuart, and her eldest granddaughters, Patty and Betsy, young ladies of twelve and thirteen. Nothing made her happier than buying presents for the family.

When they left Philadelphia on Monday, their caravan was joined by Mary Morris and her daughters in their own family coach. Only two more nights on the road remained until journey's end. Finally, on Wednesday, May 27, they arrived at Elizabethtown Point. There they were met by Robert Morris and the newly inaugurated president himself, who must have leaned down to embrace his sorely missed little wife and the excited children, with perhaps a grateful handshake for the faithful Bob Lewis.

The spanking new, brightly painted presidential barge, built for Washington's reception by civic leaders, was forty-seven feet long; in case of rain, the back of the deck was covered by an awning of festooned red curtains. But rain isn't mentioned in any account of this exhilarating day, the culmination of what Martha regarded as a "very agreeable journey." The smartly dressed New York pilots in their white smocks and black-fringed caps, thirteen in all, shipped their oars and waited for their guests to board the craft for the fifteen-mile trip. The servants, carriages, horses, and baggage would follow by ferryboat.

At the coxswain's command, the oars flashed in unison as they crossed Newark Bay, went up Upper New York Bay, received yet another thirteen-gun salute from the Battery at the tip of Manhattan Island, entered the East River, and docked smartly at Peck's slip after a trip of a little more than an hour. Crowds of cheering New Yorkers awaited them there, along with Governor George Clinton, who couldn't resist delivering a welcoming speech to Martha. He escorted the Washingtons and their friends from the landing to No. 3 Cherry Street just a couple of blocks away, where Congress had rented a house for the presidential family and staff.

Not one to sing her own praises, Martha wrote her niece, "The paper will tell you how I was complimented on my landing." Thanking God that "the President"—her first written use of George's new title—was very well, she plunged immediately into the capital's social whirl without any time to rest or settle in. The day after her arrival, she was the hostess at an official dinner for leading members of Congress; on Friday evening, the presidential mansion was crowded with New York's social and political elite, both women and men, at her first public reception. So much for her expectation of leading the kind of private, domestic life she had enjoyed during the Revolution.

Much to her surprise, at the end of her long trip from Virginia to New York, Martha Washington discovered that, like George Washington, she belonged to the nation and that she too had become part of American history.

CHAPTER ONE

Little Patsy Dandridge

*H*istory's Martha Washington was born Martha Dandridge in rural New Kent County, Virginia. She was called Patsy (often spelled Patcy) by her family and friends as a matter of course. In those days, Patsy, Patty, and Pat were the nicknames for Martha, just as Margaret was commonly shortened to Peggy or Peg and Mary became Polly or Poll.

A true child of the colony, she was at least a fourth-generation Virginian on her mother's side. For more than a hundred years, her maternal ancestors had been respected landowning gentry, but they were not grandees with uncounted acres. They lived in a web of relationships based on marriage, kinship, business, and neighborhood. Without strong community ties, no individual could have survived the rigors of early colonial life. Patsy Dandridge was part and parcel of English Virginia and the world of its tobacco planters.

Starvation, disease, hostile Indians, and years of financial losses—for its first twenty or thirty years, the little colony planted in 1607 at Jamestown teetered on the edge of extinction. Then the vagaries of European fashion turned Virginia's future as golden as the mines of Spain's Latin American colonies. Almost overnight, tobacco became all the rage—whether smoked in pipes or daintily inhaled as snuff—and Virginia lands seemed predestined for its cultivation. To most of the world, tobacco and Virginia became synonymous.

Prime tobacco land meant wealth and prestige. Some colonists came with leather satchels bulging with coins, others as indentured servants who had signed away four to seven years of their own hard labor to repay the costs of their passages; but rich and poor alike aspired to landownership. And not just any land. Immigrants wanted acreage on one of the four great tidal rivers of the Chesapeake Bay—the James, York, Rappahannock, or Potomac—as European settlement moved northward. This was the Tidewater, the land between the coast and the fall line, where the first waterfall on each river prevented ships from sailing any farther upriver.

With the labor of indentured servants, Virginia planters cleared hundreds, then thousands, then hundreds of thousands of acres for tobacco cultivation. By the mid-1600s, fleets of English merchantmen set off across the Atlantic each summer, fetching up in the Chesapeake Bay by early fall. They sailed directly up the hospitable rivers—no need here for port cities—anchoring to take on board tightly packed hogsheads or bundles of dried, golden brown tobacco leaves and to deliver hoes, plows, axes, scythes, and other manufactured goods.

Thirty miles or so from its mouth, the York River splits in two: the southern branch is the Pamunkey River, named for the Powhatan tribe that lived along it. Although the Pamunkeys were forced to accept the authority of the colonial government, they still retained considerable land on the frontier when New Kent County was created there in 1654.

No one knows exactly when or under what circumstances Martha Dandridge's maternal forebears came from England to try their luck in Virginia. In 1664, her great-grandfather William Woodward first appears in the documentary record. That summer, Queen Cocka Coeska, leader of the Pamunkeys, sold him 2,100 acres of river land in New Kent County. In a petition to the Governor's Council, she declared her desire to have him as a neighbor and translator for herself and her people.

Family lore holds that Woodward had moved out to that "howling wilderness" sometime in the 1650s as an Indian trader. To English colonists, the great forests were alien and frightening places, where not only the wind and the wolves howled, but the native inhabitants as well. In their eyes, trees were to be chopped down, wolves to be killed, and Indians civilized, beginning with learning the English language and giving up their own "foule noise." Woodward must have been an unusual Englishman, for he learned the Pamunkeys' language and gained their confidence. So very unusual was this linguistic skill that he was always identified as "William Woodward, the Indian Interpreter." Although not a colonial official, he was employed for specific negotiations between the Indians and the governor.

Even the name of Martha Dandridge's great-grandmother, the woman who married William Woodward, is unknown, as are those of so many colonial matriarchs. The seventeenth century was concerned with brute survival and the acquisition and protection of wealth. Men owned land, held office, and fought wars: many of their names survive in a document somewhere. Not so with women. Nearly four hundred years of indifference, fires, floods, and vanished burial plots means that a goodly percentage of Virginia foremothers are unknown.

Mrs. Woodward may have been Martha West, a descendant of Lord Delaware; whether or not she was Martha West, this great-grandmother was almost certainly Virginia born. The Woodwards married sometime in the mid-1600s. Like almost all early planters, even the most successful, they doubtless lived in a modest frame home of two rooms with an attic. Cultivated fields were interspersed with forests teeming with game—squirrels, rabbits, deer, and turkeys, as well as predators like gray wolves. Wolves posed such a menace to settlers' livestock that Virginia's ruling council offered a bounty for killing them, requiring delivery of the ears as proof.

The Woodwards had five children, including a daughter named Martha. Colonial women's birth dates are even more elusive than their names, but Martha Woodward was born sometime between 1657 and 1665. She is the first of Martha Dandridge's female ancestors that we can identify with certainty. About 1680, this Martha married Gideon Macon, a Huguenot planter who had immigrated in 1672. Like thousands of other Protestants who fled persecution in France, he brought welcome capital and skills to Virginia. The Macons built a house called Mount Pleasant on Macon's Island in the Pamunkey River; their plantation incorporated the land that Martha inherited from her parents.

They had six children between 1681 and 1701; their eldest was another Martha. In early 1702, Gideon died. Within a year, the widowed Martha Woodward Macon, now in her late thirties or early forties, married a wealthy bachelor, Captain Nathaniel West of West Point, a neighbor and perhaps her cousin. Their only child was a daughter named Unity, born about 1703, who will figure in our story later. Widowed, remarried to a Scottish merchant, and widowed again, Martha Woodward Macon West Biggers moved back to Mount Pleasant, where she resided until her death in 1723.

In January 1703, her daughter Martha Macon married Orlando Jones. His mother was a native-born Virginian, Anne Lane; his father was an Anglican clergyman, the Reverend Rowland Jones, who had emigrated from England in the 1660s. The elder Jones was one of the founders and the first rector of Bruton Parish.

Orlando studied at the new College of William and Mary, became a planter near Williamsburg on Queen's Creek, a navigable stream (at least at high tide) leading out to the York River, and served as a burgess. As the eighteenth century brought greater prosperity, Orlando and Martha Macon Jones lived in a brick house with five or six rooms, which included nineteen chairs, pictures on the parlor wall, and a few pieces of silver. Plantation labor had changed, too. Indentured Englishmen had become less common in the tobacco fields, replaced by enslaved Africans. By this time, fully a quarter of all colonial Virginians were black, the majority of them toiling on large plantations. Even a small planter like Orlando owned twenty-one slaves.

Not only was Orlando and Martha's house more comfortable and stylish than their parents' had been, they lived right outside the growing new capital, where they could enjoy at least the rudiments of urban life—a few shops, craftsmen, markets, and taverns.

In Virginia, a rural colony with a widely spread population, all the other so-called towns amounted at most to a warehouse, a tavern, and a house or two.

Marshy, disease-ridden Jamestown was destroyed once too often by fire; in 1699, it was replaced by Williamsburg as the new capital. On the relatively high neck of land between the James and York rivers, the College of William and Mary, built to keep planters' sons close to home, and the simple brick Bruton Parish Church were incorporated into a handsome plan of wide, sand-covered streets and brick government buildings. Still far from complete, *this* town was built to last.

The Joneses' first surviving child was a son named Lane, born in 1707, followed by a daughter, Frances, in 1710, a break in the line of Marthas. Martha Macon Jones died in 1716, when Fanny was only six. Life in colonial Virginia was uncertain, and the chances of a child growing to adulthood with two living parents were rare indeed; living grandparents were even less common.

Like most colonial widowers (not to speak of widows), Orlando Jones soon remarried; it was simply too difficult to maintain a household and rear children alone. Reflecting this reality, many colonial documents refer to "now husband" and "now wife" to distinguish from earlier spouses. After three childless years, Orlando also died and left the guardianship of his children to his second wife, Mary Elizabeth Williams Jones. His will directed her to sell his "tenement," or rental house, on Duke of Gloucester Street in Williamsburg. Although he further directed that the family remain on the plantation, the young widow had other ideas. A year after the sale, she married the purchaser, a Huguenot watchmaker named John James Flournoy.

Despite their many blood relatives, Fanny and Lane Jones found themselves, willy-nilly, living in town with their stepmother and her new husband. Babies arrived in rapid succession, and the white frame house was soon bursting at the seams. Initially, Mary Jones Flournoy was obligated to care for her stepchildren. But by their early teens, Fanny and Lane were clearly anxious to leave the household.

The Flournoys probably kept the Jones children for several years against their wishes because of the money. As guardians, they had a legal right to use the income from the Queen's Creek plantation and its slaves to maintain the household where Lane and Fanny resided. Orlando's sister Anna Maria Jones Timson sued twice to gain custody of her niece and nephew, as well as their estate, but she was unsuccessful. When he was eighteen, Lane legally emancipated himself from the Flournoys' guardianship and moved out to Timson's Neck with his aunt.

Poor Fanny was forced to remain behind for ten more months. At sixteen, she also sued to emancipate herself. The Flournoys were cleared of any financial wrongdoing when the estate was finally settled, but they sold their house and business and moved west to Henrico County, out of our story. We can surmise that Fanny was left with an abiding suspicion of stepparents and the conviction that good aunts had a duty to help out their orphaned nieces.

No one knows where Fanny Jones went to live in 1726. Because she chose a New Kent County planter as her guardian, it seems likely that she moved out to the Pamunkey River neighborhood. All Fanny's grandparents were dead, and her aunt Anna Maria's house was overcrowded. Besides her guardian, there were a number of Macon aunts and uncles in that neighborhood.

The most interesting possibility is that she lived with or paid long visits to a maternal aunt, her deceased mother's younger half-sister, Unity West Dandridge. A considerable heiress in her own right, Aunt Unity was only a few years older than Fanny. In 1719, she had married William Dandridge, an English immigrant twenty years her senior. By 1726, they had three little children, the eldest a daughter named Martha.

The pool of customary names among English settlers was small and the desire to honor family members great: names were repeated in each generation, and two or three cousins often bore identical names without a middle name to distinguish them. All those Marys, Elizabeths, Marthas, Annes, Franceses, Williams, Georges, Thomases, Roberts, Johns, and Daniels make for endless confusion. As one of the early editors of George Washington's papers put it: "To name generation after generation the same is an evil habit"—and one the Dandridges indulged in repeatedly.

Unity and William Dandridge lived at Elsing Green, a fine brick house in the new Georgian style on the north bank of the Pamunkey. By this time a successful merchant, military man, and member of the Governor's Council, William had arrived in Virginia in 1715, bringing his fifteen-year-old brother, John, with him. Like most new colonists, they were the descendants of yeoman farmers and skilled craftsmen in England—people of what were called "the middling sort." The Dandridge brothers prospered in the colony, and William's marriage to Unity West gave them social cachet.

The courtship of Fanny Jones and Jack Dandridge was almost inevitable. She would already have known him as her half-aunt's brother-in-law, and they furthered their acquaintance during the late 1720s after she left Williamsburg. Blood kinship or kinship by marriage was always a plus in colonial matches, both financially and emotionally. Hard for a modern reader to follow, genealogical snarls were easily disentangled by colonial Virginians. In those days of early death and frequent remarriage, most people had several half- and steprelatives and kissing cousins by the score.

Though never as successful as his older brother, Jack Dandridge did well. He was deputy clerk of New Kent County, soon to become clerk; a militia officer who would eventually become colonel; and the owner of five hundred acres on the Pamunkey. While he was courting Fanny, he built a house called Chestnut Grove on his small plantation across the river from Elsing Green.

In the eighteenth century, the word *plantation* defined an agricultural property that was devoted to the cultivation of a single crop for the export market. In Virginia, that crop was tobacco. Plantations encompassed everything from estates with thousands of acres, hundreds of slaves, and grand mansions to little more than jumped-up farms where the owners worked in the fields. Chestnut Grove fell somewhere in the middle of this range but was still considered genteel.

Fanny and Jack married in 1730, when she was twenty and he was thirty. She brought a respectable dowry to the upwardly mobile young man—a piece of land in King William County and at least ten slaves left to her by her father. In the custom of the times, the newlyweds would have moved into their new house and set up housekeeping at once. Chestnut Grove was a comfortable two-story frame house with three pine-paneled rooms on each floor, warmed by fireplaces at each end of the house; the kitchen was in a separate small building. Its setting was handsome, on a curve of the lazy Pamunkey, surrounded by chestnuts and an orchard of fruit trees.

Like all good Virginia ladies, Fanny was soon pregnant—"breeding," as her condition was frankly known. The Dandridges' first child was a daughter they named Martha for her grandmother and great-grandmother (and possibly great-great-grandmother). She was born between twelve and one o'clock on June 2, 1731, in her parents' bedroom on the first floor of Chestnut Grove.

A brunette with hazel eyes and fair skin, baby Patsy had little time to enjoy being an only child; her brother John (Jack) was born slightly less than nine months later. William made his appearance in 1734, Bartholomew (Bat) was born in 1737, and the sister who became her best friend, Anna Maria (Nancy), was born two years later. By the time she was eight, Patsy had four younger siblings. Then the live births stretched out, with Frances arriving in 1744, Elizabeth (Betsy) in 1749, and Mary in 1756. What with miscarriages and stillbirths, Fanny Jones Dandridge was either pregnant or nursing almost continuously for a quarter of a century.

Patsy was uncommonly lucky to have both her parents living throughout her girlhood. As the eldest daughter in a household without a retinue of servants, she was surely mama's little helper with her younger brothers and sisters, all of them born at home. No wonder motherliness was one of her distinguishing attributes as a woman or that she always enjoyed the company of young people.

The New Kent County in which the Dandridges lived was pure

country, fields bordered by forests, without a town worthy of the name. As a girl growing up on a small plantation, she had a matter-of-fact knowledge of sexuality, reproduction, and bodily functions. There was an earthiness to country life, with steaming manure heaps by the barn, chamber pots and privies, the fall slaughter of pigs and cows, the breeding of horses with bloodlines much discussed, the sounds of her parents' lovemaking in the deep silence of the night, the birth of spring livestock—not to speak of the human babies born on the place. Patsy never fell into the chilly, tight-lipped clutches of prudishness. Good-humored and laughing, she enjoyed all the pleasures life offered.

There were perhaps fifteen or twenty slaves at Chestnut Grove, an estimate based on acreage. New Kent is one of Virginia's "burned counties," whose courthouse records were long ago destroyed by fire. At a place like the Dandridges', slaves working in the tobacco fields were the key to family prosperity. Very few of them would have been spared for household duties—at most, a cook and maid/laundress on a regular basis. While Fanny and her daughters did a good deal of the housekeeping, they had to know how to do everything, even the heavy jobs they delegated to the servants. And there was plenty of work every day for all of them.

Besides the mundane tasks like sweeping and mopping, here are some of the things Patsy learned to do at her mother's side: kill, pluck, and draw fowls, from the smallest hen to the largest turkey; track down setting hens, gather their eggs, and candle them; make dyes; spin, weave, and dye wool and linen; make clothes, sheets, towels, pillowcases, mattress covers, quilts, curtains, bed curtains, tablecloths, napkins, underwear, menstrual pads, diapers, and nightwear; stuff pillows and mattresses; beat dust from the rugs; turn mattresses and even out the feathers; gather useful herbs, plants, berries, and roots in the woods; concoct home remedies and beauty aids; salt and smoke hams, bacon, beef, and fish; make vinegar, sauces, syrups, and jellies; preserve fruit and vegetables; cook large meals over the fire in an open hearth; bake in a brick oven; make soap from lye and household grease; make furniture and silver polish and use them; wash clothes weekly in a huge boiling kettle without shrinking or discoloring them and spread them to dry; crimp ruffles and press clothes with heavy irons heated in the fireplace; darn, mend, and patch; and knit, knit, knit—woolen stockings wore out fast. The most common verb in this long list is "make," and that's what colonial women did. Small planters purchased a few imported luxuries, but not most of the necessities of daily life.

As toddlers, girls and boys were dressed alike in linen shifts and "napkins," as diapers were called; both wore long dresses for more formal occasions. Breeches for the boys and petticoats for the girls had to wait until they were reliably toilet trained; the shifts made changing wet or dirty diapers easy. The leading strings sewed to their garments at shoulder level were handy for teaching children to walk, pulling them out of danger, or controlling a temper tantrum. At five or six, however, children were customarily dressed in miniature versions of adult clothes, like little women and men.

Even before Patsy graduated from shifts to dresses, she began to learn genteel deportment when her soft little body was encased in stays, the boned corsets worn by girls and women to impose erect posture and to restrain easy movement. Never again would she be seen in public without them; uncorseted freedom was for slatterns and sluts.

Proper manners, posture, gestures, curtseys, bows, voice modulation, conduct toward social superiors and inferiors—all were signs of elite status, and the gentry trained their children young in such essential behavior. Their ideal was the British aristocracy; whatever their family origins, Virginia planters had become self-conscious members of the upper class.

Patsy would also learn other lessons important to a lady's role— to manage her wide skirts gracefully either walking or sitting, to decorate her home appropriately, to dress stylishly, to set a table correctly and symmetrically, to be sociable and gracious to guests, to carry on a conversation with the most ill-assorted company, to sing the popular airs of the day in her pleasant voice, and to do fine sewing, like needlepoint and embroidery.

Although she had probably been on horseback since she was a baby, Patsy had to learn to ride with style. The Dandridges had no carriage, just a wagon, so they rode most places. A poor seat on horseback—awkwardness, slouching, failure to control one's mount—was an embarrassment. Patsy might ride astride on the plantation, but she had to master the difficulties of riding sidesaddle for public occasions.

Virginians loved to dance and indulged themselves in that pleasure as often as possible. Peripatetic dancing masters made a circuit from neighborhood to neighborhood, gathering all the planters' children at one of their houses for lessons that would continue for two or three long days. These martinets didn't hesitate to box the ears of inattentive students without a word of protest from their parents, and in the evening the adults danced along with the children. Patsy's group for such vital lessons doubtless included her cousins, brothers, and neighbors. To the perplexity of outsiders, dancing helped create social cohesion in Virginia, as well as contributing to physical fitness; dancing well was essential to acceptance by society.

The intricate steps of minuets, French dances, reels, and country dances were taught thoroughly and practiced frequently. Dancers had to "mind the music and the step" very carefully indeed. Long lines, circles, or squares of dancers moved in rhythm through intricate patterns in limited spaces. Pity the awkward booby who turned left instead of right or tripped over his own feet. The grace, beauty, and courtliness of dancers were on display, an opportunity for social success or public humiliation.

Dancing was far more essential in the eighteenth century to a Virginia girl's education than reading, writing, or arithmetic, but Patsy's schooling in those more mundane areas was not neglected. Probably her mother was her teacher, since the Dandridges were not wealthy enough to employ a resident tutor; she received a solid basic education, better than that of some planters' daughters, inferior to that of most of their brothers. For the rest of her life she was a reader, enjoying novels and poetry and perusing daily the Anglican Book of Common Prayer and the Bible, especially the New Testament. She had a solid grasp of arithmetic, which she later used to financial advantage.

Patsy's letters were filled with variations in spelling and grammar. But so were most people's. Spelling, capitalization, and verb usage were not yet standardized in England, still less in the colonies. Form was important, and she wrote a passable hand, the lines fairly straight and even.

There was a wide gap in the rhetoric taught girls and boys. The admired style of the day—pretentious, florid, overflowing with ornamented sentences and lofty principles—was almost completely a masculine purview. Like most women, Patsy wrote letters that were short, direct, and to the point. No ornamental flourishes, no highfalutin sentiments, no musings on abstract subjects. Writing for her was a means of communication, not an opportunity to parade her learning.

Religion was fundamental to Patsy's upbringing. The Dandridges were regular churchgoers, riding four miles along dirt roads through overhanging woods, welcomed by the ringing bell well before the imposing square brick tower of their church came into view. St. Peter's stood alone in the woods, coming alive on Sundays when all the neighborhood arrived, tying their horses to the trees that surrounded the church. Her father was a vestryman, one of the powerful board of laymen who directed parish activities. Patsy became a devout member of the Church of England; daily prayers were one of her lifelong emotional supports.

Church attendance was about more than religion in those hardworking times. Sundays and court days were the highlights of rural social life. Both before and after church (and during, for many of the menfolk who remained outside), neighbors took the opportunity to visit and do business in the churchyard. Sociability also ruled at court days, the monthly sessions where county officials, including John Dandridge, dealt with legal matters at New Kent's courthouse. Invitations flew, and both church and court were followed by dinners, barbecues, fish feasts, visits of a day or a week, dances at a neighbor's house. It was primarily at these house parties that marriageable young women like Patsy spent time with potential suitors.

Williamsburg, though, was the center of colonial social life, boasting about a thousand permanent residents by 1748. During the spring and fall court sessions, which were often combined with a meeting of the legislature, the city's population almost doubled as planters and their families flooded in for business, politics, lawsuits, or simple pleasure. These "Public Times" were crowded with entertainments and social events—balls, assemblies, teas, dinners, horse races, theater.

The town was laid out on a plan worthy of a far grander place. The carefully leveled main street, Duke of Gloucester, was six poles wide—wide enough for two or even three wagons to pass abreast. It stretched straight as a string for almost a mile, bounded at one end by the college and at the other by the ruins of the burned Capitol building, in the process of being rebuilt. Bruton Parish Church and the Governor's Palace were situated on a crosswise axis. The two-story brick palace had inspired some wealthy planters to imitation in their own elegant new mansions. It faced the Palace Green, with falling gardens that sloped down to an ornamental canal overhung with trees; the iron front gates opened onto a forecourt with four long oval parterres of clipped yaupon holly, the beds planted with pastel periwinkles.

To most colonial Virginians, Williamsburg was an exciting metropolis with its grand public buildings, taverns (some with assembly rooms for social events), and racetrack. A number of the wealthier planters, not including John Dandridge, owned brick or frame town houses, enclosed with fences to keep the town's pesky dogs and hogs out of their gardens. What with an apothecary, jeweler and silversmith, wigmaker, shoemaker, general store, printer, saddler, blacksmith, milliner, gunsmith, cabinetmaker, and more, sandy Duke of Gloucester Street seemed to offer no end of tantalizing shops. It was the biggest town that Patsy had seen in her young life.

Besides the dances and other social events in New Kent, she probably accompanied her parents to a ball or two in Williamsburg. At home and in the capital, she would encounter prospective husbands and take her place in Virginia society as a beautiful young woman. Patsy Dandridge's childhood and education were behind her at seventeen, her character essentially formed. The first chapter of her adult life was about to open.

CHAPTER TWO

Courtship

*P*retty Patsy Dandridge was plenty old enough to think of marriage in 1748. Fashions in beauty change with every generation, and seventeen-year-old Patsy's looks were just right for hers. She was what the English called a pocket Venus, a petite, cuddlesome armful. Barely five feet tall, she had the tiny hands and feet that were considered marks of gentility. With dark brown hair and strongly marked eyebrows, smooth white shoulders sloping down to full breasts, bright hazel eyes, and a ready smile displaying beautiful white teeth (a rarity for the time), she epitomized the feminine ideal for many Virginians.

She had long since met every eligible bachelor and widower in her neighborhood and farther afield. But in the eyes of potential husbands, her beauty, social graces, sex appeal, and personality didn't quite offset her biggest deficiency—money. For Virginia planters, as for the gentry in Britain and throughout the British colonies, marriage was not a matter to be decided by individuals on the basis of love alone. It was a serious family affair, in which money, landownership, social position, religious affiliation, dowry, and parental consent balanced and often outweighed personal attraction—especially for the daughters of the family. The Dandridges' fortune wasn't as large as their family, and they couldn't provide a substantial dowry.

So essential was money in gentry marriages that the *Virginia*

Gazette of Williamsburg frequently included the amount of women's dowries in their wedding announcements; that information must have been provided by the families themselves. One example among dozens says it all: In 1737, the *Gazette* stated baldly that Beverley Randolph's bride Betty Lightfoot was "an agreeable young Lady, with a Fortune of upwards of 5000£." Agreeable indeed, with such a sum to command.

Nevertheless, people usually managed to find a compatible spouse within their own social circles, and happy marriages were probably as common then as now. Patsy would surely find an attractive and companionable husband from among the neighboring New Kent planters of comparable means or her many Pamunkey River cousins—a Dandridge, Macon, or Woodward.

A New Kent neighbor did come courting, but her parents must have been both shocked and delighted by the identity of Patsy's suitor. Contrary to all probability, Daniel Parke Custis came from the very top tier of colonial society—the descendant of Virginia's most prominent families and the son of one of the richest men in the colony. A bachelor twenty years Patsy's senior, he was an active dark-haired man of average height, standing five feet six inches (although he sometimes claimed an extra inch), somewhat stout, with large dark eyes that radiated kindness.

During the eleven years that he had lived in New Kent County, running one of his father's plantations just a few miles down the Pamunkey from Chestnut Grove, Patsy had come to know him well. His life had crossed her family's at countless points—court days, militia musters, social events, church (he served on St. Peter's vestry with her father), the Public Times at Williamsburg—and he had obviously noticed the little girl growing into a lovely young woman. At thirty-seven, he was only a year younger than her mother, but the age difference between him and Patsy was not an impediment; young girls often married older men.

There was, however, one major obstacle to Patsy and Daniel's marriage—his father, John Custis IV, the master of several plantations and thousands of acres, as well as a house in Williamsburg where he lived. Daniel hadn't chosen voluntarily to remain single at nearly forty, a curiosity in a society that married early and often. Old Colonel Custis's eccentricities were as vast as his wealth, particularly on the subjects of marriage, parental authority, money, and social rank. Daniel had not been allowed to take up planting until several years after his peers. His attempts at matrimony, including a proposed union with the heiress Evelyn Byrd, had been thwarted by his father for monetary reasons. Both marriages of Daniel's older sister Fanny had failed because her father refused to turn over her dowry; perhaps from sheer disappointment, she had recently died.

After a lifetime of paternal domination and dutiful behavior, Daniel was reluctant to inform his father of an engagement he was sure to hate. If a Byrd wouldn't do, how could a Dandridge? Patsy must have been upset and offended as Daniel continued to keep their intended marriage a secret. He enlisted the aid of family friends James Power, an attorney, and John Blair, a leading colonial official, who convinced him that the longer he waited, the worse his father's reaction would be.

It's hard to see how it could have been much worse. John Custis flew into a blind rage and demanded that his son forget Patsy Dandridge. But Daniel was deeply in love and determined, for once, to have what, or rather whom, he wanted. Astonished at his dutiful son's defiance, Custis abused Daniel, Patsy, and her father up and down the town of Williamsburg in the most embarrassing way. As he thundered to friends, he had not spent a lifetime amassing a fortune to have it spent by any daughter of Jack Dandridge. Neither Patsy Dandridge's pedigree nor her wealth matched the Custises', and the old colonel meant to force his disobedient son to break off the engagement.

A controlling temperament wasn't the only reason for John Custis's opposition to this marriage. His antagonism was also rooted in two generations of unhappy family life. His mother had died when he was a child, his father remarried, and he had spent his teens studying in London, far from family and friends. When he returned to Virginia, he set up a bachelor household. In his late twenties, he fell

madly in love with a beautiful heiress, Frances Parke. In his infatuation, he penned passionate letters to "Fidelia," following the preva-
lent style for classical pseudonyms. His sweetheart's family life
made his own look cozy.

Both rich and rakish, her father, Daniel Parke, had married Jane
Ludwell of Green Spring plantation when they were in their teens;
within a few years, he left her and their two little daughters behind
while he followed his military star abroad. Despite Jane's pleas for
him to return home or at least to send money, Daniel had revisited
Virginia only once in fifteen years. That visit was far from a success,
since he brought along a mistress masquerading as his cousin and a
bastard son, whom he left behind with the long-suffering Jane. As
governor of the island colony of Antigua, he was murdered by riot-
ing local planters because of his policies, licentiousness, or both.
Parke was very wealthy, but the complications caused by the recognition of an illegitimate daughter in his will would trouble his descendants for years to come.

John Custis and his Fidelia married in 1705, but their chances
of happiness were effectively nil. Both were astonishingly bad-
tempered and determined to rule the roost. Soon their violent private and public altercations were the subject of common gossip
throughout the colony. Pity the poor children brought up in such a
terrible household: no doubt Daniel and his sister came in for their
share of parental rage and verbal abuse.

Stories about the Custises' relationship are legion, the details
perhaps apocryphal, but their unhappiness real. At one point, it is
said that they refused to speak to each other for months (probably
an improvement over their endless quarrels), sending messages
through the butler. Or that while driving together in a gig and ar-
guing furiously, John turned the team toward the shore of Chesapeake Bay and drove out into the water. Fanny demanded to know
where he was going, and her angry husband replied, "To hell,
Madam." She is said to have responded, "Drive on, Sir." They created their own little hell on earth.

Ultimately, the turmoil reached such a pitch in 1714 that the warring Custises signed a legal contract, mutually agreeing not to call each other "vile names or give . . . any ill language." Within months after signing this sad document, Fanny died of smallpox at the age of twenty-eight, leaving behind a five-year-old daughter and three-year-old son. Custis never remarried, devoting himself to raising rare plants in his Williamsburg garden and making his children miserable—all to avoid any more mistakes in the name of love.

Increasingly frustrated by his son's determination to marry Patsy, John Custis threatened Daniel with disinheritance in 1748. He swore that he would leave all his unentailed estate to Jack, his mixed-race child by "young Alice," one of his slaves. This little boy, who was about ten years old and recently freed, was one of the very few people the irascible old man cared about. But to his father's surprise, Daniel stood firm.

John Custis's confidants during this emotional period were Anne and Matthew Moody, tavern keepers near the Queen's Creek ferry outside Williamsburg. Almost every day, Custis rode out to his plantation and stopped at the Moodys'. They were the audience for his violent outbursts, benefiting as he began giving them pieces of valuable Custis family silver and furniture. When they demurred (according to their own account), Custis threatened to throw the silver out into the road rather than allow that Dandridge girl to enjoy it.

Through these nerve-racking months, there is no doubt that Patsy helped strengthen Daniel's resolution. Without her fortitude, he might well have let this chance for happiness drift away like all the others. Neither Daniel's arguments nor the support of Power and Blair seemed to be making any headway with his father.

Never one to wait around helplessly, Patsy somehow contrived to talk with the crusty old tyrant herself. Just how she managed it, we don't know. Like many bullies, Custis was impressed by strength of character: he actually found the spunky little lady engaging. It is tempting to imagine the scene in which the petite young woman, by now eighteen, reasoned with the bewigged seventy-year-old colonel.

Soon afterward, when James Power visited Custis's home, a brick house (two rooms down and two up, separated by passageways) in the middle of a very large garden on Francis Street, he found the old man in a calmer frame of mind. After all, the Dandridges were socially acceptable planters, not riffraff, and the size of the Parke/Custis fortune made a large dowry unnecessary. Seized by a bright idea, Power handed over a little horse and bridle he had just bought for his own son to Jack, pretending that they were a gift to the boy from Daniel. In 1749, for one of the few times in his long life, John Custis changed his mind. He consented to his son's marriage to the woman who had the nerve to stand up to him.

Power immediately wrote to Daniel Custis out in New Kent County: "This comes at last to bring you the news that I believe will be most agreeable to you of any you have heard—that you may not be long in suspense I shall tell you at once—I am empowered by your father to let you know that he heartily and willingly consents to your marriage with Miss Dandridge—that he has so good a character of her, that he had rather you should have her than any lady in Virginia—nay, if possible, he is as much enamored with her character as you are with her person, and this is owing chiefly to a prudent speech of her own. Hurry down immediately for fear he should change the strong inclination he has to your marrying directly."

John Custis made a will in Daniel's favor, making generous provision for little Jack, and died in November 1749 before he could change his mind again. Patsy and Daniel postponed their wedding for a few months of respectful mourning, meanwhile winding up the elder Custis's tangled bequests.

On May 15, 1750, when Patsy was a couple of weeks shy of her nineteenth birthday, she married Daniel Custis at home in the parlor at Chestnut Grove. Weddings in colonial Virginia were very different from the traditions that would later develop in nineteenth- and twentieth-century America. Everyone simply gathered in the parlor and hall without any sort of procession. Brides wore their brightest-colored and most beautiful silk gowns. The very idea of their friends dressing in matching gowns or the groom in mournful black would have sent them into fits of laughter. The wedding party and guests, men as well as women, were like a rich, silken flower garden in the vibrant colors and combinations that suited their fancies.

Almost every wedding was celebrated at the bride's home. Churches stood by themselves out in the country with no place nearby for the festivities to follow. Although the Church of England required that weddings take place in the morning, most Virginia marriages took place in the afternoon or evening, a local adaptation to allow their many guests time to travel several miles by horseback, wagon, or coach. The ceremony was followed by dinner and dancing. At some point, the newlyweds would slip off to the room reserved for them, but the rest of the guests would continue to frolic long into the night.

The next morning, the bride and groom endured a good deal of covert observation, giggling, and sly nudges; in letters to their friends, guests often commented on whether or not the lady looked happy after her (presumably) first sexual experience. The festivities might continue for several days, with walks, games, card playing, flirting, eating, drinking, and yet more dancing. Like most plantation houses in 1750, Chestnut Grove was rather small. At house parties and weddings, women slept four or five to a bed, with the overflow occupying trundle beds or pallets. Men dropped off wherever they could—on chairs, cots in the hall, rugs, haystacks in the stable. But Virginians never minded a crowd as long as the entertainment was lively.

After a week or so, the newlyweds usually moved directly into their own homes. A honeymoon trip was unknown in the colonies. Where would they have gone if they had thought of such a thing? Hotels were nonexistent, and taverns were rough and dirty at best, places of drunken masculine bonhomie, with beds often shared with strangers as well as bedbugs and fleas. Home was really the only place where they could spend time together, fully enjoying their new closeness. At White House, the Custis plantation, Patsy and Daniel settled into the home where they would live throughout their marriage. It was only four miles from Chestnut Grove, but light-years away in the wealth and power it embodied.

CHAPTER THREE

Young Mrs. Custis

It was quite a Cinderella story: Patsy Dandridge was now a wealthy woman with social position. Daniel Custis had inherited nearly eighteen thousand acres of prime farmland, houses in Williamsburg and Jamestown, nearly three hundred slaves, and several thousand pounds in English treasury notes and cash. But Patsy brought her husband an equally valuable gift—happiness. Motherless since he was a toddler, frustrated and humiliated by his father throughout his life, he was almost thirty-nine when he married and at last found an emotional haven.

Reaching from beyond the grave, John Custis had left a provision in his will for a tombstone inscription as wounding as anything he had shouted in a lifetime of rages:

Under this Marble Tomb lies the Body
of the HONORABLE JOHN CUSTIS Esq.
of the City of Wiliamsburgh and Parish of Bruton
Formerly of Hungars Parish on the Eastern Shore of Virginia and
County of Northampton the Place of His Nativity
Aged 71 Years and yet liv'd but Seven Years
Which was the space of time He kept
A Bachelors house at Arlington.
This inscription carved at his express orders.

This final barb thrown at his hated wife, thirty-five years dead and presumably beyond insults, must have been enormously hurtful to his son. The many years Daniel had lived with his domineering father and the succeeding years at his beck and call were dismissed contemptuously—his very existence of no importance in John Custis's bitter summation of his life.

No wonder Daniel reveled in living with a charming young woman who raised emotional support to an art form. Throughout their marriage, they remained at White House, a two-story frame house downriver from Chestnut Grove. Though no larger than the Dandridges' home, it was distinguished by the beauty of its setting. The house sat on a slight rise, its broad lawn sloping down to the wide, curving Pamunkey, opening to a serene view of golden marsh grasses and meadows on the far side of the river. There Daniel could enjoy the loving smile, kind eyes, and soft voice of his new wife. It must have seemed like heaven.

Virginia hospitality was famous throughout Britain's colonies, and Patsy was a born hostess who soon turned her hand to making a bachelor establishment fashionable. Like all the great planters, Daniel ordered luxuries, as well as manufactured items, from the London, Liverpool, Bristol, and Glasgow merchants who sold his crops. In 1749, he began keeping a memorandum book of the orders he sent annually via the tobacco ships. In it, he scrawled lists of goods—everything from china, satin suits, and nutmeg to scythes, grinding stones, and axes. Along with household inventories, this book with its faded ink, deeply water-stained by some long-ago soaking, is the key to picturing Patsy and Daniel's White House.

As the Custises were setting up housekeeping, the plantation elite was swept up in an enormous consumer revolution, a spiraling demand for European luxury goods in the colonies. Their forebears, even the richest, had lived simply; they had been too busy fighting for land and wealth to waste much time on display, and luxuries had been difficult to come by. By the 1750s, however, the leading planters were well established financially, and their trading system had matured. Most of them had done business for years with their own favored British merchants, who brokered their tobacco crops every year and were more than happy to seek out expensive items for their clients, permanently securing their business and encouraging them to build up the large debts that would be their downfall. Daniel Custis was exceptional in staying out of debt even as he enjoyed the new amenities of planter life.

The fluid social situation of the early colony had also hardened. Virginia's class system was now more rigid and clearly demarcated—from large planters, small planters, and merchants, through craftsmen, the poor, and indentured servants, down to African slaves, the fastest-growing and least privileged group in all Virginia. Through aping British gentry fashions (even if they were a few years out of date), the elite competed socially with their peers and set themselves still further apart from the common sort.

At the center of planter hospitality was a separate dining room. Just a generation earlier, a room dedicated solely to eating meals was all but unknown in the colonies. Then, tables (as well as the best bedstead in many houses) had been placed in the parlor or the other common room, called the hall. During meals, the table was set with a motley array of pewter, pottery, and even wood; common drinking vessels were passed around; knives were the usual eating utensil, and prudent visitors carried their own in case there weren't enough to go around; spoons were often shared as everyone dipped into the serving vessels; and the few chairs in the household were supplemented by stools, benches, and chests. And those were the planter households!

The new fashion called for individual chairs, plates, flatware, glasses, and napkins for each diner. Chairs were expensive, highly prized status symbols. Besides those at the table, extras were proudly lined up around the dining room walls and down both sides of the entry hall, their stately march a testament to their owners' opulence and good taste. Planters bought an abundance of all the necessary items to provide for their dinner guests, but matched sets of everything were most desirable—a concept that would have dumbfounded previous generations of Virginians. Symmetry and balance ruled eighteenth-century taste.

Twelve yards of crimson damask arrived from London to cover the seats of the mahogany dining room chairs at White House. Not only was damask an elegant fabric, but crimson was a much more prized and expensive hue than common red. Half a dozen large damask tablecloths and a dozen napkins to match soon followed. The table could be laid with their set of gilt china or stylish blue-and-white Chinese export dinnerware. A matching tea set in the same patterned porcelain appeared at the new ritual of afternoon tea.

Silver—its reflective surface greatly admired in those dimly lit households—gradually replaced utilitarian pewter, brass, tin, and steel. Most novel of all, forks were now included in table settings along with knives and spoons. Forks were the first true dining revolution since the Middle Ages, in use so far only among the upper classes. Daniel inherited many silver display pieces that had belonged to the Parke family, but the Custis silver remained firmly in the hands of his father's tavern-keeping friends, despite a suit to reclaim his heirlooms. At last, giving up, he ordered a variety of serving silver, all engraved with the Custis crest. As fashion dictated, White House silver included coffee- and teapots, salvers, serving stands, candlesticks, pepper box, and sugar tongs, as well as flatware.

Never extreme in her dress, Patsy liked elegant fabrics, bright colors, and fashionable, but not exaggerated, styles. Daniel had to learn her taste; early in their marriage, he started to order green satin for a ball gown, only to scratch it out and amend it to her favorite blue. Patsy took pleasure in the luxury of buying a dozen pairs of kid gloves at a time or an ivory fan in the latest London fashion. Every year when the tobacco ships arrived, she unpacked her purchases from their chests—silk stockings for her slim legs, a black satin hat, white or flowered calico for a summer dress, purple and crimson pumps, a quilted crimson petticoat against winter's drafts, a scarlet riding habit.

With the happiness of a new husband, Daniel enjoyed lavishing gifts on Patsy. Probably the most delightful—and extravagant—of his gifts was a "chair," lined with smooth blue English cloth, "for Mrs. Custis's use." We can almost hear the pride with which he first wrote that phrase. A chair was a small one-person carriage with out-size wheels, whose high-perched seat resembled, or sometimes actually was, a chair. It took a good driver to manage this sporty vehicle and the well-bred horse that drew it. Patsy could tool around the neighborhood in her new chair or visit Williamsburg in a London-built coach drawn by a team of six. There was also a schooner tied at their dock, though she was less than enthusiastic about traveling by water.

But all these pleasures had to be paid for. A landowner who ignored his fields for endless parties or, worse yet, gambling would soon find himself bankrupt. Daniel applied himself closely to business, managing his home plantation and attending closely to overseers' reports from his other properties. He also kept careful watch on his English investments and lent money to other planters, land rich and cash poor, to be repaid when their crops were sold.

In the starkest economic terms, all planters' wealth rested on the backs of enslaved Africans. The flood of white indentured servants to the early colony—largely English, Irish, or Scots—had dwindled to a mere trickle by the 1750s. Africans had almost completely replaced them as plantation labor. Nearly a century before, Africans' ambiguous legal status had been decided: blacks in Virginia were no longer servants whose terms of indenture ended after a certain number of years, but slaves for life. Not only were they themselves permanent captives, but their descendants would inherit the status of their mothers.

The value of indentured servants lay in their labor and whatever special skills they possessed, limited by the number of years specified in their contracts. Their transportation and sale in the colonies was not hugely profitable for the sea captains who brought them on the outward voyage to America; the return voyage with holds packed with hogsheads of tobacco was the major source of income.

Because the African slave trade was built on the permanent possession of labor and the increase of generations, however, it became a source of massive international wealth in itself. European powers went to war more than once to control the profitable trade. In the colonies, slaves were a valuable commodity for merchants and an important portion of every planter's net worth, their humanity ignored.

Daniel had inherited nearly 300 enslaved blacks. More than 150 of them worked in the fields and residence at White House. On the Queen's Creek plantation outside Williamsburg, about 75 slaves toiled, with another 50 divided among three smaller quarters (as outlying plantations managed by overseers were known) in King William, Northampton, and Hanover counties. The field crews of men and women planted, hoed, weeded, suckered, picked, dried, and packed the tobacco that the colonial economy rested on. The men and an occasional woman plowed the fields; drove carts and transported hogsheads of tobacco; birthed and butchered live-stock; fished and hunted; dug ditches and repaired roads; framed, built, shingled, repaired, and painted plantation fences and build-ings. Other jobs shared out among women, old people, and the young were gathering and chopping the endless firewood needed for kitchen hearths and cold winters; gardening; feeding, tending, and herding livestock; cooking, cleaning, polishing, and generally tending to the planter family; and so on and on.

There is no indication that Daniel had any doubts about the jus-tice of unfree labor. Nor did Patsy, it would seem. Like most British colonists (there were slaves in every colony), she apparently believed that slavery and the slave trade were part of the natural order of things. Slave labor was the bedrock of plantation success, and her upbringing had taught her to prize that success. North or south, only a very few Americans, primarily Quakers, had just begun to question and speak out against human bondage.

Patsy always treated the slaves in her power well, speaking pleasantly, granting favors easily, allowing sick leave, and looking after the elderly. Not for her the excesses of Daniel's aunt Lucy Byrd, who viciously whipped the maids whenever she was feeling out of sorts. But Patsy also expected able-bodied slaves to know their places and work hard. To her, slacking or running away was a dereliction of duty and a danger to the proper social order.

With little experience overseeing servants, Patsy found herself at eighteen the mistress of a large household staff that eventually grew to twelve slaves. They included two men who waited at table, a cook and her assistant, a washer, ironer, spinner, two seamstresses, and a lady's maid; additional servants were brought in as the Custis children were born. Despite her youth, Patsy proved very efficient at creating an orderly household, just as her mother had trained her.

Prints and maps on the walls, brightly colored upholstery, highly polished furniture and silver, and two tall, silvery-looking glasses made the parlor and dining room attractive and welcoming. In the winter, the house would have been cozy with its rugs, curtains closed against drafts, and fireplaces crackling warmly. Night came on early, the signal for candles and lamps to be lit. Patsy would have sewed, read, or just chatted with her husband in their island of light in the black, black night of the country before they retired to bed, its drawn curtains creating a warm and private place.

In a Virginia summer, coolness was all. Rugs were rolled up and stored, upholstered furniture disappeared under smooth linen slip-covers, and windows and doors were left open to create refreshing cross-drafts. Mirrors and chandeliers were covered with gauzy cotton to keep them from being marked by the ever present flies. Summer or winter, keeping the house clean was a constant chore or, rather, series of chores, what with flies, spiders, mosquitoes, roaches, and their leavings; dust and pollen that drifted in the open windows; rats and mice (special wire traps were ordered from London); dirt, mud, and barnyard filth tracked into the house; and soot and ashes from smoky chimneys.

Breakfast, tea, and supper were rather small meals, usually including breads, cakes, and some combination of leftovers. But dinner was the meal where a housewife showed what she and her staff were made of. Dinner was served in midafternoon, about three o'clock, after the planter returned from riding over his fields and his wife had completed her domestic duties. Patsy and Daniel would have cleaned up, arranged their hair, and donned dressier clothes. At White House, dinner was served by two slave men-servants, Breechy and Mulatto Jack, outfitted in livery of dark cloth trimmed with silver lace and horn buttons, replaced a few years later by scarlet suits trimmed with mohair braid. The meal was a little theater piece.

Guests—often a number of guests—arrived unexpectedly or by invitation several days a week. In the early years of the colony, the amount of food at dinner had corresponded roughly to the number of people eating. Now fashion demanded a very large array of foods every day, arranged on the sideboard and table in formally balanced patterns. Two full courses with wine throughout—the tablecloth removed after each course—would include soup; several meats, fricassees, great meat pies, fowls, and fish; gravies and sauces; fresh and pickled vegetables; bread, rolls, biscuits, and butter; pies, cakes, jellies, creams, tarts, and fruit compotes. The meal would end with the polished wood of the table exposed as the servants offered sugared fruit, crackers, pieces of Gloucester or Cheshire cheese cut from eight- or ten-pound imported wheels, and nuts, accompanied by still more wine and toasts to old King George II, absent friends, all the ladies, and any number of variations on these popular themes.

Besides the abundant foodstuffs from garden, pasture, river, and woods, Patsy added imported delicacies to her cuisine. Fine wines (their favorites were the white Rhenish and Canary wines and red Port, all of them rather sweet), beer, green tea, capers, olives, almonds, spices, raisins, currants, sugar, and anchovies were ordered regularly from England. So too were six pounds each of brown and white sugar candy to satisfy her sweet tooth. Good manners didn't require that diners stuff themselves, but it must have been difficult to resist such profusion.

Patsy was soon pregnant. Pregnancy, especially the first, was an exciting and hopeful time, the happy news quickly imparted to friends and relatives in person or by letter. There was no nonsense about expectant mothers secluding themselves: as long as she felt well, Patsy would have continued her household duties, and she and Daniel would have attended social functions. Special pregnancy stays helped maintain her erect posture without interfering with her swollen belly.

Joyful as pregnancy was, it was also shadowed by fear for the life of the mother, especially for a woman as tiny as Patsy. Childbirth was one of the leading causes of death among colonial women. The danger was particularly grave for first-time mothers, who sometimes died in labor, after hours or even days of futilely attempting to bring forth a very large or breech baby. Even if the mothers survived, their first babies often died from the trauma of their births.

Birthing was women's work, the husband firmly but kindly excluded from their bedchamber. When her time came, Patsy would have "called her women together": the midwife, her mother, aunts, friends, and maids. The women clustered around the laboring woman, soothing and encouraging her, mopping her sweating forehead, holding her hands, providing cloths for her to clench in her teeth to stifle shrieks of pain. She would have remained partially upright during most of her labor, squatting on a low midwife's stool, sitting at the edge of a chair, standing from time to time, sitting on the lap of one of her helpers. What a relief for them all when a healthy baby finally dropped into the hands of the waiting midwife, who cleaned off the infant, cut the umbilical cord with a sharp knife, and made sure the child was wrapped warmly. On November 19, 1751, Patsy gave birth to a boy they named Daniel Parke Custis for his father.

After giving birth, she probably spent a month or so in "confinement," resting in bed from her ordeal, regaining her health, and nursing little Daniel. Most elite women were aware of the importance of breast-feeding to their infants' health and often found a great deal of joy in "so sweet an office." Only if Patsy had been very ill or had insufficient milk would she have called on a wet nurse from among the slaves. She probably continued nursing her son until he was a year or two old; weaning marked a major passage in a child's life, as well as a mother's, since she was likely to become pregnant again soon after taking the child from the breast. As the lady of the house, Patsy could revel in her baby in ways that poorer women could not. She could enjoy a clean, sweet-smelling infant, his clothes washed and diapers changed, because a slave nursemaid was brought into the house with Daniel's birth and tended to his daily needs before handing him back to his mama.

Little Daniel was his father's delight, referred to in the yearly orders to London as "my son," emphasis no doubt on the possessive. We can picture horseback rides with his father or carriage rides with his mother, the minute gentleman attired in his baby dresses topped with sailor jackets and a jaunty feathered hat ordered from London, uncut curls blowing in the breeze.

A month before Daniel's birth, another young boy had died in Williamsburg. John Custis had freed Jack, his "favourite boy," as townspeople referred to his son, bought a small property for him, and entrusted several slave boys and money to the care of a nephew who was to turn them over to Jack when he came of age. John Custis's will instructed Daniel to house the boy, but it seems clear that Jack remained in town, most likely living with the Moodys at their tavern. Anne was fond enough of him to keep a portrait of "black Jack," which later descended to her son. Wherever he lived, Jack fell ill with a pain in the back of his neck (perhaps meningitis) and died within twenty-four hours, shortly after midnight on October 9. His property, including the young slaves, remained firmly in the hands of his trustee. The records make no further mention of Jack's mother.

Although he wasn't a burgess, Daniel Custis would have joined the other leading planters and their families in the social seasons of Williamsburg. He and Patsy probably stayed at his father's convenient house, its gardens still lovely with Dutch tulips, pink dogwoods, horse chestnuts, and yews. Its four acres included a stable for the Custis coach and a kitchen, with room in the outbuildings for the servants they brought to town with them.

In April and December, Market Square was taken over by town fairs, with their stalls hawking every sort of merchandise, produce, and livestock. More entertaining were the "games and contests, cockfights, puppet shows, dancing and fiddling, and country activities" that attracted crowds from throughout the Tidewater. Planters strode through the crowds, arrayed in silks and satins, fine as fighting cocks with their ruffles and lace, lords of their little universe. Horse racing, card playing, dicing, and the heavy gambling that went with them added spice to it all.

Then there were the balls at the Governor's Palace, the black velvet night of Williamsburg illuminated by candles in the windows of
every house. As the hundred or more guests converged, the palace
glowed with light, brighter than any other building in the colony.
Its public rooms—the grand hall adorned with flags and bayonet-
tipped muskets, the parlor and dining room on the first floor, the
formal reception room on the second floor, and the broad stairway—
were lit by uncountable candles in lavish chandeliers and outsize
globe lamps. Patsy would have joined the other women, probably in
the parlor, shaking out their skirts, rearranging powdered tresses,
and changing their street shoes for silk slippers, so delicate that they
might be danced to shreds by the end of the evening.

A new lieutenant governor took office in November 1751, usher-
ing in a fresh social and political era in Virginia. Robert Dinwiddie
was an experienced colonial administrator, a stout middle-aged
Scot who wore the plainest of white bobbed wigs; his family came
with him—a much younger wife, Rebecca, and two little girls.
Daniel waited nearly a month after his son's birth to ride into the
capital and pay his formal respects.

The public celebration of coronations, battle victories, peace
treaties, and royal births and birthdays was an essential element
of imperial policy; British colonies around the world joined the
motherland in reiterating their common heritage and loyalty
through these grand events. Dinwiddie followed that policy with
verve. At Williamsburg there were fireworks and general illumina-
tions, militia parades with drums rat-a-tatting and fifes shrilling,
cannons booming and volleys of muskets cracking, crowds of ordinary folk in the Market Square gathered around a great bonfire and
drinking bumbo (rum punch) from the large barrels provided for
them, and fashionable assemblies and balls for the gentry at the
Governor's Palace.

Dinwiddie unveiled the new ballroom wing at the palace with the
celebration of the king's birthday in November 1752. This elegant
addition at the rear of the palace included a grand rectangular ball-

room and an adjoining supper room. Tables for cards, dice, and backgammon were set up in the other rooms of the palace. The new formal gardens adjoining the ballroom—eight diamond-shaped boxwood parterres planted with periwinkles and English ivy, towering topiary cylinders of clipped holly, trained beech arbors, and a maze—brought an English country estate to mind. Even though she was five months pregnant with their second baby, Patsy and Daniel probably joined the other revelers at that celebration; no fashionable planter could bear to miss it.

Along with the governor's ballroom, the rebuilding of the Capitol was completed the following year, providing another large assembly room. Theater too was a major source of entertainment. Williamsburg had been a theater town on and off for more than thirty years, but the new playhouse, completed in 1752 on Eastern Street behind the Capitol, housed two successive companies of professional English actors, who played to packed houses. These troupes arrived with copies of the most popular plays of the London stage (scripts were often hard to come by in America), chests full of costumes, and brightly painted sets. Colonial audiences adored spectacle, and theater managers obliged them by "improving" the old standards with processions, dances, songs, crowd scenes, and duels with naked swords. So realistic were the sword fights that the empress of the Cherokees, in town for the inauguration of the governor's ballroom, almost sent her guards onstage to prevent a killing during a performance of *Othello*.

An evening at the theater—seven shillings, five pence for a box seat—was well worth the cost. To open, the troupe's lead actor delivered a poetical prologue filled with local references. Then the actors performed a well-known crowd-pleaser. During the times that Patsy and Daniel were in Williamsburg, such dramas as *Richard III* and the broadly comical *Lying Valet* were presented. This would be followed by an interval with instrumental music and songs, a jig or other solo dance, and perhaps a comic turn. The evening ended with an afterpiece, usually a short, raucous farce.

Back at White House in April 1753, Patsy gave birth to Frances Parke Custis, named for both her grandmothers. The middle name

Parke was given to all the Custis children as a condition of inheritance under Daniel Parke's will. Ten months later, little Daniel fell ill with a fever. The warm, muggy air, sluggish streams, and swamps of the Tidewater bred swarms of mosquitoes, giving rise to numerous fevers. Everyone contracted malaria, but most people survived, suffering recurrent episodes of chills, sweating, and fever, known as the ague, throughout their lives. Daniel, however, died shortly after his second birthday.

Death was a sadly commonplace family affair, and the little boy probably died in his mother's arms. Patsy herself may have laid out the body of her son, washing and dressing him in a white linen shroud. Since corpses were not embalmed, the carpenter would have worked through the night to make the small hexagonal coffin, the common shape at the time. The family burial ground at Queen's Creek, where the elder Daniel's mother and sister lay, was a few miles from White House. So the family would have driven over to meet the minister and other mourners, all bundled up against February's chill. Ropes creaked as slaves lowered the coffin into the cold ground; the parents would have thrown the first handfuls of earth and watched as their eldest child was buried. The next order to London included a "Tomb for my son," no marble being available in Virginia.

No doubt it was during this afflicting period that Patsy Custis developed her lifelong anxiety about her children, which went hand in hand with her intense love for them. She delighted in their company but was always fearful of illness, accident, or death. Losing her firstborn son—she always favored boys—forever made her an overanxious mama.

At about the time of little Daniel's funeral, Patsy became pregnant again, and John Parke Custis (called Jacky), named for both his grandfathers, was born in the fall of 1754. In the summer of 1754, while Patsy was pregnant, the colony of Virginia briefly took center stage in world affairs, leading the British Empire into yet another war against France. The rivalry for international power between Great Britain and France had been played out for the past half century in a series of wars that raged throughout Europe and around the world. Their respective colonies were the bargaining chips when peace treaties, usually short-lived, were made. This time, the competition began over the rich Ohio Valley, whose lands were marked out for conquest by both British and French colonists. The region lay to the west of the British colonies of Virginia and Pennsylvania and to the south of French Canada—all bent on expansion. It was a question of who could get there first, seize the area, establish forts, make Indian allies, and bring in their own settlers.

One of Governor Dinwiddie's instructions was to block the French and encourage British settlement in the Ohio area. To affirm British claims, he sent out two small expeditions led by a little-known young officer named George Washington. These skirmishes against the French included the killing of a French officer who may or may not have been a diplomatic envoy, each nation affirming the opposite version. The incident set off a new war, which quickly spread to Europe and other European colonies. Called the Seven Years' War in European history, it was known by Americans as the French and Indian War, signaling their developing sense of national priority.

The French were always better at Indian diplomacy than the British, and they soon sent their Indian allies to attack Virginia's frontier settlements—marauding, sacking, burning, killing, carrying off prisoners. British refugees poured back over the Blue Ridge Mountains with tales of terror. New Kent County was far from the western frontier and danger, but the entire colony was in an uproar, and war became the center of everyone's attention.

Great Britain responded in 1755 by sending a force of British regulars under the command of General Edward Braddock. In one of the classic tales of American history, Braddock led his army out to meet the French again, only to be ambushed. This costly loss with its heavy casualties, including his own death, led colonists to discount unduly the effectiveness of the British army in American warfare. Braddock's aide George Washington led the surviving soldiers to safety. All of a sudden, at twenty-three, Lieutenant Colonel Washington was a somebody in Virginia.

The Custises no doubt discussed the colony's rising military star.

If they knew him personally, it was not very well. A younger son of a middling planter near Fredericksburg, he had never had the money or the occasion to spend much time in Williamsburg, where they would have met. They did have an interesting connection through Washington's half-brother, Lawrence, and Patsy's uncle William Dandridge, who had served together as officers in the ill-fated British attack on Spanish colonial Cartagena fifteen years earlier. And, of course, there were the gentry intermarriages of acquaintances and cousins of cousins that kept everybody informed about who was who.

Political clamor and military alarms aside, life in the Tidewater continued to revolve around tobacco growing and family matters. In 1756, Patsy gave birth to another daughter, Martha Parke Custis, who had the Parke family's dark good looks—large brown eyes and curly black hair. At about the same time, Patsy's mother, Fanny Dandridge, age forty-six, produced her last child, a change-of-life daughter. That August, proud papa John Dandridge went to Fredericksburg, where he dropped dead of apoplexy, as a stroke was then called. The weather was so scorchingly hot that his body had to be buried immediately in the town cemetery; there was no time to take him home or to summon the family before the body decomposed. His loss was felt deeply by both families along the Pamunkey. Patsy's oldest surviving brother (John Jr. had died as a teenager), twenty-two-year-old William, took over the management of Chestnut Grove for his mother and younger siblings.

Daniel's orders to Britain now included items for the Dandridges, such as silk pumps of a color appropriate "for Second Mourning," probably either purple or gray, for his mother-in-law. He proudly ordered for the three fine Custis children as well—fashionable hats, leather and silk shoes, a quilted cap, stays, an expensive "Dolly," necklaces, kid gloves, ten shillings' worth of toys, ribbons for the girls, and a saddle and bridle for Jacky. Running about in her pretty red shoes, Fanny was old enough to begin learning her letters, so he sent for a slate and pencils. Alas for such plans. In April 1757, Fanny died just before her fourth birthday, joining her brother in the family plot at Queen's Creek.

Death was too common a visitor in colonial homes to allow grieving parents to withdraw from their daily lives. Patsy and Daniel had to continue about their regular routines, attend to the needs of their surviving children, and receive guests at White House. Within the three months following Fanny's death, a traveling portraitist, an Englishman named John Wollaston, came to stay with the Custis family. In the eight years since his arrival in America, he had made the rounds of New York, Maryland, and Virginia, painting more than three hundred three-quarter-length portraits of everyone who was anyone in the colonies. Reflecting the tastes of his elite clientele, he bestowed special attention on the "rich fabrics touched with subtle highlights" of their finest outfits.

At White House, Jacky and little Patsy, two and a half and one, posed together in all their adult finery, he with a pet redbird perched on his wrist, she with a rose in her lap, pearls and ribbon in her wispy baby hair, the tip of a red shoe peeking out from beneath her gown. Wollaston painted separate portraits of Daniel and Patsy attired in their best, she in a silver lace and beribboned blue gown with a yellow petticoat and stomacher, her dark hair combed straight back and entwined with pearls, picking a white blossom edged with pink from a flowering bush. The price for all three works was a costly fifty-six pistoles, a Spanish gold coin that circulated in the British colonies; Wollaston's high prices reflected his popularity among the gentry.

The Custises' return to normality was brief. Three months after Fanny's death, both Jacky and the robust Daniel fell ill on July 4. Patsy immediately sent to Williamsburg for medicine, and when there was no improvement the next day, Dr. James Carter, one of the capital's leading physicians, came out to attend the patients. For three days, he administered a course of medications that suggests some sort of virulent throat infection—scarlet fever, a streptococcal infection, diphtheria, quinsy. Rather than dosing his terribly ill patients with the usual purges and emetics that formed colonial doctors' stock practice, Carter concocted medicinal pastes with honey to be smeared on their gums and tongues. These pastes were absorbed slowly rather than swallowed straight down. If Daniel and

Jacky were suffering from severely ulcerated or swollen throats, they would have been unable to swallow.

Jacky survived, but Daniel died on July 8, after only seven years of married happiness. It was a terrible way to die, slowly suffocating as his throat closed up, and Patsy must have been with her husband and son throughout those awful days. The day of Daniel's death, she sent to the carpenter to build a black walnut coffin for his speedy interment. Oddly enough, in a time of hovering illness and swift death, many people waited until they were on their deathbeds to make a will and frequently left it too late. Daniel Custis was one of that number, dying intestate and leaving the inheritance of his family to fall under the rules of English common law. He was buried alongside his mother and his two children at Queen's Creek.

Patsy had little time to express her grief, other than in action. A local seamstress was called in to alter a gown and make mourning dresses for her; a tailor came to make black mourning suits for Jacky and the male house servants. In Daniel's account book, the date of his last memorandum was 1757, shortly before he died. Turning the page, the reader suddenly sees Patsy Custis's neat and well-formed handwriting as she took up her husband's responsibilities two weeks after his death, listing the items the plantations needed from England. She plunged straight in, ordering two seines, or large nets, for shad fishing in the Pamunkey. Her description of the desired nets is carefully detailed—thirty-five fathoms long and twenty feet deep, made of "the best three Thread laid Twine," well fixed with leads and corks, "the slack Lines made of the best Hemp and full large," along with spare slack lines. She went on to other mundane items such as starch, cotton for the slaves' clothing, pins, thread, and castile soap.

Then she turned to "One handsome Tombstone of the best durable Marble to cost about £100 [very expensive]—with the following Inscription and the Arms sent in a Piece of Paper on it, to wit 'Here Lies the Body of Daniel Parke Custis Esquire who was born the 15th Day of Oct. of 1711 & departed this Life the 8th Day of July 1757. Aged 45 Years.'" In her letter to Robert Cary, her English factor, she included two locks of hair for the jeweler, probably in a separate sealed piece of paper. She ordered two gold mourning rings in honor of Daniel and little Fanny, their tresses to be covered by clear crystal.

So, in a mixture of prudence and bravely borne grief, Martha Dandridge Custis marked the end of her first happy marriage. With two children to watch over, she had a future to plan and a long life ahead.

CHAPTER FOUR

The Widow Custis and Colonel Washington

*U*nlike most widows in colonial Virginia, Patsy Custis was rich and independent, free to make any decision she pleased about her own future. In contrast, slave women were forced to keep working despite their sorrow; poor women might be reduced to beggary, their children taken away and apprenticed; the middling sort often ran their husband's businesses, taverns, or farms if they had sons old enough to work the fields; planters' widows had money and social position, but their property was sometimes controlled by male trustees set in place by the wills of distrustful husbands.

Free of such galling conditions, Patsy controlled an immense property. English common law ensured the dower rights of the widows of property-owning men; such women automatically inherited one-third of their husbands' estates for their own lifetimes, and Patsy had no trustees to interfere with her decisions. By August 1757, she was hard at work ensuring her own and her children's financial well-being. Ordinarily, an inexperienced young widow might look to her father, brothers, or brothers-in-law for assistance. But her father was a year dead, her husband an only son, and her brothers even less experienced than she.

Her youngest brother, Bat, an attorney of twenty, acted as her go-between in early August, seeking general advice from two of the colony's leading attorneys. They approved of her intention to administer the estate herself, offering practical advice on maritime insurance for tobacco shipments and the suggestion that she hire a trustworthy steward.

Patsy followed through with the insurance but acted as her own steward, retaining the overseers already at work. Throughout August and September, she settled accounts, arranged for a power of attorney, and informed the Custises' British factors of Daniel's death. The tone of her letters is strikingly businesslike. These Londoners, Liverpudlians, and Glaswegians were businessmen, after all, not friends. She notified them all that she would be managing the Custis estate, requesting an up-to-date account from each of them. Expressing her hope that their association would be "agreeable and lasting to us both," she made it clear that she expected them to sell her tobacco at a good price. The implication that she would otherwise take her custom elsewhere couldn't be missed. Patsy understood financial power and didn't hesitate to use it.

She continued Daniel's practice of lending money at interest to cash-strapped planters. With more than £1,000 of ready money in the house at his death (a tidy sum, worth about $15,000 to $20,000 today), she did a considerable amount of business, keeping careful records of all her loans. When the accounts of a Williamsburg attorney for a long-standing Custis estate suit failed to satisfy her, she had the horses hitched up and drove into town to confront him face-to-face—to his shrill and voluble indignation.

Luckily, Patsy had plenty of common sense. As the oldest child of a large family and the wife of a wealthy planter, she was accustomed to command in household and domestic matters. But she had no enduring desire to inhabit the rough world of men's affairs with its wheeling and dealing, anxiety over crops and prices, and management of a large labor force, both enslaved and free.

Besides, in colonial society it was considered wildly eccentric for a widow or widower to remain unmarried, and she could expect to turn over her responsibilities to a second husband sooner rather than later. Her late unmourned father-in-law was a rare exception: two or three marriages in a lifetime were the norm among Virginians at every social level. A decent period of mourning was expected, but the timetable could be startlingly short to modern eyes. A perfectly respectable courtship might begin within a month or two after a spouse's death and the marriage take place a couple of months later.

Patsy's own tastes, so decidedly domestic and sociable, made her eager to remarry. Still in her twenties, she could expect to bear more children. Two children were not nearly enough for her large heart. Mrs. Custis would not remain unmarried for lack of suitors. Control of such a large estate was temptation enough, but the prospect was further sweetened by her beauty and good humor. Baldly put, she was the colony's ultimate marital prize, and she could expect single men to start calling soon after Daniel's death.

Among the Virginia gentry, everyone knew everybody else's business, and gossip was the universal spectator sport. All Williamsburg, and therefore all the important planters in the colony, knew to the last shilling how much money Patsy Custis controlled. They knew, too, that she had no bothersome trustees to interfere with her remarriage. No doubt several gentlemen thought about wooing her themselves or urged their kinsmen to make the attempt: a wealthy marriage was advantageous to an entire family.

As an intelligent woman, though, she had to be careful in her choice of a second husband. At this time, she was a *feme sole* in English common law, free to make her own decisions about her property. Wealthy widows were the most economically and personally independent of all American women. As soon as she married, however, she would become a *feme covert,* her legal status, wealth, children, and place and manner of life controlled by her husband. Colonial husbands enjoyed almost unlimited legal power over their wives, even in the event of a separation. Overbearing or spendthrift stepfathers were unfortunately commonplace, a danger to be avoided by a woman with beloved children and their wealth to protect. Her own mother's unhappy girlhood experience with stepparents no doubt came to mind. In March 1758, eight months after her husband's death, two suitors began actively pursuing Patsy—Charles Carter and George Washington.

Like Daniel Custis, Charles Carter was a member of the ruling plantation elite, a son of the immensely wealthy Robert "King" Carter. Charles had been educated in England before taking over several thousand acres of prime tobacco land, as well as pursuing successful mercantile ventures. He was one of the colony's political leaders: he had represented King George County in the House of Burgesses since 1735 and routinely chaired important committees. Financially and socially secure, he would be a careful steward of the Custis family interests. At nearly fifty, he was still a fine figure of a man who dressed in the latest fashions and sported a modishly curled wig. His second wife had died just six months earlier, and he sorely missed the pleasures of marriage.

Charles Carter's elegant house on the Rappahannock was just ten years old; it was large and imposing, two stories with a seven-bay front on the river. Built of dark brick boldly set off by the contrasting light stone used for quoins and door and window surrounds, Cleve was a tribute to the sophistication and success of the Carter family.

Best of all, Charles was truly in love with Patsy. In a gossipy letter, one of his friends wrote that "C. C. is very gay" since "he has attacked the widow Custis." Carter himself wrote to his brother that "Mrs. C__s is now the object of my wish." The enforced celibacy of a widower made him miserable, and he eagerly anticipated "taking a Belov'd Wife." He was frank about his emotional and sexual desires: "I am trying to restore to myself all the happyness I once could boast in the Arms of my dear Belovd Partner." He praised Patsy's beauty, amiable mind, and "uncommon sweetness of Temper" and hoped to "raise a Flame in her breast." Charles's suit suffered from two drawbacks. He was twenty-three years older than she, old enough to be her father, and she had already been married to an older man. He also had a round dozen children, ten of them living at home, ranging in age from two to twenty. There were two older married daughters, the eldest nearly as old as Patsy, and a grandson. Although Patsy wanted more children, she found the size of his family daunting, warning Charles frankly that she doubted her ability to do them all justice as a stepmother.

Her other suitor appeared on the scene at about the same time. A bachelor eight months younger than Patsy, he was far less socially and financially eligible than Charles Carter, but he had youth and powerful physical magnetism on his side. As the son of a second-tier planter who had died when he was a boy, George Washington had received a somewhat sketchy education. At sixteen, he had begun to make his way in the world as a surveyor before becoming a colonial military officer. His original inheritance consisted principally of a 260-acre farm on the Rappahannock and ten slaves, but his masterful mother was ensconced there with no plans to vacate, claiming all the land's profit for her own upkeep. During the five years he had served in the military, George gained increasing respect and social status in Virginia, as well as a measure of fame throughout British America, but his financial circumstances were far from secure.

In 1752, however, his older half-brother, Lawrence, died, leaving him secondary heir to Mount Vernon, a Washington family plantation of some 2,200 acres on the Potomac. With the death two years later of Lawrence's daughter, the place would eventually come to George, but it remained in the possession of Lawrence's widow throughout her lifetime. Remarried and living in Westmoreland County, she and her second husband agreed to lease Mount Vernon to him.

Since then, they had continued this arrangement as George tried to balance his military career and agriculture, leaving Mount Vernon in the care of his younger brother Jack during the growing season while he took the field with the Virginia Regiment across the Blue Ridge Mountains. The estate had not flourished, and he was growing increasingly frustrated with his divided interests. When the British government refused to grant his Virginia commission regular army rank, thus relegating him permanently to second-rate military status, the life of a full-time planter took on a new appeal.

Suffering from bouts of the bloody flux (dysentery), he had gone to Mount Vernon to recuperate. Lonely and depressed in his sparsely furnished house, George started to fear that he was dying. On March 5, 1758, he headed for Williamsburg to consult one of the capital's leading doctors, stopping to visit his mother and the Speaker of the House on his way south. Often repeated family lore holds that on this journey George happened to encounter Patsy Custis at a neighbor's house on the Pamunkey River, fell in love on the spot, and began his courtship on the spur of the moment. Neither the route he took, the details in his financial ledger, his health fears, nor his deliberate character support this fairy-tale version of events.

Their courtship probably began much more prosaically. George arrived at Williamsburg on March 14 or 15. The morning of the fifteenth he visited John Amson, the respected physician whose advice he sought. He seems to have recovered his health and good spirits almost immediately after the doctor's reassurance that he stood miles from death's door. The legislature was in session, and the town was crammed with the gentry enjoying the spring social season; George would have joined his friends for dinner or a convivial glass of wine, catching up on all the news of the capital. If gossip about Patsy Custis's availability hadn't already reached him at Mount Vernon, he would have heard that day about the very tempting widow who was the talk of the town.

The next day, he rode out to visit the widow Custis on what might be called a reconnaissance mission. For nearly a year, George appears to have been thinking about getting married. By eighteenth-century standards, it was high time for him to settle down. That past April, he had ordered goods from London for an extensive enlargement of his small farmhouse, including 250 windowpanes, a marble mantelpiece, fine wallpapers, and mahogany dining room furniture, followed by further orders for china, a card table, and two dozen packs of cards. All the evidence points to a man planning to give up the bachelor life. With an elegant home suitable for the entertainment of his peers, a genteel wife was needed to complete the picture.

George was always susceptible to women, falling in and out of love since his teens, enthusiastically describing his latest passion in letters to his friends. He had tried to woo sixteen-year-old Betsy Fauntleroy when he was twenty but had been dismissed by the young lady. In New York City, he had spent a few days on the way to and from Boston in the company of the heiress Polly Phillipse, but their romance was more in the minds of mutual friends than in George's.

With his military reputation and the inheritance of Mount Vernon secure, George had just begun to be considered an eligible match two or three years earlier. Unfortunately for his own interests, he had tumbled into love again at about that time with a married woman, Sally Cary Fairfax, the wife of his close friend and neighbor George William Fairfax.

George had long hero-worshipped the Fairfax family of Belvoir, the estate downriver from Mount Vernon. Related to the English aristocracy, they were wealthy, sophisticated, and very influential in Virginia. Lawrence Washington's marriage to one of the Fairfax daughters had given his brother social entrée, and the Fairfaxes remained George's friends and patrons after Lawrence's death. Childless and at loose ends, Sally was a charmer two years George's senior who frustrated and enticed the naive young man with an on again, off again flirtation. There were many good reasons for George to get married, perhaps chief among them the wish to break the spell of a woman who kept him dangling helplessly.

What did George see when he was greeted by Patsy Custis in her parlor? Now twenty-six, she was still the same pretty woman who had fascinated Daniel Custis into defying his terrifying father nearly a decade earlier. Short, slim but buxom, her radiant smile her greatest beauty, she had matured through love and loss, experience and new responsibilities. But she still possessed the ineffable charm that made a man dream of comfort and home and the peace of his own fireside with her at his side.

Besides her children and servants, her seventeen-year-old sister, Nancy Bassett (married just a month before Daniel died), and her brother-in-law Colonel Burwell Bassett, the master of Eltham, a plantation downriver on the York, were probably with her when Colonel Washington came to call. George kept very detailed records of his expenditures; on the sixteenth, he noted munificent tips to the Custis servants, no doubt trying to make a good impression, and a far smaller amount to the Bassett servants. Had they been at Eltham, the ratio would have been reversed.

What did Patsy see when George Washington walked into her

parlor? Towering over most men by half a foot, George was exceptionally tall for the time—about six feet two and a half inches, more than a foot taller than Patsy—and well proportioned at 190 pounds. Just turned twenty-six, he was also exceptionally athletic, powerful, and graceful, as much at home on the dance floor as on horseback and equally unafraid in either setting. In a society and time when everyone rode well, George stood out as a truly magnificent horseman. His powerful physical appeal was not diminished by his appearance. Reddish brown hair, blue gray eyes, a strong nose, and slightly pockmarked fair skin were well within the bounds of contemporary English notions of acceptable but not handsome looks, bespeaking the leader rather than the fop.

The visit stretched out, the presence of the Bassetts making it possible for him to stay for dinner and perhaps the night. And whatever polite nothings were exchanged as they talked, possibilities became unspoken probabilities almost overnight. George was strongly encouraged by the lady to return a week later to continue their acquaintance. After completing most of his business in Williamsburg, he came back to White House on March 25, perhaps broaching the subject of marriage on that visit. Then he hurried back to the frontier to rejoin his regiment.

When did Patsy become aware of George's infatuation with Sally? Chances are that he never confessed those feelings to her, but she probably guessed early in their courtship. He would have told her all about his beloved Mount Vernon, where he wished to live, and about his friends in the neighborhood. Things said and left unsaid, an averted glance, a constrained tone of voice, would have given away his secret to a sensitive woman.

George Washington had everything to gain from marrying Patsy Custis. Sally Fairfax was out of reach. After a youth spent under a stern mother's rule, he yearned to share a home with a warm and nurturing woman. And essential to all his dreams, the Custis money would allow him to make the plantation a success. Patsy combined a near genius for creating a happy household with the necessary financial wherewithal.

Patsy's choices were nearly limitless. Charles Carter was madly in love with her, with no lingering romantic dreams to cause problems. There may have been other suitors at this time as well; if none of these men seemed right for her, she could wait for others to come calling in the future. In fact, she didn't need to marry at all unless she truly wanted to.

But it seems clear that Patsy fell passionately in love with George almost immediately and decided to please herself in her second marriage. She didn't lose her head completely: she took the time to get to know him better before making her final decision. She discovered an honorable gentleman who would never embarrass her, a kind man who would love the children, hers and theirs, a man faithful to his word who would safeguard the Custis inheritance. His lack of fortune needn't have concerned her since she had plenty of money for them both. She was also a woman confident of her own allure, unafraid of rivals for his affection. In George Washington, she saw a man with whom she believed she could live lovingly and happily. And she was right.

Pausing briefly at Mount Vernon in April, George started his workmen on the long delayed improvements to the house that he had begun planning a year before. His pride and sense of self-worth made it essential that he ensconce his wealthy bride in a respectable house, preventing gossips from whispering that she had made a great comedown in marrying him. Most of all, he wanted his wife to love Mount Vernon as much as he did.

Rather than starting anew, he decided to add a full second story atop the modest old house, raising the existing half story to the third floor. That decision was crucial for the appearance of the house through all subsequent enlargements and renovations. As it stood, the house had four rooms downstairs, separated by a hall, with small bedrooms and cramped storage space above. The renovations increased its size to eight full rooms, a respectable size for a planter family.

Returning to his troops, he left the rebuilding project under the supervision of his friend George William Fairfax. No doubt he informed both Fairfaxes of his marital hopes at the same time. He and

Sally had exchanged letters from time to time while he was at war on the frontier, but now she forbade any further correspondence, perhaps suffering a twinge or two as her devoted admirer wooed another woman.

Of all the letters that Martha and George Washington wrote to each other over the years, the destruction of the correspondence of the spring of 1758 is most distressing. We have no idea of the tone, sentiments, or frequency of those courtship letters as the young couple moved closer to a decision to marry. At the end of April, there was still no formal engagement, but on May 5, George felt hopeful enough to order a ring from Philadelphia.

Conveniently, the governor called the colonel back to the capital soon afterward. On May 28, George was at the palace in Williamsburg, meeting with him. Then, having attended to business, he set out on the now familiar road to White House on June 5 to pursue his courtship in person. Patsy and George's actual engagement probably dates from that visit.

As he returned for the last time over the mountains, George's thoughts were still torn between the latest campaign against the French and the future at Mount Vernon. Patsy's were taken up with wedding plans, a continuing care for the Custis property, and the preparation of her children for the changes to come. Her annual order to London included clothes ("to be grave but not Extravagant nor to be mourning"), shoes, gloves, a piece of fine lace, a silver chain, perfumed hair powder, and a bureau dressing table and mirror. She also sent a favorite evening gown to be dyed a more fashionable color. That summer, Daniel's tombstone finally arrived from London, and she employed a mason to lay the brickwork for his monument—a farewell to a loving husband as she entered the next phase of her life.

That July, George was elected one of the burgesses from Frederick County, where he owned land, a step up the ladder of colonial leadership. The men of the Fairfax family and his fellow officers were out in force, campaigning for him among area voters. He had failed in a previous attempt to win the seat, but this time the frontiersmen knew him better and his more sophisticated friends treated them, paying for the barrels of booze that voters then expected from political candidates, and he prevailed.

After George William Fairfax returned to Belvoir, Washington continued to correspond with him about the endlessly fascinating details of Mount Vernon's renovation, including a grand new staircase, the uneven wooden floor of the upstairs passageway, and smoky chimneys. With equal parts excitement and anxiety, he urged his friend to make the workmen hurry and finish. On September 11, 1758, he received a letter from Fairfax about construction progress and crops, noting that an enclosed letter from his wife would give further details. But Sally's real purpose was to torment or reproach him about his coming marriage to the lovely widow Custis.

Poor George. His baffled, incoherent response the next day shows just how young and emotionally vulnerable he was. He rushed to assure her "how joyfully I catch at the happy occasion of renewing Corrispondance which I feard was disrelished on your part. . . . In silence I now express my Joy.—Silence which in some cases—I wish the present—speaks more Intelligably than the sweetest Eloquence." Brushing aside her suggestion that his anxiety for an end to the conflict might be attributed "to the animating prospect of possessing Mrs. Custis," he went on to a transparent declaration of his lingering love for Sally. "Tis true, I profess myself a Votary to Love—I acknowledge that a Lady is in the Case—and further I confess, that this Lady is known to you.—Yes Madam, as well as she is to one, who is too sensible of her Charms to deny the Power, whose Influence he feels and must ever Submit to. I feel the force of her amiable beauties in the recollection of a thousand tender passages that I could wish to obliterate, till I am bid to revive them.—but experience alas! sadly reminds me how Impossible this is."

Unable to resist once more pulling the emotional strings that bound George to her, Sally wrote a long response, apparently pretending to be in doubt about the meaning of his letter. George replied, "Do we still misunderstand the true meaning of each others Letters? I think it must appear so, tho I would feign hope the contrary as I cannot speak plainer without—but I'll say no more, and leave you to guess the rest." Loyalty to his friend, her husband, kept him from a potentially disastrous step. Later in the same letter, he commented on the Fairfaxes' amateur theatricals, a presentation of Joseph Addison's popular tragedy *Cato*. The star-crossed lovers in that play, Juba and Marcia, were popular symbols for unattainable love. Assuring her how happy he would have been to play a part, he declared that he would have found himself "doubly happy in being the Juba to such a Marcia as you must make."

This exchange, for all its seeming disloyalty to George's fiancée, may have been good for the eventual success of his marriage. It called attention to Sally's willingness to trip frivolously on the edge of infidelity—unwilling to commit herself, equally unwilling to set her infatuated lover free. The two women couldn't have been more different. Patsy was too kind ever to enjoy teasing someone who loved her.

Tempted as he was by Sally, George was committed to a life with Patsy. When he returned to Williamsburg in December 1758, he resigned his commission to become a full-time planter. Patsy Custis and George Washington married at White House on January 6, 1759, and stayed there with her children and a large party of wedding guests. The bride was opulently attired in a deep yellow brocade overdress enhanced by silver lace at the neck and sleeves; the skirt opened in front to show a petticoat of white silk interwoven with silver. Her dark hair was probably entwined with her favorite pearls, and her tiny shoes were purple satin with silver trimmings. Now that he was a civilian, the groom wore a suit rather than a uniform.

His peers thought George exceptionally fortunate in his marriage. Virginia's governor noted that "Colonel Washington ... is married to his agreeable Widow." His former second in command in the Virginia Regiment wrote: "I ... beg leave to present my hearty Congratulations on your happy union with the Lady that all agree has long been the just object of your affections—may you long enjoy all the felicity you propos'd by it, or that Matrimony can possibly afford—Be so good as to offer my Compliments in the most respectful and obliging Terms to Your Lady (a new Stile indeed) and tho' she has rob'd me and many others of the greatest satisfaction we ever had or can enjoy in this Service yet none can be more sollicitous for her happiness."

After the wedding festivities ended and the last guests left White House, the Washingtons settled into married life, tucked away cozily in the country for nearly two months of a cold, unusually snowy winter—the bitter weather providing them the opportunity to deepen their growing intimacy. Alike in their views of the future, Patsy and George began a partnership that they expected to carry them happily throughout their lifetimes as colonial Virginia planters.

CHAPTER FIVE

Gentry Life at Mount Vernon

When George Washington went to the capital to take his seat in the House of Burgesses on his twenty-seventh birthday, Patsy and the children probably moved into the Custis house in Williamsburg to be with him. For about a month of that frosty winter, they enjoyed the pleasures of the social season at the capital before moving to northern Virginia in time for spring planting.

As the Washingtons entered the more public period of their lives, Patsy became Martha Washington. Although her husband and family still called her Patsy, she was starting to assume a more formal role, and her little girl was the latest Patsy.

Moving to Mount Vernon was not inevitable: they could have remained in New Kent County after their marriage. The growing season was longer there, the soil richer and better suited to tobacco, trade with Great Britain far more convenient. The major Custis holdings were concentrated in neighboring New Kent and York counties, and Martha's family and friends were near at hand. But George had always planned to live at Mount Vernon, the home of his father and elder brother. Living there was his dream, and neither then nor later could Martha deny him his heart's desires.

For all George's efforts, Mount Vernon was still very much under construction, partially furnished, and sadly lacking all the imported luxuries indispensable for a genteel lifestyle. The furniture and household goods at White House and the Williamsburg house were all available, and Martha selected the items to include in her share of the estate, deciding what to take with them and what to send for later. Among the things she chose, delicacies to eat and drink would surely have been carried to Mount Vernon right away—stone pots of raisins, two Cheshire cheeses, a barrel and twenty-two loaves of sugar, ten dozen bottles of wine, one tierce (a giant cask holding about forty-two gallons) of rum, brandy, cider, nutmegs both plain and candied, a half pound each of cloves and mace, three pounds of comfits, six pounds of white sugar candy, eight pounds of almonds, two bags of salt.

From the Custis houses, she took a mahogany desk, a table and cabinet, two chests, three looking glasses, and six beds with their "furniture," that is, counterpanes and bed curtains. The amount of linen Martha considered necessary for her new home included twenty-four pairs of sheets, fifty-four tablecloths, ninety-nine napkins and towels, twenty-five pillowcases. For the dining room, she took two cases of knives and forks, a tea chest, at least sixty glasses, and uncountable numbers of dishes—two sets of china, a tea set, a crate of earthenware, and much more.

When they set off for Mount Vernon on April 2, 1759, Martha Washington had never been farther north than King William County on the opposite shore of the Pamunkey or more than twenty miles from the house she was born in. Despite her disinclination for travel, she made this first move as willingly as she would cover thousands of miles in the years to come. She married George Washington because she loved him, and she went with him wherever he wanted to go.

Martha and the children rumbled along in the Custis coach while George rode on horseback. Household goods, trunks, and her household slaves would have jolted slowly behind in heavy wagons. But in his haste to get the family on the road to their new home, George had neglected to make arrangements for their arrival. The house had been locked up, its furniture covered or stored, the pantry bare. On the road, he suddenly realized this omission—or, perhaps, Martha reminded him by a tactful inquiry. Because he loved the place so much, even (or especially) in the middle of a construction project, he hadn't thought about the impression that the scant comfort of a bachelor household would make on his bride.

He hurriedly sent a messenger ahead to John Alton, his plantation manager, to get the house key from the Fairfaxes at Belvoir. Cleaning, airing, building fires, putting up beds in the hall and dining room (the upstairs bedrooms weren't complete), setting out and polishing tables and chairs, buying some eggs and chickens for the travelers' dinner to be prepared "in the best manner you can"—all had to be accomplished before their arrival the next day. Alluding to his special pride, George directed that "the Stair case ought also to be polished in order to make it look well."

On April 6, the heavy coach lumbered up the long, straight western approach to Mount Vernon, the drive bracketed by formal parterre gardens. Probably the children—perhaps even Martha—peered out the open carriage windows to catch a first glimpse of their new home. They would have arrived well before dark; only fools traveled those primitive roads at night. When they drew up in front of the door, they found a simple welcome. Construction wasn't complete, but Martha could see the comfortable and gracious house that was emerging.

Mount Vernon didn't pretend to the Georgian high style of Charles Carter's Cleve or William Byrd's Westover. George's decision to enlarge his brother's frame farmhouse, rather than pull it down and start over with an entirely new design, meant that his house would always be asymmetrical—rambling and comfortable rather than elegant. It reflected a man in touch with his roots, proud of himself and his family, proud of his attachment to the land.

Two and a half stories high, Mount Vernon was painted white, the paint mixed with sand to give the impression of rusticated stone; the afternoon sun would have been kind to the house's western front, giving it a golden glow. As Martha entered the downstairs passageway for the first time, she went from bright springtime sunlight into the shadows of the thirteen-foot-wide hall. George had transformed the passageway with wooden paneling and dramatic cornices painted a rich, deep yellow ocher. To the right of the front door was the ample walnut staircase, presumably polished to the desired high gloss.

George probably led her straight through and out the matching door at the east end of the hall. The beauty of the wide vista the house commanded—the sloping lawn bordered by tall trees, the Potomac (more than a mile and a half wide at Mount Vernon) rushing along in its spring flood, the dense forest on the Maryland shore—was breathtaking to everyone on first sight and all the more to the woman who would be mistress of this estate.

During those early days and weeks, she and the household servants brought from White House set Mount Vernon to rights—sparkling clean, furniture arranged and polished, appetizing meals appearing at the appointed times. For them all, especially Jacky and little Patsy, the shock of the move would have been lessened by the presence of the familiar black, brown, and tan faces of the household slaves—Old Doll ruling over the kitchen with the scullion Beck at her side; Breechy serving in the dining room, newly togged out in Washington's crimson-and-white livery; Betty bent over her mending; Sally sprinkling scented powder in Martha's hair and fastening her corset. The children had their own servants—ten-year-old Julius, twelve-year-old Rose, and Moll to oversee and care for the lot of them. Southern planter families were emotionally dependent on the slaves they owned for their very sense that all was right with their world.

Martha apparently never doubted that she could bind George to her in a loving relationship that would deepen throughout the years of their marriage. Whatever she may have guessed about his feelings for Sally Fairfax, it took a woman of rare self-confidence not to cross-examine him or create jealous scenes. There has never been the slightest suggestion of such ill-advised tactics. Martha greeted Sally's overtures with sunny good nature, accepting the Fairfaxes as lifelong friends. George's anguished fascination cooled into friendship as he became accustomed to the joys of his own lovely wife, who was devoted to him alone and had no interest in capturing the affections of other men.

Martha fully enjoyed the social life of her new neighborhood, filled as she saw it with "mirth and gaiety." Besides the Fairfaxes, there were other friends in the nearby countryside—George's cousin Sarah and Abram Barnes, Martha and John Posey of neighboring Rover's Delight, Margaret and the Reverend Charles Green of Truro Parish, Ann and William Digges of Warburton Manor across the river in Maryland. Just ten miles up the Potomac was the new little port city of Alexandria. Wharves and warehouses ringed the shallow river bay that was the center of commerce. Unpaved streets led up the steep hill to the growing town strung along Fairfax Street. Shops, an Anglican chapel, taverns with their assembly rooms, and workshops attracted merchants, ship captains, doctors, lawyers, milliners, dancing teachers, and more who built brightly painted frame cottages. Scottish merchants grew rich and built handsome residences; among the Washingtons' friends in Alexandria were Ann and William Ramsay and Sarah and John Carlyle, who had built the grandest mansion in town. Fish feasts, barbecues, tea parties, horse races, balls, informal neighborhood dances, and visiting were the entertainments that punctuated Martha's daily routine.

During her early years at Mount Vernon, the trip north seemed a bit daunting to the Dandridge family. Only her sister Nancy Bassett and her husband came to stay every year or two with their growing family. But Martha often accompanied George on his trips to Williamsburg for politics and pleasure, visiting her mother and other family members. Since the first meeting that brought Martha and George together, he and Burwell Bassett had become firm friends. Whether alone or with his wife, George nearly always stayed with the Bassetts at Eltham when he visited the capital and also called on his mother-in-law, of whom he was quite fond.

The relationship with his own mother was laden with difficulty for both of them. Self-centered and acquisitive, Mary Ball Washington was preoccupied with her eldest son to the virtual exclusion of her other children. That preoccupation expressed itself in fears for George's safety, pleas not to put himself at risk in military action, and demands for assistance, usually monetary, even though she continued to occupy and enjoy the profits of his property on the Rappahannock. For example, while he served with Braddock on the frontier, on the verge of battle with the French, she requested that he find a German serving man and a barrel of butter for her. His refusal is a model of tact, but the man who sent loving greetings to his brothers usually addressed his mother as "Honored Madam" and closed as "your Dutiful son." The warmest he ever reached was "affectionate and dutiful."

Apparently, Martha didn't meet her mother-in-law until the year after she had married George, and Mary Washington never took much notice of her. George dutifully visited her by himself three or four times a year, but as far as we know, she never came to Mount Vernon after his marriage. When the entire family accompanied him to Williamsburg, they were punctilious about visiting his mother en route, but Martha never developed much of a relationship with her. When visiting in Fredericksburg, they generally spent the night at the large house of George's sister, Betty, and her husband, Fielding Lewis. George's brothers and their wives sometimes exchanged visits with the Washingtons, especially Jack and Hannah Washington.

George dove into what would be his lifelong preoccupation and passion—agriculture in all its aspects, both experimental and practical. The Custis fortune made it possible for him to add acreage, stock, slaves, and buildings to Mount Vernon during the next fifteen years. Eighty-four slaves were Martha's dower share of the estate. About half of them, all fieldworkers, were left to work her dower lands in southern Virginia under the supervision of overseers. Most of the house slaves and tradesmen—that is, skilled workers—and some field slaves, amounting to about forty-two people in all, were brought north to work at Mount Vernon over the course of the first year of their marriage.

Although George now wrote the orders to the British factors, the furnishing and embellishment of Mount Vernon was very much a joint affair, talked over and decided in their evenings together. The first item on the Washingtons' first order to Robert Cary of May 1, 1759, was a tester bedstead of seven-and-a-half-foot pitch. The color scheme chosen for their bedroom was Martha's favorite blue. That fall, they received the beech bedstead with plain mahogany foot posts and cut cornice, along with seventy yards of copperplate printed chintz (blue on white) for the bed hangings and chair covers. Lawn for linings, curtain hooks and brass cloak pins to fasten back the bed curtains, a matching chintz quilt lined with lawn, cloth-covered window cornices, fashionable festooned window curtains, and two Wilton ingrain bedside carpets (fine wool woven in two different patterns, one pattern bordering the other) completed the Washingtons' desire for their room to be "uniformly handsome and genteel." Their orders continued to flow to London throughout the years.

Dolls, toys, books, and musical instruments delighted Jacky and Patsy, four and a half and three when they came to Mount Vernon. Summertime or early fall, when the tobacco boats came upriver, must have seemed like Christmas, Easter, and several birthdays combined. When one of Cary's ships anchored out in the Potomac, countless barrels, boxes, and trunks packed tightly with English goods were rowed in by longboat to their wharf. Unpacking their treasures was an annual celebration interspersed with disappointment at broken china, unfashionable or ill-fitting clothing, or liquor barrels whose contents had unaccountably evaporated during the voyage.

In the first year of their marriage, George upgraded the Custis vehicles. Unpaved, rough roads quickly took their toll on coaches, almost literally shaking them to pieces. In April, he purchased a small chariot, perhaps to replace Martha's older chair. In the fall, while he was in Williamsburg, he had the Custis family coach repainted. A few years later, he ordered a new coach from London, painted a fashionable green. Besides the team that pulled the coach, they eventually brought up a dozen Custis horses—sorrels, bays, and roans.

Martha and George soon settled into a pleasant routine. Both of them got up before dawn for a light breakfast. He then set off on an inspection ride around the estate or perhaps a foxhunt with the neighbors while she read the Bible and prayed before beginning the day's housekeeping chores and sewing. Her children were both an entertainment and a responsibility as she played and sang with them and taught them their first letters.

Dinner was served at about three in the afternoon in the small dining room with its elegant crimson wallpaper, marble mantel, inset landscape painting, and mahogany furniture—all brand-new. George rode in from the fields, changed clothes, and powdered his hair (he never wore a wig, even for the most formal event) before coming in to dinner. Guests were common, invited or not, and there was always room and welcome for unexpected arrivals. Neighbors who rode or drove open carriages were sent home in the Washingtons' coach if they were surprised by inclement weather. One admiring guest noted that they kept "an excellent table and a stranger, let him be of what Country or nation, he will always meet with a most hospitable reception at it."

Everyone visited in the afternoon, walking about the grounds or going for a horseback or carriage ride. In her scarlet riding habit, Martha rode sidesaddle. A simple tea was served in the late afternoon, in fine weather on the broad lawn overlooking the Potomac. After the lamps and candles were lit in the evening, they adjourned to the parlor, where they talked, read, wrote letters, played cards or backgammon, danced, or sang. Martha liked to sing the tunes of the day, and George inscribed her copy of *The Bull-Finch*, a large collection of popular English songs, "Martha Washington. 1759," the first time he wrote her new name. Sometimes he read aloud from one of the newspapers to which he subscribed, and they discussed the news—what little there was in early 1760s Virginia. After a light supper, they retired to their room on the first floor at about nine o'clock, to begin the same routine the next day.

On Sundays, they usually went to church, generally down to the small wooden Truro Parish building near George Mason's Gunston Hall. At times, they also went to the little chapel in Alexandria. Guests and children went with them (Anglicans all), and friends encountered at church were invited for dinner. Martha took communion regularly; George was a member of the Truro vestry. Both churches mounted building campaigns during these years, and by the 1770s, the Washingtons owned square wooden family pews, somewhat like horse boxes with seats on three sides, in both Pohick Church to the south and Christ Church in Alexandria. Both were elegant brick edifices in keeping with the growing prosperity of Virginia.

George wrote that fall of his newfound happiness with Martha: "I am now I beleive fixd at this Seat with an agreable Consort for Life and hope to find more happiness in retirement than I ever experiencd amidst a wide and bustling World." No second thoughts in his mind—and certainly not in hers.

The tenor of their life together was placid with joys and sorrow, gains and losses. George steadily added acreage to Mount Vernon and moved from tobacco to the cultivation of wheat and other crops. Overall, the plantation provided them comfort and luxury, but he sometimes had to borrow from the estates of his wealthy stepchildren to keep afloat in the bad years. They experienced worry, depression, dismay, and unhappiness from time to time. After a trip south, Martha wrote her sister, "I have had a very dark time since I came home. I believe it was owing to the severe weather we have had." But the happy times far outweighed the sad.

Measles, whooping cough, malaria, dysentery, assorted fevers, colds, influenza, aches, and strains—like all colonists, they suffered illnesses. Martha dosed the family with the harsh and generally useless remedies of the day—emetics, purges, bark (quinine), mercury. But some of her remedies were herbal, based on everyday observation. Pinworms in children's intestinal tracts were commonplace, in her opinion the source of most childhood illness. In criticizing a niece's child-rearing practices, she wrote, "I have not a doubt but worms is the principle cause of her [the child's] complaints. Children that eat everything as they like and feed as heartely as yours does must be full of worms."

Worms were something she could easily deal with. Her sovereign remedy for worms in children was passed down through the Custis family. It called for "1 oz seeds of wormseed / half an oz Rhubarb / 1 tablespoon small cloves of garlic. put the ingredients into a pint bottle. fill it with best wine or whiskey, let it stand a few days, shaking it well, then strain it. for a child of 5 years a small teaspoonful, less for younger children." The combination of a worm killer, an effective laxative, and the liquor would have purged Jacky's and Patsy's youthful guts of the most persistent worms.

If an illness lingered, the Washingtons sent for a doctor from

Alexandria to administer harsher and even more useless treatments, such as bleeding (sometimes a couple of pints were drawn) and blistering. But Martha and George were generally healthy and active, as were Jacky and Patsy. Both of them lost siblings—her teenage sister Fanny while they were courting, his elder half-brother Augustine in 1762, followed by her little sister Mary, the same age as her own Patsy. Nancy Fairfax Lee, George's former sister-in-law, died in 1761, leaving him the undisputed master of Mount Vernon.

With her children, Martha was very attentive, even overanxious. On a visit to Hannah and Jack Washington at their plantation, Bushfield, Martha took her "little Patt" with her but left Jacky "at home for a trial to see how well I coud stay without him." That first two-week separation wasn't a success. She worried incessantly— every barking dog or strange noise made her think that a messenger had come with bad news. As she wrote to her sister Nancy, "I often fancied he was sick or some accident had happened to him." She concluded that she couldn't leave the children again for any length of time until she had someone responsible to care for them.

In the summer of 1761, Walter Magowan, a well-educated Scot like many colonial tutors (though the accent could be a worry), came to live at Mount Vernon and teach Jacky and Patsy, now seven and five. Martha wrote proudly to her sister that the children were learning their books "very fast." Jacky would naturally, to the minds of the time, receive a more comprehensive education than his little sister. Magowan requested Greek grammars and texts, histories, a geography, a bookkeeping manual, and a ream of writing paper for Jacky. For seven years, he oversaw the children's education and formed a congenial part of the Mount Vernon family.

For children of the gentry, music and dancing were as important as the alphabet. George himself couldn't sing or play an instrument, though he was a tireless dancer, but he found "nothing more agreeable" than music. At the same time that Magowan came to teach the basics, George sent to London for a small harpsichord, known as a spinet, for Patsy's use; three years later, her big brother would receive a violin and a German flute (a transverse flute, not a recorder). John Stadler, a German immigrant "Musick Professor" and a highly accomplished musician, made a circuit of Virginia plantation houses during this time. Spending three or four days a month at Mount Vernon, he gave singing lessons to Martha and the children. She may have trilled out some of the songs in the *Bull-Finch* like "On the Marriage Act," which declared "But Adam and Eve, then they first enter'd Course / E'en took one another, for better, for worse" or the untitled but requisite "God save great George, our King / Long live our noble King / God save the king." Songbooks contained only lyrics, many of them to be sung to a few familiar tunes; one of a music teacher's tasks was to help students fit lyrics to music.

While Martha soon gave up the lessons, Stadler continued teaching Patsy and Jacky singing, adding instrumental music, for several years. The routine for dancing lessons was much the same. A dancing teacher lorded over a group of students at Mount Vernon one month, at George Mason's Gunston Hall the next. For a few days each month, neighboring children gathered to spend several hours each day learning to dance like little ladies and gentlemen, joined by their parents in the joyous evening romps.

One shadow on their happy life was their failure to have children of their own. For the first few years, given Martha's fertility as Mrs. Custis, they must have expected welcome news each month. They probably gave up hope soon after she turned forty. No one knows why she never became pregnant again. George may have been sterile from birth or from disease; he had suffered a mild case of smallpox in Barbados as an adolescent, and smallpox can cause sterility. Martha may have suffered some injury during the birth of Patsy, her fourth child. George himself believed the problem lay with his wife.

A newcomer arrived to live at Mount Vernon in late 1764— Lund Washington, a distant cousin from the Chotank area of Stafford County and former manager of a neighbor's large estates. Five years younger than George, Lund was a pleasant bachelor of twenty-seven who was hired to manage the Mount Vernon farms. As George had expanded his acreage and operations, he felt the need to have an experienced assistant, especially when he traveled.

With a tutor, estate manager, and housekeeper living in the house, Martha now dared to leave the children at home while she accompanied George on occasional trips. In August 1767, they set out for Warm Springs, Virginia (now Berkeley Springs, West Virginia). Their friends Sally and George William Fairfax went with them. There must have been quite a caravan rolling up the dirt roads into the Blue Ridge Mountains—a carriage for the ladies, the men on horseback, and a couple of wagons for servants and supplies. The trip took nearly a week as they climbed higher into cool air and heavy forests.

The several mountain springs were both genteel resorts and health spas, bringing together wealthy planters from throughout the South, only a few of them really ill. Besides "taking the waters"—drinking glasses of the warm, mineral-flavored water or immersing themselves in the springs—the Washingtons and Fairfaxes rode to nearby beauty spots, strolled, played cards, dined with friends, and generally enjoyed themselves in a place where the rules of dress and behavior were somewhat relaxed. Some visitors settled for little makeshift cabins, but their friend George Mercer had built a house where they stayed. They brought their own cook, and he prepared healthy meals from the produce the locals brought in for sale—squash, corn, cucumbers, potatoes, beans, cabbages, greens, watermelons, peaches, and apples. George amused himself by looking at the stock of the ubiquitous horse traders and ended by buying four horses—two grays, a black, and a bay.

Martha had been feeling poorly and out of sorts that summer, and the trip refreshed her greatly. One of her bathing dresses is still preserved at Mount Vernon, although it's probably from a later period. Loose, light, and ankle-length, with a simple tie at the neck and loose three-quarter-length sleeves, the pale-blue-and-white woven linen gown looks a lot like nightwear. The ease and comfort of such a dress must have been heavenly for a woman who wore stays every waking moment. When she waded into the spring, she didn't have to worry about watching after the skirt—the hem had little lead weights sewn in to keep it modestly in place.

Lund knew just how anxious Martha would be about Jacky and

Patsy while she was vacationing. At least twice during the month, he wrote long letters to George about crops, building projects, and laborers, but he was always careful to report on the children. He sent the news for Martha that "her Children are as well as I ever saw them & have been during her absence." In the second letter, he again emphasized their continued good health and sent a message: "They desire their Love to their Mama & you."

These golden years, as Martha would later remember them, flowed on seemingly untroubled at the local level. But their counterpoint was escalating economic and political divergence between the American colonies and the mother country. Both she and George were loyal subjects of their king, proud of their English heritage. No one at first imagined that the end of the French and Indian War in 1763 would lead directly to the violent break of the American Revolution. Most Virginians had expected to enjoy a halcyon time of peace and prosperity. Their traditional enemy, France, had been soundly defeated, forced to give up all her North American colonies, and her Indian allies were subdued. The seas were safe for British ships again without fear of capture or destruction, agriculture and trade were booming, and all should have been well. As George wrote to an English acquaintance: "I deal little in politics, and what to advance under the article of news I really know not. This part of the country, as you know, affords few occurrences worthy of remark."

But like other loyal colonists, George would soon be forced to deal in politics. George III, who had ascended the throne in 1760, had no intention of leaving these jumped-up colonials in peace. A century of imperial wars had depleted the national exchequer and led to a monstrous, albeit unevenly imposed, tax burden in Great Britain. Working through a series of docile chief ministers and shifting parliamentary support, the young king determined to recoup some wartime outlays by taxing Americans.

Colonial leaders resisted each attempt to impose taxes and tighten royal control in a series of increasingly acrimonious disputes beginning in 1763. They sent agents like Benjamin Franklin to represent their interests in London, waged newspaper warfare, established intercolonial ties, wrote countless letters and broadsides, and formed committees to enforce their refusal to buy British goods. Boston took the lead, followed by New York City, both their genteel leaders and their mobs of ordinary citizens profoundly suspicious of British intentions and authority. Virginians watched and waited; radicals like Patrick Henry were ahead of the rest. The Proclamation of 1763, the Sugar Act, the Currency Act, the Stamp Act, the Quartering Act, the Declaratory Act, and the Townshend Acts—through the 1760s, the British Parliament passed and then repealed a string of measures, which seldom added to their revenues, eroded imperial control over the colonies, and drove more and more Americans toward defiance and ultimately revolution.

The end of the 1760s just as surely brought upset and changes in family life at Mount Vernon. In 1768, Walter Magowan went to London to be ordained as an Anglican priest, there being no bishopric in the American colonies. When he returned to Virginia, he became rector of a parish; both the pay and prestige were superior to continued service as a tutor. At fourteen, Jacky was old enough to be sent away to school. Even with a resident tutor, he had constantly taken off from his studies to go riding or shooting. Martha spoiled him, but so did his stepfather. It's hard to imagine that any coercion could have turned him into a scholar. After all, he didn't *need* to study very hard: when he came of age, he would be a very rich man indeed.

After asking for recommendations from among his acquaintances, George wrote to the Reverend Jonathan Boucher, an English clergyman who kept a boarding school in Caroline County, south of Fredericksburg; Boucher's sister assisted him in looking after the boys under his care. They determined to send Jacky there in the summer.

But as they weighed terms and possibilities for Jacky's schooling, a calamity befell the family. Beautiful little Patsy, just turning twelve, experienced a violent seizure, the first of many to come. It seems clear that she suffered from epilepsy, and puberty is one of the trigger points for the malady's first manifestation. Beginning in January 1768, her fits grew worse over the years, both in violence and in frequency. Patsy's care became the center of Martha's life and ironically made it easier for her to send Jacky away to school.

Epilepsy was untreatable by any medical knowledge of the day. The Washingtons spent much time and money consulting a variety of doctors (at least eight of them over the years), trying changes in lifestyle, mountains of medicines, and treatment with "simples," that is, herbal remedies. Dr. William Rumney, an Englishman in practice in Alexandria, treated Patsy regularly for five years, coming down to Mount Vernon every few weeks to examine his patient and bring capsules, powders, pills, and decoctions. Throughout her ordeal, antispasmodics such as valerian and musk were the primary medicines prescribed—to no avail. At one point, poisonous but often used mercury and severe purging were ordered, Martha nursing and watching her daughter throughout. Another time, a blacksmith came and put an iron ring on Patsy's finger, based on an English folk belief that such rings prevented seizures. Later, they spent a month at Warm Springs, hoping the waters might be beneficial.

As Patsy grew up, Martha tried to provide as normal an adolescence for her daughter as she could. They visited relatives and neighbors, even though they sometimes were forced to return home if her seizures were too severe. Friends were important to the young girl. Millie Posey, a neighbor girl whose mother had died, practically lived at Mount Vernon during these years, joining in Patsy's dancing lessons. Sally Carlyle came out from Alexandria and stayed a few days a month, sharing in music lessons. Patsy enjoyed the fashionable clothes and accessories of a great planter's daughter, attending a dance or two during her good spells, but during the bad times she sometimes had two fits a day. At heart Martha knew that Patsy's condition was hopeless. As her husband wrote, "The unhappy situation of her daughter has to some degree fixed her eyes upon [Jacky] as her only hope."

In July 1768, after about a six-month hiatus in his lessons, Jacky moved to school with a servant and two horses. School didn't prove too taxing, as he frequently came home on long visits. For all his own English education, Boucher had no training as a schoolmaster and didn't manage to drill much Latin, Greek, or even arithmetic into his bored student's head. Most Virginia gentry schools were kept by Anglican rectors, and most of them were similarly lackluster.

In April 1769, George and Martha went down to Williamsburg for the spring legislative session. Her youngest sister, Betsy Dandridge, was with them; she had been visiting at Mount Vernon, and they were taking her back home. By now George represented Fairfax County, a sign of his rise in the world since his marriage. Although not yet a colonywide leader, he no longer disavowed an interest in politics, closely following the developing crisis with Great Britain. His particular mission at this time was to present the Virginia Resolves, written by his friend and neighbor George Mason, opposing taxation without representation and British infringements on Americans' rights. After heated discussion, the royal governor dissolved the assembly. Its members promptly reconvened at the Raleigh Tavern and agreed to an organized boycott of British goods until the taxes were repealed. Martha stayed at Eltham with the Bassetts, consulting still another doctor about Patsy, waiting eagerly for a report on the meetings before going back home to put the boycott into effect in their own lives.

Finding local substitutes for such British-manufactured goods as cloth, thread, pins, needles, hoes, scythes, wallpaper, stoneware chamber pots, hats, paper, windowpanes, and paint wasn't easy for people who were so accustomed to receiving annual deliveries from England. But Martha and George were committed to this political statement. The workshops at Mount Vernon had always produced quantities of homespun cloth, mostly for slaves' clothing. During the next years, they expanded their output. Martha trained and oversaw the estate's spinners, seamstresses, and knitters. Weaving was traditionally men's work in Britain and the colonies, and George oversaw the hiring of itinerant weavers to convert the spun flax and wool thread into the linen and woolen fabrics used and worn at Mount Vernon.

Jonathan Boucher accepted a parish in Prince George's County,

Maryland, outside Annapolis, and moved his school there. In the summer of 1770, sixteen-year-old Jacky, or Jack, as he now preferred to be called, rode to the new location. His mother had agreed to his continuing as a student with Boucher, though she steadfastly opposed the clergyman's blithe suggestion that he guide the boy on a grand tour of Europe in another year or two. George was for a time intrigued by the idea, but Martha's common sense told her that such an extended trip with the indulgent minister could only lead to disaster for her son.

Annapolis was very convenient to Mount Vernon and as the capital of Maryland offered bountiful social opportunities. Jack came home often to attend dancing classes, go hunting, or just spend time gladdening his mother's heart. Kindhearted and loving, he was genuinely attached to Martha and Patsy, and they adored him in return.

Jack studied a little and socialized a lot. He became something of a fop, spending money on embroidered waistcoats and wrist ruffles, rings and silver knee buckles. As a matter of course, he had his own manservant and horses with him, went to the Annapolis races, bought lottery tickets, and enjoyed such expensive tropical treats as oranges and pineapples. Boucher wrote at one point, "I must confess to you that I never in my Life knew a Youth so exceedingly Indolent or so surprisingly voluptuous; one wd. suppose Nature had intended him for some Asiatic Prince."

In the spring of 1772, one worry was taken off George's mind when his mother, now in her sixties, agreed to move into a small white frame house in Fredericksburg on Charles Street within easy walking distance of his sister Betty's house. He bought the house for her, and she lived in comfort there until her death. Within a couple of years, he sold the farm on the Rappahannock, which was too far away from his central properties for effective management.

In May 1772, Jack brought home a young painter from Annapolis with a recommendation from Boucher. Charles Willson Peale was a former saddler who had studied with Benjamin West in London. Jack wanted the artist to paint a miniature of his mother, and she, of course, wanted images of both her children, now in their teens. Within a couple of days, even the reluctant and unenthusiastic forty-year-old George, "having yielded to Importunity," donned his colonel's uniform from the Virginia Regiment (it still fit after thirteen years!) to pose for his first portrait. Martha's insistence led to the creation of the only image of George Washington before he became truly famous.

Fortunately, Peale was a technically proficient painter with the gift of capturing his subjects' personalities. At forty, Martha was still lovely, dimpled and slightly smiling, growing a bit plump, her dark hair pulled back with pearls. Jack at seventeen was fair, still very boyish, with light brown hair, flushed pink cheeks, a small mouth, and a slightly receding chin. Two years younger, Patsy is beautiful, with dark hair, big brown eyes, and strongly marked brows, but there's something wistful about this portrait, as though it's shadowed by her suffering.

In early 1773, the Washingtons began to think of sending Jack on to college. The College of William and Mary didn't have a very good reputation, in George's opinion, and he consulted Boucher about the rival merits of the University of Pennsylvania in Philadelphia and King's College (renamed Columbia University in 1784) in New York City, which the cleric far preferred.

In the meantime, Jack had been making his own plans. One of his school friends was Charles Calvert, the son of Benedict Calvert of Mount Airy, a planter and collector of customs for the Patuxent district of Maryland. The Calverts were the descendants of Lord Baltimore, the original proprietor of the colony, still wealthy and powerful at the end of the colonial era. The current Lord Baltimore didn't live in the colony; his brother-in-law Robert Eden served as governor. Married to the daughter of a previous governor, Benedict Calvert was an illegitimate but recognized member of the family, his social status secure but his wealth not comparable to that of the rest. Under Boucher's lax administration, the boys were allowed to visit the Calverts' town house or ride over to Mount Airy at will; Jack spent more and more time flirting with the two eldest Calvert girls.

Benedict Calvert wasn't about to discourage the attentions of the Custis heir. Although he was only eighteen, Jack fell in love with the Calverts' beautiful second daughter, Eleanor, and became secretly engaged. Nelly, as she was called, was only fifteen or sixteen at the time. It's hard to be exact about her age because the sources give different birth dates.

As his stepfather firmed up college plans, Jack decided to reveal his engagement. He came home on vacation in March, along with a party of prominent Marylanders that included Governor Eden and Benedict Calvert, who were passing through the neighborhood. For nearly a week, the Washingtons joined in the entertainment of these distinguished visitors. After they left for Williamsburg, however, Jack at last told his secret. Probably he approached his mother first. When he told his stepfather, George was as furious as he could have expected. There must have been some hot words on the subjects of duty, responsibility, and impropriety. It wasn't just that Jack was too young to get married, he had ignored Virginia mores by not consulting his family before becoming engaged, even though his fiancée came from a well-connected gentry family. It's clear, though, that Martha and George had different reactions to the engagement. For all his indignation, she was undoubtedly pleased.

On April 3, George wrote a letter to Nelly's father that fairly crackles with chagrin and anger. Jack's imprudence horrified Washington and, as he wrote frankly, he considered it "a Subject . . . of no small embarrassment to me." Although he assured Benedict Calvert that the connection with Nelly's family would be extremely pleasing, Jack's "youth, inexperience, and unripened Education is, & will be insuperable obstacles in my eye, to the completion of the Marriage." Waiting two or three years would give the young couple time to discover if their affection was fixed—if not, better to find out before marriage than after. Laying out Jack's great financial expectations (surely no surprise), he expected that Calvert would do "something genteel by your Daughter," a polite request for a respectable dowry.

So far, not too bad for Jack. The brief final paragraph of the letter tells it all: "At all times when you, Mrs. Calvert, or the young

Ladies can make it convenient to favour us with a visit we should be happy in seeing you at this place. Mrs. Washington & Miss Custis join me in respectful Compliments." Martha was clearly in favor of the match; she and Patsy were agog to meet the girl who had captured their darling Jack's interest.

Jack rode off to Annapolis to deliver the letter to Mount Airy personally—happy, no doubt, that the engagement was at least provisionally accepted and looking forward to spending more time with Nelly. A week later, he returned with Calvert's answer. His prospective father-in-law had no intention of letting such a big catch off the line. And, to do him justice, he may also have seen how much they loved each other. He acquiesced in the decision to postpone the marriage for the time being but made it clear that he was holding Jack to his promise. Because he had ten children to provide for, Nelly's dowry would be "inconsiderable," but their happiness, he declared, was more important than financial considerations. In fact, "Nothing in my power shall be left undone to promote so pleasing an Union." He ended by inviting them all to visit at Mount Airy and promising that he would bring his family to Mount Vernon soon.

On Saturday, April 10, Jack delivered this letter and another from his schoolmaster avowing his ignorance of the clandestine courtship, no doubt to his stepfather's simmering disapproval and his mother's and sister's happiness. The next day was Easter Sunday. When the family went to church at Pohick, Jack probably thanked God that his strike for freedom had succeeded so well.

The next day, George and Jack went up to the Annapolis races, primarily to visit Mount Airy and begin building a new family relationship. When George returned, he could reassure his wife that the Calverts were highly respectable and the lovely Nelly "of exceeding good Character"—not that Martha seems to have had any doubts about the matter. Before she ever set eyes on the girl and very much against her husband's wishes, she had agreed to the engagement and informed Nancy Bassett happily of the event. In a letter on the same day to Burwell, George acknowledged Martha's approval, adding, "I shall say nothing further therefore on the Subject," be-

Chestnut Grove, New Kent County, Virginia. Martha Dandridge's birthplace, sketched ca. 1934. *(Virginia Historical Society)*

Colonel John Custis IV,
Daniel Parke Custis's father,
ca. 1725.
(Washington and Lee University)

Martha Dandridge Custis, by John Wollaston, 1757.
(Washington and Lee University)

Daniel Parke Custis, by
John Wollaston, 1757.
(Washington and Lee University)

John Parke ("Jacky") Custis and
Martha Parke ("Patsy") Custis,
by John Wollaston, 1757.
(Washington and Lee University)

George William Fairfax, ca. 1760.
(Virginia Historical Society)

Sally Cary Fairfax, ca. 1915,
after early portrait.
(Virginia Historical Society)

Conjectural drawings of the evolution of Mount Vernon: the original house, the enlargements of 1758–1759, and the final expansion of 1774–1787.
(Mount Vernon Ladies' Association)

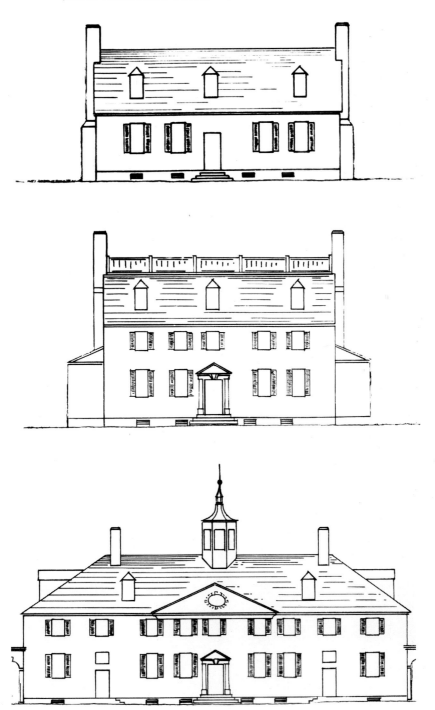

George Washington, by
Charles Willson Peale, 1772.
(Washington and Lee University)

Martha Washington, by
Charles Willson Peale, 1776.
(Mount Vernon Ladies' Association)

John Parke Custis, by
Charles Willson Peale, 1772.
(Mount Vernon Ladies' Association)

Martha Parke Custis, by
Charles Willson Peale, 1772.
(Mount Vernon Ladies' Association)

Washington's headquarters, Cambridge, Massachusetts.
(Private collection)

Washington's headquarters, Newburgh, New York.
(Private collection)

fore saying a great deal more about Jack's immaturity and lack of knowledge.

On April 24, Elizabeth and Benedict Calvert arrived on a return visit with their two eldest daughters, Betsy and Nelly. The importance of this visit in Martha's eyes can be seen in the trouble they took to invite distinguished dinner guests, including Lord Fairfax, to meet the Calverts. In effect, this was an engagement party, as Jack and Nelly were introduced as an affianced couple. Young friends from the neighborhood had also been invited for dancing in the evenings. After four days of enjoyable entertainments and informal companionship, the families were on easy terms.

But George persevered in his fruitless attempts to make Jack over. After being allowed to visit his sweetheart twice more, Jack was hauled off to New York City to attend King's College. He and his stepfather rode away on May 10, stopping often on the journey to visit and be entertained by friends and acquaintances from Maryland to New York. Jack was duly installed at college with his usual special privileges, including his servant and horses.

Stopping again at Mount Airy on his way home, George no doubt pressed Martha's urgent wish for a visit from Nelly during Jack's absence; he arrived home on June 8. After three days of anticipation, Nelly arrived accompanied by a Calvert family retainer. Not only sweet and charming, Nelly was a dark beauty of the same type as Patsy Custis. They were about the same age and could have passed for sisters.

As usual, the house was full of company, including Patsy's doctor on one of his regular visits. After he left, George thought she was "in better health and spirits," her mood probably lifted by Nelly's presence. During the first week of Nelly's stay, visitors came and went for dinner or the night, including Jack and Hannah Washington with two of their children, giving Martha the chance to introduce her son's fiancée to the family. One scorcher of a day followed another. Except for attending services at the new Christ Church in Alexandria, Martha and the girls stayed close to home, probably sitting in the wide hallway, the doors at either end open to create a breeze, chatting, sewing, and getting better acquainted.

Saturday, June 19, continued hot and dry, and they probably spent the day indoors. After a convivial family dinner, they all rose from the table sometime between four and five o'clock. Patsy and Nelly were talking about Jack, and Patsy went into her bedroom to get his latest letter. There she was seized with "one of her usual Fits." Nelly ran to her and shouted for help. Her mother and stepfather hurried in, and she was lifted onto the bed. This seizure was her last: she died "in less than two Minutes without uttering a Word, a groan, or scarce a sigh."

For seventeen years, Martha had nurtured and protected her fragile daughter, who was her constant daily companion. In her husband's words, she was reduced "to the lowest ebb of Misery." He was so worried about her that he begged his brother-in-law to convince Martha's mother to come and live permanently at Mount Vernon to console her. Fanny Dandridge didn't leave her New Kent home, but Nelly Calvert comforted Martha during this time of anguish.

There were practical matters to deal with—a coffin to be built overnight by an Alexandria carpenter, the ceremonial black pall to cover the coffin retrieved from an acquaintance, the minister to be summoned. Even though Patsy had died on Saturday, she had to be buried the next day because of the blazing weather. Her body was probably laid out in the parlor.

After church services the following day, the Reverend Lee Massey, rector of Truro Parish, came to Mount Vernon in time for dinner. The subdued company was increased by the presence of the Fairfaxes. After dinner, Massey read the funeral service and Patsy was buried in an old brick vault close to the river. The day was warm and thunderous, but fortunately the rain held off. The Calverts allowed Nelly to remain with the grieving Martha for another week, sending her older sister to join her. Nelly's presence when Patsy died and during the week following created a lifelong bond between her and Martha.

A couple of weeks later, the Washingtons suffered another loss when George William and Sally Fairfax left for England to press a complicated legal suit. George and Martha stood on the Belvoir dock, waving forlornly as their closest friends sailed downriver to visit her parents before going abroad. Naturally, George had agreed to take charge of their affairs, subsequently renting Belvoir and selling off much of its furniture. They all knew the Fairfaxes would be gone a long time, but as it turned out, they never returned.

Cementing their new relationship, the Calverts returned with Betsy and Nelly on July 10; they stayed a couple of days and then left their daughters for a longer visit. Even though Martha was in mourning, she took great pains to keep the girls entertained with horseback rides, visits to neighbors and Alexandria, barbecues, and dances with neighboring young people in the evenings. Although she didn't often travel, she joined George in taking them home after a three-week visit, remaining at Mount Airy for four days.

Later in August, Nelly returned to Mount Vernon again, in the care of Governor Eden and a party of friends. Martha continued to provide for her entertainment during the three weeks she stayed before the governor picked her up on the way home. Nelly spent about half the summer—a total of fifty-four days—at Mount Vernon, ensconcing herself firmly in Martha's heart. Martha loved her from the beginning for Jack's sake, but she also came to regard Nelly as another daughter, whose presence during that summer lessened the pain of Patsy's loss.

Jack had been at college for three months when he was granted a vacation in late September; he was to meet his stepfather in Annapolis during the races and enjoy a quick reunion with his fiancée. When they arrived home on October 2, George's understanding was that Jack would enjoy a good long vacation and then return to college to study harder. Soon after their return, he confidently ordered books for his stepson, including Adam Smith's *Theory of Moral Sentiments* and John Locke's *Two Treatises of Government*.

It took him a while to realize that all those books would go unread. In October 1773, the Washingtons and Jack set off for the fall legislative session and social season at Williamsburg, stopping to visit Mary Washington and the Lewises on their way south before arriving at Eltham. George had to present his guardian's accounts to the court and wind up Patsy's estate, the investments of which were divided between her mother and her brother. While he was busy in Williamsburg, Martha spent most of the time with her relatives, no doubt being comforted for the loss of her daughter and encouraged in her plans for her son.

With some of Jack's inheritance, George bought more land for him—two tracts close to the rest of his land, Romancoke and Pleasant Hill. The latter included a commodious two-story brick house, which he may have expected Jack and Nelly to live in after their marriage. In a way, George kept daydreaming about making Jack more like himself. The thousands of Custis acres were rich and productive; any decent tobacco planter would want to take charge of his own land and keep a close eye on the crops once he came of age. Jack was pleasant, compliant, and passive—probably agreeing to everything and not saying, even not realizing, perhaps, that he and Nelly wanted to stay close to their parents and not move so far south. Jack had no more interest in farming than in Greek or Latin.

During their time away from home, Martha finally brought her husband to realize that it was pointless to return the unwilling student to college. Jack wanted to get married as soon as possible, and more important, that's what Martha wanted. He was her last remaining chick, as well as the sole heir to a large fortune, and she wanted grandchildren. After their return to Mount Vernon, George finally wrote to the president of King's College on December 15. Wistfully reiterating his wish for Jack to receive "useful knowledge," he accepted that "these hopes are at an end; & at length, I have yielded contrary to my judgment, & much against my wishes, to his quitting College." He had acceded to "his [Jack's] own inclination— the desires of his mother—& the acquiescence of almost all his relatives . . . as he is the last of the family . . . & therefore have submitted to a Kind of necessity."

On February 3, the day rainy and drear, George and his cousin Lund arrived in time for the wedding that evening. Martha did not attend because her mourning garb and evident sorrow would, she felt, cast gloom on the festivities. For the first years of their marriage, the young Custises had no home of their own but divided their time between Mount Airy and Mount Vernon.

Washington's doubts about the wisdom of Jack's early marriage made sense, but in fact it was Martha, wiser in the ways of the heart, who was right. For after Jack married, he showed no signs of regret or infidelity but devoted himself happily to his wife. Jack never really took hold of anything in his life except Nelly Calvert, and his marriage gave him stability. Once he'd accepted Jack as he was, George could relax in his company for the first time since he was a little boy.

The relationship was made easier, as well, by George's turning his formidable energies toward political affairs. He had less time to occupy himself with Jack's failings as he pondered events in far-off New York and Boston. News of the Boston Tea Party, the destruction of a valuable cargo of British tea by protesting Bostonians in December 1773, soon reached Virginia. As he and Martha read the newspapers and entertained well-informed visitors, the discussion usually turned to British colonial policy and what it might mean for Virginia's interests.

None of these concerns could keep George from beginning an extensive enlargement of Mount Vernon in April, something he had been thinking about for a while. He planned to add to both sides of the existing house—at the north end, a great room, which could serve as both formal dining room and ballroom; at the other end, a private study and bedroom for him and Martha. The driveway would be changed as well. Instead of the commonplace straight drive leading up from the public road, he planned an elegant serpentine driveway with the two branches meeting in a circle at the front door. The gardens would be replanted to enhance the dramatic effect he was aiming for.

Martha was certainly consulted about these plans, no doubt spending hours listening as he debated the pros and cons of one option or another; but building was George's passion, not hers. For him, the house was both a consuming interest and an expression of his position and self-esteem. Martha's devotion was to people, not property. For her, the important question about the house was the number of relatives and friends she could fit into it.

In May 1774, Martha and George went down to Williamsburg.

During the first week of their stay, he lodged in the capital city and attended sessions of the House of Burgesses while she stayed at Eltham with Nancy. The Bassetts had passed two enjoyable weeks with them at Mount Vernon the month before. Nancy was Martha's dearest friend, and the distance between them pained her.

That week, further news from Boston reached Williamsburg. The affronted British Parliament had passed the Coercive Acts (called by Americans the Intolerable Acts), a series of provisions meant to bring Bostonians to heel. Notification of these new laws was brought to Boston by a military force in May: the port was to be closed to all trade on June 1 until reparations for the lost tea and taxes were paid—in effect abruptly stopping all business in the city and throwing hundreds of men out of work. Other provisions tightened imperial administrative and judicial control, and perhaps most provocatively, British soldiers would be quartered in Boston homes. Loyalty and confidence in the mother country started to falter even in Virginia, the most British of the colonies in culture and tradition. But nothing yet seemed completely irrevocable; after all, previous crises had been resolved.

Although the times were filled with controversy, there was still room for civility. The royal governor of Virginia, Lord Dunmore, had succeeded Lord Botetourt three years before; his wife, six of their children, and several servants had recently come out from England to join him. Lady Dunmore, the daughter as well as the wife of an earl, was beautiful, elegant, and very chic. Virginians may have been edging slowly toward revolution, but they still admired the English aristocracy and were eager to meet them socially.

After a weekend at Eltham, George brought his wife to town on Monday for social events in honor of Lady Dunmore. Martha enjoyed dinners with colonial officials, including the governor and his wife, a ride and breakfast out at their farm, and a grand ball given by the House of Burgesses to welcome Lady Dunmore. The countess's gown was the most gorgeous ever seen in Williamsburg. It did come straight from London. As she led off the ball with a minuet, followed by the popular country dances, she was so graceful that one observer said with a sigh, "We had never seen dancing before."

Martha no doubt enjoyed every glamorous minute while well aware that only the good manners of Virginians allowed the social events to go on during the same week that they were moving closer to rebellion against the government Dunmore represented.

On Tuesday, the burgesses unanimously passed a proposal to declare June 1, the day the port of Boston would be closed, a day of fasting, humiliation, and prayer. On Thursday, after the Washingtons returned from the governor's farm, Lord Dunmore dissolved the assembly in response to the resolution and the fear of even more aggressive measures. On Friday, the day of the ball for Lady Dunmore, the burgesses met in the Apollo Room of the Raleigh Tavern and passed resolutions in support of American liberties and against the Coercive Acts. They also agreed to boycott tea and other British goods and to write to the other colonies proposing a general congress. George Washington was one of the signers.

With no legislative business possible, the Washingtons spent nearly another month in a combination of business and pleasure, including the fireworks in the capital in honor of Lady Dunmore, before they returned home in late June. The Custises came to spend July with them before George rode back to Williamsburg for the rebellious Virginia Convention, which began August 1. He took Jack along with him to look over his plantations, while Nelly apparently stayed at Mount Vernon with Martha. The members, who included most of the burgesses, agreed not to import any British goods whatsoever (except medicines) beginning November 1. They elected seven delegates to represent the colony in September at "the General Congress at Philadelphia," George Washington among them.

He was beginning to emerge as one of the natural leaders of the American colonies in their swiftly deepening split with Great Britain, and Martha fully supported his involvement. Politics at Mount Vernon was not a hush-hush matter kept from the ladies' delicate ears. Martha and George Washington discussed anything and everything.

On August 30, 1774, two of George's fellow commissioners—Edmund Pendleton and Patrick Henry—came to spend the night before going to Philadelphia, along with the formidable George Mason. The evening must have passed in intense political discussion. The next day dawned very hot and windless. After dinner, Washington, Pendleton, and Henry rode away to attend what was to be called the Continental Congress. Their charge was to discuss joint action vis-à-vis their mutual rulers.

Edmund Pendleton wrote, "I was much pleased with Mrs. Washington and her spirit. She seemed ready to make any sacrifice and was cheerful though I knew she felt anxious. She talked like a Spartan mother to her son on going to battle. 'I hope you will stand firm—I know George will,' she said. The dear little woman was busy from morning until night with domestic duties, but she gave us much time in conversation and affording us entertainment. When we set off in the morning, she stood in the door and cheered us with the good words, 'God be with you gentlemen.' "

During George's absence, Martha would have read the newspapers faithfully and corresponded with him regularly. A new spirit of colonywide cooperation and resistance toward Britain was in the air. Twelve of the thirteen colonies sent representatives to Philadelphia, and they laid out the unconstitutional acts and encroachments of British authorities. The congressmen agreed to enter into a nonimportation, nonconsumption, and nonexportation association and to prepare addresses on their grievances to the people of Great Britain, the inhabitants of British America, and King George. Another Congress was scheduled for the following year. George arrived home on October 30, and he and Martha spent the fall about their usual pursuits, while following political events closely.

Patsy's death, Jack's marriage, and the deepening chasm between Great Britain and her colonies signaled the end of the long Mount Vernon idyll for Martha Washington. Their last full year of peace was 1774. For the rest of her life, through the American Revolution and her husband's two terms as president, she longed to recapture those peaceful days before George Washington stepped irrevocably onto the stage of American history.

CHAPTER SIX

Lady Washington and the American Revolution

With the rift deepening between Britain and the colonies, George rode to Richmond in March 1775 for the second Virginia Convention, returning at the end of the month. Once again, he had been chosen as part of the Virginia delegation to the Second Continental Congress in Philadelphia. During April, Jack and Nelly were back at Mount Vernon when many of Virginia's leading politicians, including George Mason, came and went, in discussion and preparation for the Congress.

Then the men of Massachusetts upped the ante. On April 19, militiamen attacked the British regulars sent out to confiscate their weapons, first at Lexington and then at Concord, pursuing the fleeing redcoats all the way back to Boston. Their dander up, they besieged the city, calling for reinforcements from other New England militias. Even before the Congress gathered to consider the options, these colonists were in arms against Great Britain.

On May 4, 1775, George Washington rolled away in the family coach with Richard Henry Lee, the latest in a stream of visitors, who was also returning to Philadelphia as a delegate. Martha waited and fretted as the Congress discussed courses of conduct; although she got some information from George's letters, she probably wasn't prepared for the news she received at the end of June.

British intransigence and the New Englanders' siege of Boston pushed the Second Continental Congress into much more decisive action than the first had taken. John Adams, the radical lawyer from Massachusetts, suggested on June 14 the need to elect a national commander; when Washington realized whom he had in mind, he left the chamber. The following day, Adams proposed that George Washington be appointed general and commander in chief of the forces outside Boston, which would be reconstituted into a continental army rather than a loose collection of New England militia units. There were other possible commanders, each with his own supporters, but Washington had military experience and stature, and he was from Virginia. Unless the conflict became truly colonieswide, including Virginia (the oldest and largest of them) and the other southern colonies, New England would surely be overcome. When the appointment was passed unanimously the next day, Washington accepted, with some genuine misgivings about his own qualifications.

In his acceptance address, as recorded by Edmund Pendleton, he requested that the Congress pay his expenses but refused to accept a salary since "no pecuniary consideration could have tempted me to have accepted the Arduous employment." To that sentence, he added one key phrase: "at the expence of my domestk ease & happi[ness]." No man enjoyed home life more than Washington, and he truly regretted giving up its pleasures.

George waited three days before writing to Martha on June 18, to give her what he knew she would consider very bad news. As always, his lengthy epistle began "My Dearest" and he called her "my dear Patcy" twice as he made his case. George wrote of his deep concern about the uneasiness he knew his news would cause her. Swearing that he had not sought the appointment, both because of "unwillingness to part with you and the family" and his sense of unworthiness, he assured her that "I should enjoy more real happiness and felicity in one month with you, at home, than I have the most distant prospect of reaping abroad, if my stay was to be Seven times Seven years." But his sense of honor and responsibility wouldn't allow him to refuse.

Hoping that the British government would knuckle under to

colonial determination fairly soon, he wrote that he had no doubt he would "return safe to you in the fall"—perhaps more as a consolation than a true belief. He begged her not to be unhappy "at being left alone"—this to a woman who lived in a house packed with relatives, friends, visitors, and servants. But to Martha, he well knew, his presence was the one essential to her happiness. Alone to her meant being without him. Hoping that she would summon her resolution and pass her time "as agreeably as possible," he almost pleaded to hear that she had accepted his decision and "to hear it from your own Pen."

George was never an overbearing patriarch: he left any decision about where Martha would stay in his absence to her own good judgment. During the few months that he expected to be gone, he begged her to go wherever she liked. Perhaps to their Alexandria town house? Or visiting her family down in New Kent County? "In short, my earnest, & most ardent desire is, that you would pursue any Plan that is most likely to produce content, and a tolerable degree of Tranquility as it must add greatly to my uneasy feelings to hear that you are dissatisfied, and complaining at what I really could not avoid."

Enclosing a new will drawn up by Pendleton, he expressed his hope that she would find agreeable the terms it laid out. Despite the fortune she brought to their marriage, legally he didn't need to consult her about his testamentary dispositions, and many husbands exercised absolute control over their wives' wealth, to the women's misery. But the confidence between Martha and George was unconditional, and he considered her a full partner in their relationship. He ended the letter with a postscript about his purchase of two suits "of what I was told was the prettiest Muslin," which she had requested in her most recent letter. As with so much of life, here the dramatic and the commonplace were inextricably entwined.

Over the next days, he and members of the Congress worked out the appointments of the army's major generals and made arrangements for his command. But George's most immediate concern was his wife. In the first week of his appointment, he wrote seven known letters; only two dealt with military matters. He wrote two letters to Martha and three to relatives to make arrangements for her safety and happiness.

On June 19, he wrote to Burwell Bassett, asking him and Nancy to visit Mount Vernon and to convince Martha to go south with them, "as I have no expectations of returning till Winter & feel great uneasiness at her lonesome Situation." Apparently, his optimism to his wife about a fall return could be dropped a bit when he wrote to his brother-in-law.

The same day, he wrote to Jack Custis, "My great concern upon this occasion, is the thought of leaving your Mother under the uneasiness which I know this affair will throw her into; I therefore hope, expect, & indeed have no doubt, of your using every means in your power to keep up her Spirits. . . . I have I must confess very uneasy feelings on her acct." The solicitous husband continued with the assurance of his pleasure at having Jack and Nelly live at Mount Vernon at any time, especially now "when I think it absolutely necessary for the peace & satisfaction of your Mother."

The next day, he wrote to his brother Jack Washington, who lived not too far away in Westmoreland County, hoping that he and his wife, Hannah, would find time during the summer to visit Mount Vernon. He was fully conscious of how much he meant to Martha and of how much she would miss him. Without false modesty, he described his absence and danger as "a cutting stroke upon her." He sent the traveling coach and its four horses back home for her use. To replace them, he bought a light phaeton and a team of two white horses, as well as three additional mounts.

Having done all he could for Martha's happiness short of coming home, he turned to the army. The Battle of Bunker Hill on June 17, though an American defeat, gave both the British and the Americans themselves a new appreciation of the colonists' strength under fire. Six days later, as Washington was leaving for Boston, he dropped Martha a short note to express his confidence in "a happy Meeting with you sometime in the Fall." He sat writing in a room full of congressmen and Philadelphians come to bid farewell to the man they counted on to resolve the present crisis. As they called for his attention, he assured his much loved wife that "I retain an unalterable affection for you, which neither time or distance can change."

Martha decided to stay at Mount Vernon while waiting: that was where George would go at once if the military action was brief and decisive or if he allowed himself any leave. As always during his infrequent absences, they corresponded regularly, generally weekly. The postal service was in flux from the royal mail to a constitutional post office, then to a continental system. Many letters went astray because of "the infernal curiosity of some of the Scoundrel Postmasters" and loyalist interception of correspondence—to Washington's indignation.

As much as he worried over "the heavy, and lonesome hours of my Wife," he missed home himself and looked eagerly for letters. Richard Henry Lee and other friends made it a point to stop by to see Martha and send on any news to Washington.

One possibility terrified some Virginians, especially Alexandrians: a British man-of-war might sail up the Potomac to Mount Vernon, kidnap Martha, and hold her prisoner. The threat seemed especially real since Virginia's royal governor had retreated to a British ship lurking near Williamsburg, within easy striking distance of any target on Virginia's rivers. But Martha refused to let any danger drive her from home. An accomplished horsewoman could easily outdistance the marines that a ship would send ashore to capture her. Although George had scoffed at the notion, he fretted about it often in his letters. No one yet had any idea what sort of war this would be, if any, and whether or not civilians would be attacked.

Throughout the fall, Martha often declared that she would go to camp if George would allow it, but to her disappointment no invitation came. She finally decided to go to the Bassetts but waited until Nelly Custis recovered from giving birth to a baby girl, who died soon afterward. Late in October, Jack escorted his mother and wife south, stopping for a few days in Fredericksburg to see Mary Washington and the Lewises; in New Kent County, they stayed at Eltham and visited the Dandridge clan. Given the exigencies of wartime, his stepfather had turned over the management of the Custis property to Jack, even though he wasn't yet of age, and Jack probably met with his overseers on this trip.

Charity was one of the bedrocks of the Washingtons' joint belief about the responsibilities inherent in their good fortune. As a matter of course, they provided food and clothing to their poor neighbors and always gave wayfarers a meal and a night's lodging. In their absence, Lund Washington was instructed to continue "the Hospitality of the House, with respect to the Poor. . . . Let no one go hungry away." Lund put it succinctly: "I believe Mrs. Washingtons Charitable disposition increases in the proportion with her meat House." Soon after arriving at Eltham, Martha heard about a poor neighbor woman with a sick husband, and she directed her overseer to "let her have a barrel of corn and half a barrel of wheat . . . and give her a fat hog."

During that summer and fall at headquarters in Cambridge, outside besieged Boston, Washington began the enormous task of creating a national army. The Congress had named four major generals to serve under the commander in chief, all of them with command experience in the French and Indian War. These appointments were as much politico-geographic as military, and the upper echelon of the army changed during the years of the war as officers' fortunes in battle rose and fell.

One of the brigadier generals, the English-born Horatio Gates, was appointed adjutant general. An officer in the regular British army, Gates had moved to a Virginia plantation near Petersburg when his career stalled. His military experience and talent for administration made him invaluable at Cambridge, where he wrote army regulations and maintained military records.

Washington began assembling his military "family" at this time, the staff officers on whom he depended to write and file letters, carry orders and confidential messages, entertain visitors, act as sounding boards for his ideas, and provide companionship during the long, dull, anxious stretches of time between battles. The young men who served as aides-de-camp during the Revolution became a cadre of surrogate sons to him and to Martha when she eventually arrived at headquarters.

During these months, George fully expected to be able to go home for a visit at the end of the year. At that time, armies settled into winter encampments and generally didn't fight again until spring or even summer, depending on the weather, a sort of informal time-out. Foraging expeditions and occasional sorties, yes—but not full-scale battles. Feeding and clothing large numbers of men in action, as well as moving troops over frozen roads and fields, was simply too overwhelming a task for the logistics of the day. These downtimes coincidentally provided an opportunity for officers to take leave.

But European armies were professional organizations of long standing, the officers and men falling into well-worn grooves, maintaining discipline and order until it was time to go into battle again. Not so for the American army, which was still just a conglomeration of state militias. By early October 1775, Washington realized that his army was at a crucial point. Without the commander's presence, there was the terrifying possibility that all his work would be for nothing. Most of the soldiers enlisted for short terms and took off as soon as their enlistments were up—just keeping the siege manned and the troops supplied was an enormous task. Washington couldn't leave now. So that year, he did what he would for all the years to come: he wrote to Martha, asking her to join him in winter camp.

Many British officers entertained themselves in camp with all-night drinking bouts, high-stakes gambling, and a plethora of easily available sexual partners. The Puritan strain in American society called for greater discretion in their camp, but some men took the opportunity to kick off—or at least loosen—the marital traces. Not their commander. Whatever George Washington's sexual experiences as a young man may have been, he had never led a dissipated life—even his love for the married Sally Fairfax had been well-nigh respectable. There would be no startling middle-aged outbreak: he was well aware that he set the example for his men, and he genuinely delighted in his wife's company and their "domestic enjoyments."

Unlike many husbands of the day, he never ordered his wife to do anything. He simply invited Martha "to come to me, altho' I fear the Season is too far advanced . . . to admit this with any tolerable degree of convenience." After all, she had never been north of Annapolis and hadn't much relished those trips; she had no experience of the bone-chilling weather in Massachusetts or the potential dangers of a winter trip there. George described "the difficulties . . . which attend the journey before her and left it to her own choice." Then he waited for her response. And waited.

The vagaries of the mail caused the long delay. It wasn't until the twenty-second of the month, nearly a week after Martha had gone down to Eltham, that Lund received his cousin's letters of October 2, 7, and 9, along with his accompanying letters for Martha. When Lund realized that George wanted his wife to come north, he sent a messenger with her letters the next morning. "I expect her home Imediately," he wrote George, incorrectly, as it happened.

But Martha wouldn't be chivied into departing before she was ready, however much menfolk might fuss and fume. Lund's messenger returned with a letter for George and the news that she wouldn't return home for another week. Having made the trip to the Bassetts, she meant to finish up there before leaving. Lund was on pins and needles, assuring George that he would do everything to get her on the road as soon as possible.

Lund was devoted to George Washington and his interests and proved his commitment time and again throughout the war years. When he wrote that "I will cheerfully do . . . every thing that lays in my power for you," it was only one of many such avowals. But he chafed under Martha's authority and the unlimited confidence George reposed in her. She could make whatever decisions she pleased, despite his objections, and he resented that power in a woman.

During the autumn of 1775, he had several occasions to complain about Martha's high-handedness. Throughout his life, George Washington valued his papers and maintained them carefully— diaries, letters, account books. His commitment to their preservation is the reason we know so much about him today. Martha herself packed her husband's papers in a locked trunk to move them to a safer place when a British attack seemed possible. Lund was aggrieved that she left him out, imagining that she had jumbled all the papers. To his indignation, she took several sums of money for her northern journey without accounting to him for them. Although George had suggested that their friend Sarah Barnes might stay at Mount Vernon as the estate housekeeper that winter, Martha vetoed it, seeming "to think it will not answer."

She wouldn't come back from Eltham, nor would she leave Mount Vernon when he thought she should. And then the final complaint: "This House has been so Crouded with company since Mrs. Washington came home that I fear many things is left undone that should have been done before she left home. I write in haste & a little confuse'd." A woman who knew what she wanted and did it confidently put Lund off his stride, but George was never fazed.

There are two sorts of travelers—those who fly out the door with the clothes on their backs and those who try to pack everything for any possible contingency. Martha was definitely one of the latter. Before she would leave home, she had to be satisfied that she had all the hams and blankets, clothes and endless hanks of knitting wool, and the million and one other things she needed for an absence of months. No one was going to push her out the door a day before she was ready to go.

Besides all her supplies, she brought family members with her to re-create their household away from home. Jack Custis went along as companion, escort, and mother's delight; Nelly was happy to make one of the party, probably hoping that new sights would take her mind off losing the baby. One of George's nephews and namesakes, his sister Betty's son George Washington Lewis, came with them because he was joining Washington's personal guard. The party finally set off about November 16. Along the way, they picked up Elizabeth Phillips Gates, wife of the adjutant general.

Martha's first journey to the northern colonies began to assume the quality of a triumphal procession. Since she first married, she had enjoyed position and status within a close-knit community. Now she was being recognized and feted by strangers as though she were "a very great somebody," as she expressed it, her carriage met and escorted by honor guards of mounted troops, her party greeted by each town's leading citizens. It was an amazing experience, her first realization that her husband had transcended his Virginia identity and become a truly American leader.

Since he assumed command of the Revolutionary forces, Washington had become a patriotic icon to Americans badly in need of a national symbol to replace the king—very much against the general's own inclination. Patriots began naming their sons George Washington, and he became the subject of laudatory poems by such writers as Philip Freneau and Phillis Wheatley.

Reams of adulatory poetry and patriotic songs were written about the commander, but visual representations of the hero were even more important in a semiliterate age. Legislative bodies, colleges, and wealthy admirers desired paintings of Washington, while engravings by the hundreds, as well as flags and transparencies for parades and patriotic displays, were necessary to satisfy the desires of the general public. Through it all, George showed a wry acceptance of the public's wish for visual images. To Martha's bemusement, her image too began to be demanded as a symbol of the republican wife.

Martha's party arrived in grand, red-brick Philadelphia, that most elegant and sophisticated of colonial cities, on November 21. With the Congress meeting there, it was in effect the capital of the colonies. As Martha wrote home, "I don't doubt but you have seen the Figure our arrival made in the Philadelphia paper." The travelers settled into comfortable lodgings to rest for a week before continuing on their long journey, becoming acquainted with Philadelphians and congressmen who came to pay courtesy calls on the commanding general's wife. To Martha's pleasure, a group of prominent citizens had organized a ball in her honor. Like any Virginian, she found celebrations and dancing as natural as breathing, completely compatible with her husband's grave responsibilities.

She had reached middle age in an extremely homogeneous society, and she had no experience of the social and cultural tensions that existed in a big city like Philadelphia with its Quakers, Presbyterians, Baptists, and political radicals of a puritanical bent. Her first hint of dissension came on the day of the ball when a delegation of four serious men called to express their "great regard and affection to her," along with compliments on her husband's "defense of our rights and liberties."

Of course, she thanked them graciously for their sentiments, but they hadn't yet come to the real reason for their call. A ball, in their opinion, was an excess in "these troubled times"; then they appealed to her "not to grace that company to which, we are informed, she has an invitation to this evening."

Martha quickly recovered from any surprise and proffered her "best compliments" to her censors, assuring them "that their sentiments on this occasion were perfectly agreeable unto her own." Though no doubt disappointed at missing the evening's pleasure, she was well aware of her husband's need to draw together troops and support from all the colonies and to respect many points of view, however restrictive they might seem. The ball was canceled after she sent her regrets to the hosts.

Among the many Philadelphians she met was Joseph Reed, a congressman who had served briefly as Washington's aide; the men corresponded regularly after Reed returned home. When the carriage got back on the road on November 28, Martha observed that "I left [Philadelphia] in as great pomp as if I had been a very great somebody." Reed wrote to Washington that "Mesdames Washington, Custis, and Gates were very agreeable ladies. . . . No bad supply, I think, in a cold country where wood is scarce." Every winter, when Martha and the other officers' wives began arriving at headquarters, that stale old joke was trotted out. It was based on the reality that colonial buildings at night were nearly as cold inside as out and that warm bedmates made for a comfortable night's sleep.

They arrived safely in Cambridge on December 11, to the great relief of General Washington. He had been worried about their finding the way safely, asking Reed to give Martha "particular instructions and advice." He sent one of his aides to escort the coach, asking him to send a messenger to headquarters a day ahead of their arrival. Although George complained that snow had turned the ground into an unpleasant white waste, she was positive as usual. "This is a beautyfull country, and we had a very plasant journey through New England, and had the plasure to find the General very well. We came within the month from home to the Camp."

Martha had a naturally calm and optimistic outlook on life, but she also worked at maintaining that attitude. As she later wrote, "I am still determined to be cheerful and to be happy in whatever situation I may be, for I have also learnt from experience that the greater part of our happiness or misery depends upon our dispositions, and not upon our circumstances; we carry the seeds of the one, or the other about with us, in our minds, wherever we go."

The village of Cambridge was surrounded with earthworks and chock-full of American soldiers, their officers occupying many of the principal houses. The men were armed with a wide assortment of weapons brought from home or acquired higgledy-piggledy. There were no standard uniforms: some wealthy officers supplied uniforms of their own fancy to their troops; in other units, men wore their everyday working clothes or leather hunting shirts and breeches copied from the Indians.

The town common had become a parade ground. Harvard was closed down, its buildings serving as barracks. From the heights around Boston, colonial soldiers watched the British tear up wharves, fences, and abandoned houses for firewood. Sounds carried too in the crisp, cold air, as both sides listened to bugles and shouted commands, alert for the noises of an unexpected foray.

At first, Martha found the preparations for war and the nonchalance of the soldiers and citizens bewildering. She wrote: "Every person seems to be cheerfull and happy here. Some days we have a number of cannon and shells from Boston and Bunkers Hill, but it does not seem to surprise any one but me; I confess I shudder every time I hear the sound of a gun." She was driven up Prospect Hill to look down at "poor" Boston and Charlestown. The latter had only a few chimneys standing, but a number of fine buildings still stood in Boston. She observed: "God knows how long they will stand; they are pulling up all the warfs for firewood. To me that never [has] seen anything of war, the preparations are very terable indeed, but I endever to keep my fears to myself as well as I can."

Martha settled into a fine Georgian two-story frame house, well furnished, the property of a Tory, Major John Vassall, which had been taken over as the commander's residence. It stood in a large fenced lot, whose garden must have been charming earlier in the year but was now blanketed with snow. She was happy to discover that although "the distance is long ... the post comes in very regularly every week"—all the way from Williamsburg. Still influenced by traditional British formality, many people settled on calling Martha "Lady Washington" for want of an official title.

As usual, her first concern was her husband's comfort, allowing him freedom from domestic details to concentrate on his military responsibilities. The household was run by a steward, its expenses paid by one of Washington's aides who also kept the accounts; she reorganized household affairs so that they ran more smoothly. His emotional comfort, however, was her primary care. Her deep devotion to her children and other family members paled before the burning intensity of her love for George Washington. He accepted her adoration without much thought. It was the atmosphere in which he breathed and lived, where he was most himself. She was at his side and on his side, sympathizing and supporting him through depression, failure, disloyalty, and anxiety about the future. With her, he needn't pretend to be perfect.

As army headquarters, the Vassall house was the commander's office as well as the Washingtons' home and staff quarters. Being the commander's wife was something like being a fraternity house mother; Martha and George were in their mid-forties, living with a large group of men in their twenties—Washington's aides-de-camp and a shifting number of other bachelor officers and visitors. The young men slept two or three to a bed and several to a room; they were always bustling back and forth on military errands, sometimes seeking out their own private entertainments of the sort not best shared with Lady Washington.

This first winter camp in Cambridge, though far more comfortable than those to come, set the pattern for the rest of the American

Revolution. The arrival of the commander's wife signaled that other officers might bring their wives to join them. Martha loved nothing more than congenial company, and the Vassall house became quite gay with dinners and visits. Jack and Nelly, who soon discovered that she was pregnant again, were great social assets.

The higher-ranking officers and their wives became part of a sociable circle, taking turns entertaining one another throughout the winter. Cambridge almost began to seem like home. That is, if one ignored the weather, the strange conglomeration of accents and manners, and the reason that had brought them all together. Martha made lifetime friends among the officers' wives, but Elizabeth Gates wasn't one of them. They came to dislike each other, especially later when Gates allowed himself to be considered a likely replacement in command by Washington's critics, egged on by "that Medusa . . . [who] rules with a rod of Scorpions," as another general described her.

Curiosity had drawn visitors to Cambridge since the beginning of the siege. With both armies out of action for the winter and Lady Washington in residence, the visits increased, including several congressmen come to look over this "continental" army that they were supporting. The entertainment of influential guests, who naturally expected dinner at headquarters and personal tours, had taken up too much of Washington's time. Martha provided a screening process, greeting and chatting with them when they entered the house before taking them to meet the general and sometimes taking over their entertainment again after their shortened interviews.

Among his line officers, George found two inexperienced, native-born leaders especially talented and congenial—Nathanael Greene and Henry Knox. While both enjoyed healthy strains of pride and egotism, they were loyal to Washington and could submerge their individual ambitions for the greater good. They were middle-class civilians of the sort who would never have stood a chance to become officers in the caste-ridden professional armies of Great Britain, France, or any of the German states.

Nathanael Greene was a Quaker from Rhode Island who had been read out of his meeting when he joined the state militia. A farmer and smith from a moderately well-to-do family, Greene lacked military experience but learned fast. Nearly six feet tall, he was strong and well built, a good-humored man who smiled often. His physical presence and charisma helped him inspire confidence in a ragtag collection of men from different colonies. He leaped in one day from private to general in the Rhode Island militia and proved his ability over time.

At camp, he was joined by his young wife, Catherine Littlefield Greene (twenty-two to his thirty-four). Nathanael was desperately in love with the very pregnant Kitty. A vivacious, sometimes reckless brunette, she became one of Martha and George's great favorites. When she arrived in Cambridge, Kitty drove up to the Vassall house, where she talked with Martha in the paneled parlor. Then they went across the wide hall to the general's office. Saucy and always ready with a quick response, Kitty was the sort of young woman George most enjoyed spending time with. He teased her about her "Quaker-preacher" husband, and she promised to name her baby for the general if it was a boy. True to her word, when she gave birth in January, she named her son George Washington Greene.

Henry Knox was one of those success stories of the right man appearing at the right time. Only twenty-five when the Revolution began, he was a self-educated bookseller from Boston. A committed patriot since the Boston Massacre, he was tall, fat, and a man of unbeatable humor and charm. Martha was so fond of him that she later made him two hairnets, also known as "queue bags"—woven bags to bind up his long ponytail, or queue.

Of all the military branches, artillery was the least glamorous and prestigious, but Henry chose it, learning about big guns and the strategy for fighting them from books. After Washington named him colonel and chief of the army's artillery, his first task was to assemble enough cannons and other artillery for his men to fire.

Martha also spent time with Lucy Flucker Knox, Henry's hefty and fun-loving wife, but she came to know her well only later. The daughter of a fiercely loyalist family (her father was royal secretary of Massachusetts), she married Henry against their wishes. While her parents remained under siege in Boston, she was with the American forces, expecting her first child.

The ladies of Cambridge came calling at the Vassall house now that there was a hostess at headquarters to receive them with oranges and a glass of wine. Martha also met the formidable Mercy Otis Warren of Plymouth, an accomplished playwright, poet, and leading American patriot. Her husband, James, was paymaster general of the army, charged with finding the wherewithal to keep the troops at their posts.

A slim, sharp-featured woman, Mercy liked Martha, three years her junior, but perhaps underestimated her intelligence because of her soft southern manner. She wrote to her friend Abigail Adams that Martha had greeted her on their first meeting "with that politeness and respect shown in a first interview among the well-bred, and with the ease and cordiality of older friendship. The complacency of her manners speaks at once the benevolence of her heart, and her affability, candor, and gentleness qualify her to soften the hours of private life, or to sweeten the cares of the hero, and smooth the rugged pains of war."

The new army officially came into existence January 1, 1776. According to Washington, it was "in every point of View . . . entirely Continental." The sign and countersign for the day were "The Congress" and "America." A crowd of soldiers and civilians gathered to celebrate at the parade ground on Prospect Hill. Unfortunately, thousands of militiamen refused to reenlist, streaming steadily out of town. For a few days, until new troops arrived, the Americans were drastically undermanned, but the British didn't attack.

In the meantime, Henry Knox had been sent to Fort Ticonderoga in upstate New York to bring back a large supply of cannons and mortars, lead and flints. With a small group of picked men, he chose fifty-odd pieces of artillery (sources disagree on the exact number) and transported the weapons through three hundred miles of snowy mountains and icy roads. Eighty yokes of oxen dragged the forty-two sledges built for the trek; the large siege mortars, one of them known as "Old Sow," weighed a ton each. Had he done nothing else—and he did a lot more—bringing artillery to Boston would have made Knox an American hero.

After months of stalemate, the American army was now armed and ready. All the talk at headquarters was how and when to attack. As the commander's wife, Martha attended closely to military news, strategies, and the shortages that so bedeviled George. A committed partisan, she boasted to her sister in a quite martial letter of the success of "our navey," which had recently taken two British supply ships loaded with coal, potatoes, wines, and other supplies—all put to good use by the Americans.

The large port of New York would undoubtedly be the site of British attack soon, because of both its strategic location and its large population of loyalists. Washington had sent General Charles Lee there "in case any disturbance should happen." If the British arrived, she hoped Lee would give them "a very warm reception." Having absorbed Washington's concerns about civilian informers and spies, Martha fully realized the danger in New York posed by the "many Tories in that part of the world or at least many are suspected thare to be unfriendly to our cause at this time."

In early March, Washington sent the American army into action. Under cover of a general bombardment, the Americans fortified Dorchester Heights, overlooking Boston, and moved in men and field pieces overnight. It was a brilliant maneuver. On March 5, the British awoke to face an entrenched enemy who could blow away the city and the fleet in the harbor. After a counterattack was delayed and then prevented by a tremendous storm, the British prepared to evacuate. Among the Tory civilians who sailed away with the fleet for loyalist Halifax, Nova Scotia, on March 27 were the Fluckers; Lucy Knox would never again see her family. The siege of Boston was over.

The city was left almost in ruins—trenches in the common, spiked cannons, piles of spoiled supplies, dilapidated and destroyed buildings, wharves and fences gone, wildly overgrown gardens. Toward the end of the siege, there had been an epidemic of smallpox, and only American soldiers with immunity, identified by their pockmarked faces, could enter safely. Because she had never had smallpox, Martha could not join Kitty Greene and other officers' wives at celebratory dinners in the city. She did enjoy a bit of sightseeing, taking Mercy Warren on an early morning carriage drive "to see the Deserted Lines of the Enemy." Besides, she was busy at headquarters with Washington's aides, making arrangements for their move.

On April 4, George Washington began moving his troops to New York City, marching through Rhode Island and Connecticut. He sent Martha, Jack, and Nelly by a different route, their coach escorted by two of his aides-de-camp. By going through Connecticut via Hartford, they avoided the racket and clouds of dust raised by an army on the march. On April 13, 1776, Washington was in New York.

Martha's party didn't arrive until four days later, delayed by Jack's illness on the road. The Custises stayed a couple of weeks before returning to Maryland. Nelly wanted to settle in safely with her mother and sisters at Mount Airy well in advance of the new baby's arrival.

Though thronged with business, including trying to convince New Yorkers that the British and Americans were truly at war, George devoted his usual care to his wife's comfort. He chose the Mortier house in lower Manhattan for their residence, probably using a separate building as his headquarters. Expecting that they would live there a while, he bought a featherbed, a bolster, some pillows, bed curtains, crockery, and pottery. Also, assuming that he would spend many future days in the field, he purchased a dining marquee (a large tent whose sides could be drawn up), a living tent with an arched chamber, walnut camp stools and tables, and other necessities for comfortable campaigning.

Martha remained a little over a month in New York. With the arrival of the army, smallpox began running wild through the city. Smallpox was very infectious and frequently fatal and left many of its surviving victims horribly scarred, their faces as cratered as the moon. The combination of a port city and an army of thousands of young men from the countryside created the ideal conditions for an epidemic. George himself was immune because of a light case he had suffered in his youth, but Martha wasn't. Without being inoculated, she couldn't stay safely in New York.

George was a strong advocate of inoculation, despite the risk of death, working tirelessly to create an army safe from smallpox. But he doubted Martha's courage to go through the frightening procedure. As he wrote to his brother Jack on April 29, "Mrs. Washington is still here, and talks of taking the Small Pox, but I doubt her resolution." How could he have been so blind? Martha would brave anything to be with him.

Summoned by Congress for consultation, George took the opportunity to escort Martha to Philadelphia, out of harm's way and with access to the nation's best doctors if she was inoculated. They arrived on May 23, staying at Randolph's lodging house rather than accepting John Hancock's offer of his home. That very afternoon, Martha plunged ahead, allowing a doctor to infect her before retiring to her room for the next three weeks.

After nearly a year in command, Washington had several changes and reforms in mind to improve the army, and he was able to convince Congress to put some of them into effect. Congressmen were considering the whole question of declaring independence; Washington considered fielding an army evidence enough of rebellion. Although he complained about being held overlong in Philadelphia by politicians, he was also keeping up his wife's spirits throughout her quarantine. The inoculation was successful. Not a pockmark marred her fair skin.

By June 6, Washington was again in New York, leaving Martha behind to recover completely; she rejoined him by midmonth. Then, on June 29, fifty British ships appeared on the horizon, carrying General William Howe and his troops. They settled into camp on Staten Island, awaiting reinforcements and a larger fleet from England.

The next day, Martha Washington and Lucy Knox were hustled out of town by their husbands, who were preparing to defend the city against vastly superior enemies. Kitty Greene stayed longer, stubbornly refusing to leave, but she too finally went home, pregnant with her second child. Martha waited in Philadelphia: if nothing more came of the British presence in New York than in Boston, she might be able to return. No need to hurry home, so far away, if there was a chance of rejoining George.

Thus it happened that Martha knew about the Declaration of Independence before her husband did. She was in Philadelphia when Congress voted for independence on July 2, when the Declaration was adopted on July 4, and when the Declaration was read and independence publicly proclaimed on July 8. Wherever she may have been staying, her closest sight of the parade, gunfire, and public reading at the State House was probably through a window. The crowds were rowdy, and few of the gentry were in evidence. George received a copy of the document on July 9. To the troops assembled on the large Broadway common, the commander read aloud the words that would change all their lives. But it would surely be no easy task.

Sir William Howe's brother, Admiral Lord Richard Howe, arrived soon after the Declaration with a large fleet and British reinforcements outnumbering the Americans by about two and a half to one. For six weeks, there were skirmishes and halfhearted suggestions of peace from the Howes, about which George wrote to his wife. Martha's hopes were buoyed by the opinion of some Philadelphians who "begen to think thare will be noe Battle after all."

Also heartened by the soldiers making their way to New York and a letter from her husband, on August 28 Martha rejoiced to Nancy: "I thank god we shant want men." Ironically, that was the date of the Battle of Long Island, an American defeat. Shortly afterward, terrible news reached Philadelphia. The American forces under Washington's command had pulled back from New York City, seriously mauled. They were retreating up Manhattan Island, and supporters of the Revolution had to face the possibility that their cause could be lost. Martha went home as soon as possible. She wouldn't be joining her husband in New York City any time soon.

Harlem Heights, Valcour Bay, White Plains, Fort Washington,

Newport—one American loss followed another until Washington was driven into Pennsylvania. Congress was terrified that the successful British army, now in control of New Jersey, would march straight to Philadelphia and punish the supporters of the Revolution. They fled the endangered city and reconvened in greater safety at Baltimore in early December.

Martha and George continued writing their weekly letters, his filled with the blackest news, though they were often delayed or went astray. In October, a packet of letters from American headquarters was stolen from an express rider as he refreshed himself at a tavern and taken to the British commander, including one for Martha that General Howe politely returned. Even in the middle of loss and vexations, George maintained his steady concern for Mount Vernon and his wife—ordering holly trees planted and sending down two likely bays for the team that drew Martha's coach. Back home, she fretted and worried about her husband. As general of the rebellious army, he would surely face death if the war was lost.

But there was also new life at Mount Vernon. Martha was delighted with her first grandchild, Elizabeth Parke Custis, described by her proud papa as "the strapping Huzze [hussy]," born August 21. Jack declared seriously that she was "as fine a Healthy, fat Baby as ever was born." Her black hair and eyes were like Nelly's. "It is as pretty & Fine a Baba as ever I saw. This not my opinion alone, but the Opinion of all who have seen Her." Her grandmama had to agree when she finally saw baby Betsy.

Winter fell unusually hard that year, the roads froze, snowdrifts piled high, and still the American army hadn't gone into winter camp by late December. From the defeats suffered and the almost miraculous escapes pulled off, Washington was learning effective tactics to use against a large professional army. He was learning to mitigate the weaknesses and maximize the strengths of American soldiers. He was on the way to creating a new sort of army, one that would survive to fight again and again until it wore down its opponents.

The string of unbroken losses at the end of 1776 had created a mood of gloom throughout a nation that hadn't yet celebrated its first birthday. It seemed possible that the Revolution would be crushed long before the next fourth of July. Washington turned that gloomy foreboding around. His surprise crossing of the icy Delaware River into enemy-held New Jersey on Christmas evening and the victorious attacks on Trenton and Princeton gave the nation new hope—particularly when British forces pulled back to their stronghold in New York City. New Jersey was in American hands again. Washington's army then settled into winter camp at Morristown, New Jersey, in January 1777.

The winter at Morristown was a preview for Valley Forge—severe cold, short supplies, muttering soldiers going home when their enlistments ran out. George was lonely and missed Martha. The erratic arrival of his letters from home was "mortifying, as it deprives me of the consolation of hearing from home on domestic matters." No one, he believed, "suffers more by an absence from home than myself."

Before the roads were quite clear, Martha set out for Morristown in late February, arriving at the camp in mid-March 1777. One way or another, her husband had mismanaged all her housekeeping arrangements, and she was forced to arrange everything anew for their convenience. Her arrival also acted as a signal for the arrival of the other women—officers' wives, sisters, and daughters, as well as visitors from the neighborhood. They gathered around Martha, sewing in hand, chatting and gossiping, commenting on or contriving romances.

Everybody enjoyed being with the Washingtons at headquarters because of their obvious fondness for each other and the good cheer they radiated. Martha doted on her "Old Man," as she called him. Bystanders were often amused when the formidable general, so often the object of dumbstruck respect, failed to notice that his "dear Patsy" was talking to him. That short, determined lady would yank on his coattails to get his attention, until he smiled down lovingly from his great height. She humanized the national hero—or rather demonstrated his humanity to those who hadn't seen it. Himself very happily married, Nathanael Greene could recognize love when he saw it: "They are very happy in each other."

Martha Daingerfield Bland, the wife of Colonel Theodorick Bland of Virginia, was in camp that spring. Like many women, she was charmed by Washington's "politeness and attention" as well as his ability to "be downright impudent sometimes." She and her husband went to headquarters nearly every day "from Inclination." Washington devoted the morning and early afternoon to military and political matters, but from dinner on he enjoyed the society of Martha and their visitors. "His Worthy Lady seems to be in perfect felicity while she is by the side of her <u>Old Man</u> as she calls him." In the afternoons, a large group often rode out on horseback through the beautifully rolling countryside.

A newcomer at headquarters was Alexander Hamilton, recently appointed aide-de-camp. Brilliant, polemical, and wildly ambitious, the twenty-year-old Hamilton seemed to be the perfect aide, secretary, and right-hand man to Washington. Born in the West Indies, he had been sent to King's College in New York, where he threw himself into the patriots' cause. Although he dreamed of further combat, he made the most of his close association with the commander in chief.

Another young man joined Washington's inner circle after Martha went home in June. In July, a nineteen-year-old French nobleman arrived at camp. Fired with the desire for glory and fed up with a miserable life ruled by his overbearing father-in-law, the Marquis de Lafayette had broken free and sailed to America. Overwhelmed by his position and wealth, Congress appointed him a major general of the Continental Army—even though he had no military experience. Washington suffered constant aggravation from congressional infatuation with foreign officers—many of them bogus, others totally unsuited to serve in a republic—all of them demanding high ranks and commands. But Lafayette was different. He had come to learn from Washington, not to peacock about. He became the son Washington had longed for and that Jack Custis could never be.

Howe brought his army from New York by ship to the head of

the Chesapeake and then marched on Philadelphia—not so much because he wanted the city as that he wanted to force Washington into battle so he could destroy the American army. Congress hurriedly departed westward for Lancaster and then farther west to York, which became the interim American capital. They demanded that their general prevent the capture of Philadelphia.

For the British to win a clear-cut victory, they needed to meet the Americans in open country where their numbers and rigorous discipline would prevail. Washington had learned that he had to pick his own ground. So far, quick movements, surprise attacks, superior marksmanship, and fast retreats had prevented his forces from being smashed by their better-armed, better-trained, and numerically superior enemies. The longer the British were forced to fight so far from home, their supply lines stretched until they twanged, the better for the American cause. Running up the cost of this operation both in pounds sterling and in casualties was creating political and popular opposition to the war in England.

The French were clandestinely supplying the rebels with money and war matériel to weaken their traditional enemies across the English Channel. American commissioners in Paris headed by Benjamin Franklin were trying to negotiate official recognition and aid. Any evidence that the American cause was viable could help tilt French officials toward a favorable decision.

Washington's two attempts to defend Philadelphia, the Battles of Brandywine and Germantown in September and October 1777, came close to succeeding, each turned to defeat by overelaborate plans and adverse circumstances. Germantown, in particular, following less than a month on the loss at the Brandywine, impressed French observers with the resiliency and flexibility of the American forces. But Philadelphia was lost: Howe and his army settled there that fall, impervious to American attack.

It was the capture of General John Burgoyne's army in October at Saratoga that finally led the French to commit to the American cause. Benedict Arnold contributed mightily to the American victory, though the credit was claimed by his commander Horatio Gates. Preening himself on the greatest American victory to date,

Gates set himself up as equal to Washington, ignoring his orders and listening to intriguers who wanted him to oust the commander. Washington would be troubled and mortified by these machinations for the next several months; as in any conflict, Martha was her husband's committed partisan. Even after George overcame his detractors, she had nothing more to do with Elizabeth Gates. When Mercy Warren asked Martha to pass on her regards to Elizabeth the following year, Martha refused, citing distance as her excuse.

That fall, Martha traveled south to visit her family. Having survived her own inoculation so handily, she had become quite an advocate. She brought Nancy's sons, Burwell Jr. and John, thirteen and eleven, back to Mount Vernon with her and saw them through the pox. When she sent them home in November, she reassured her sister that "they have been exceeding good Boys indeed."

A month later, thirty-eight-year-old Nancy was dead. Although she had been ailing off and on for three or four years, her death was a complete shock. Martha was distraught, because "she was the greatest favorite I had in the world." She wrote to Burwell Bassett on December 22, lamenting and condoling with him. But she hoped that her sister had "made a happy exchange—and only gone a little before us."

Although she wished to be with him and the children, it was impossible for her to leave just then. Nelly Custis was at Mount Vernon, about to give birth any day, and Martha had to be with her, Jack, and little Betsy, who had "grown as fat as a pigg." Her second granddaughter, Martha Parke Custis, called Patty, was born at Mount Vernon on December 31, 1777, the only Custis baby not to be born at Mount Airy in Maryland.

Besides the birth of her second granddaughter, a much more important fact prevented her from going south. Winter encampment and reunion with her husband was at hand: "The General has wrote to me that he cannot come home this winter but as soon as the army under his command goes into winter quarters he will send for me, if he does I must go."

CHAPTER SEVEN

Valley Forge and Eventual Victory

Washington chose Valley Forge as his winter encampment because of its proximity to Philadelphia—to satisfy Pennsylvania politicians, to block the road to York, to spy on Howe, to be ready to act if the British moved, to attack and harry British foragers, to interfere with farmers bringing supplies to Philadelphia. His troops marched through the snow to reach Valley Forge in mid-December 1777. This was the nadir of the patriot cause, but Valley Forge was also the place where a true continental army was born.

Lafayette wrote to his adoring wife, who probably would have swooned with delight at an invitation to join her husband: "Several general officers have brought their wives to camp, and I am very envious, not of their wives (who are rather dull), but of the pleasure they have in being able to see them. General Washington has also just decided to send for his wife, a modest and respectable person, who loves her husband madly."

Soon after Patty Custis's birth, Martha left for the north. Jack, Nelly, and their two little girls remained behind at Mount Vernon. Still mourning her sister and best friend, she arrived at Valley Forge in early February 1778, met as usual by one of the commander's aides-de-camp. It was the third year that she had joined her husband in camp. American soldiers had come to look expectantly for the arrival of her carriage—the signal that the fighting was definitely over for the year. Lady Washington was cheered by the troops when she made her annual appearance. Not the least excited of them was George Washington, who fretted for days before her arrival. Valley Forge indelibly created the image of the nurturing commander's wife who did all she could to relieve the soldiers' needs. She became a mother figure matching Washington's patriarchal role—a pleasant, kind woman who visited the hospital and showed "motherly care" for the soldiers, sick and well.

Despite sporadic British attempts to portray the American general's wife as a closet Tory, Martha was publicly and privately dedicated to her husband's cause and his army. As she wrote to Mercy Warren, "I hope and trust that all the states will make a vigorous push early this spring . . . putting a stop to British cruelties, and afford us that peace liberty and happyness which we have so long contended for." She went on to gloat over the capture of Burgoyne and his army, languishing in Massachusetts while waiting to be exchanged: "It has give me unspeakable pleasure to hear that [they] air in safe quarters in your state. Would bountifull Providence aim a like stroke at Genl Howe, the measure of my happyness would be complete."

Valley Forge was the place where George Washington became the true symbol of the American cause. No other individual could measure up to his public reputation and acclaim: there were many congressmen, but none of them had a nationwide reputation; there were many generals, but none could match his presence. Without the army he led, all would be lost. That winter, he created an army of soldiers committed to winning the war, not leaving as soon as a short-term enlistment ran out. The very suffering that they went through together created an esprit de corps. That winter, he fought ferociously to feed and clothe his men and to create a professional army.

Hunger and deprivation, bloody footprints left in the snow by shoeless soldiers, an encampment ravaged by disease—that was Valley Forge. The congressional supply system had improved for a while, but by the time Martha arrived in February, soldiers were again on the verge of starvation. They were no longer freezing in tents, but they needed a regular food supply.

The men were housed in the wooden barracks they had built, their rags and tatters a joke as they huddled about roaring fires. At least there was plenty of wood in the valley and ample water. Valley Forge wasn't far out on the isolated frontier. It was a small settlement only twenty miles from Philadelphia and surrounded by farms in all directions. American foragers began supplying the camp from those farms, to their owners' unhappiness. Relations improved when a market was set up across the Schuylkill River, where neighboring farmers and traders could bring their goods. Better to choose the goods to offer than have them requisitioned—even though the payment was still continental paper money.

Meanwhile, the British army lived comfortably in Philadelphia. Howe's 23,000 soldiers (to Washington's original 11,000 to 12,000, decreased by some 2,500 deaths over the course of the winter) had settled in for the winter, enjoying themselves mightily. A Hessian captain wrote: "Assemblies, Concerts, Comedies, Clubs and the like make us forget that there is any war, save that it is a capital joke." British officers organized a very good amateur theater, acting in it along with their mistresses. Food and drink were plentiful for an army with hard cash to spend.

Martha was happy to be with George, but far from happy with their accommodations. At least he had moved out of the tent where he had stayed while his men were building their wooden huts. The small Isaac Potts house, its rough natural stone the color of dull autumn leaves, was a tight squeeze for all the aides, but it was plentifully supplied with fireplaces. Guests had to be satisfied with cots set up wherever there was a clear space or sharing with the aides. The one fair-size room on the ground floor became an office-cum–sitting room, filled with writing tables and chairs.

Trying to make the place tolerable for his wife was Washington's concern. In a letter to Jack Custis, he regretted that "we are in a dreary kind of place, and uncomfortably provided." At some point in the fall, his baggage had gone astray, and he needed those supplies for the house, "among other things a bed, end irons, plates, dishes, and kitchen utensils." He ordered them found and brought in wagons to headquarters.

The greatest lack was a dining room: besides the aides, any other high-ranking officer or notable visitor took for granted an open invitation to dine at headquarters. At one time, four congressmen attached themselves to headquarters as volunteers, incurring an officer's disdain: "The rations they have consumed considerably overbalance all their service done as volunteers, for they have dined with us every day almost and drank as much wine as they would earn in six months."

A large portion of Washington's expenses went to provide food and drink for the fifteen or twenty men, along with the occasional woman or two, who assembled at his table for a simple dinner every day. This was a time for the weary soldiers to relax, discuss the events of the day, debate strategies, and plan ahead. They sat together for two or three hours, drinking toasts in Madeira after the table was cleared. As good as she was at making do, Martha couldn't cope with all those guests without a dining room. As she wrote in a letter to Mercy Warren, "The Generals apartment is very small. He has had a log cabben built to dine in which has made our quarter[s] much more tolerable than they were at first."

Right behind Martha, the Baron von Steuben, a Prussian professional soldier with a self-bestowed title and rank, arrived at Valley Forge with the skills that made him one of the most useful of all Washington's officers. During that long, cold winter and spring, he drilled the American troops until the rankest amateurs became a cohesive, professional army. Drill became the main amusement of the camp as divisions tried to outdo one another—provoking hoots and catcalls, boasts and strutting, bets and challenges. Steuben's training did wonders for formerly bored and dispirited soldiers.

Accompanying Steuben was a French volunteer, Pierre-Etienne Duponceau, who became one of Martha's staunch admirers. He observed that "her presence inspired fortitude." Those who visited her in despair "retired full of hope and confidence."

Martha found welcome companionship among the other officers' wives. The Washingtons' favorite, Kitty Greene, was as usual the center of a social group at Nathanael's quarters, where all the foreign officers tended to congregate. She was especially popular because she spoke some French, a language she had studied for just that reason. The irrepressible and bossy Lucy Knox, getting fatter by the year, was at camp that winter, as was Rebecca Cornell Biddle, wife of the commissary general in charge of foraging. Colonel Clement Biddle was a Quaker who, like his friend Nathanael Greene, had been read out of his meeting for becoming a soldier. General William Alexander, a wealthy New Jersey landowner known as Lord Stirling in America because of his claim to a Scottish earldom (disallowed by the British), had brought his mild and friendly wife, Sarah Livingston Alexander (Lady Stirling), and their flirtatious daughter Lady Kitty, who charmed Washington by requesting a lock of his hair.

Martha and the other ladies formed a social circle of the sort she so much enjoyed in Virginia. But the way they occupied their days while conversing and drinking tea was a little different. When visiting, ladies usually did fine needlework, leaving mundane knitting and sewing for home. Needlepoint or embroidery lasted one visit at headquarters: Martha led the way in putting aside fancywork in favor of knitting, darning, and making shirts; the other ladies were quickly shamed into joining her. Dry woolen socks without holes were an infantryman's greatest joy. All those socks were knit by hand; there were no factories to produce them, and a long day's march in leaky boots produced prodigious holes in the men's socks, along with painful blisters. Such wounds easily became infected in the filth they lived in; and once gangrene set in, amputation had to follow. All winter long, Martha and her friends turned out endless pairs of socks for the soldiers.

Once the candles were lit in the evening, the Washingtons and their friends entertained themselves. Duponceau recounted, "In the midst of all our distress, there were some bright sides to the picture. . . . Mrs. Washington had the courage to follow her husband in that dismal abode; other ladies also graced the scene . . . the evening was spent in conversation, over a dish of tea or coffee." The great pleasure of the evenings was singing. "Every gentlemen or lady who could sing, was called upon in turn for a song," and Duponceau soon learned the English favorites.

Officers weren't the only men in the army to enjoy the company of women. Most eighteenth-century standing armies included a contingent of women (and children) who traveled with the troops and lived with them in camp. Both the British regulars and the German mercenaries brought women with them and picked up more from among American loyalists.

In the colonies, militia call-ups had traditionally been for a limited period, generally close to home. With a national army and long-term enlistment far from home, the new army soon included what were called "camp followers." At Valley Forge, for example, where the army eventually consisted of some 8,500 men, 450 women officially accompanied the troops, as well as additional unregistered women and probably more than 300 children.

The poorest enlisted men were unable to provide for their wives when they left work and home. So some of the women pulled up stakes, packed what belongings they could carry, including children, and went to war with their men. Although Washington fumed at the harum-scarum appearance of a bunch of unkempt women swarming into towns alongside a marching army, he understood their importance to the men. The American army provided rations and supplies (and later smallpox inoculation) for the families of the soldiers.

These women cooked, cleaned, mended, sewed, laundered, nursed the sick and wounded, and sometimes took over a gun when their husbands fell. They provided essential functions for the army in general as well as their own families. Washington tried to prevent unmarried women from attaching themselves to the army, but human nature triumphed over his commands. To the great pleasure of the rowdy soldiers, some prostitutes traveled with the army, providing readily available sex.

The officers continued to concoct entertainment of one sort or another. On Washington's forty-sixth birthday in 1778, a military band (mostly fifes and drums) serenaded the general at his headquarters. He was now well into middle age, seen as a grand old man by his army. The camp enjoyed a performance at the bake house of the beloved classic *Cato*, performed by the younger officers. The theater-loving Washington had granted permission for the play, although Congress had forbidden theatrical performances during the war.

Cato was particularly admired in America, emphasizing as it did the superiority of virtuous agrarian life over metropolitan corruption and high-minded republican rule over Caesarism, or dictatorship. No American patriot could doubt that Cato and his supporters corresponded to the Continental Congress and its army or that the usurping Caesar corresponded equally to George III with his suppression of the rights of a free people. Hardly anyone suspected that George Washington would ever be tempted to make himself dictator. Certainly his army recognized him as Cato, not Caesar.

Painfully dull for modern tastes, *Cato* features high-minded speechifying with hardly a moment of action. It includes such ringing lines as "It is not now a time to talk of aught but chains or conquest; liberty or death" and "What a pity is it that we can die but once to serve our country." Its rhetoric seemingly influenced such American patriots as Patrick Henry and Nathan Hale.

In early April, four prominent Quaker women, including the diarist Elizabeth Bowen Drinker, arrived at Valley Forge. They came to ask Washington to help secure the release of their imprisoned husbands. A numerous and influential group in Pennsylvania, most Quakers held fast to their religious beliefs: they refused to join non-importation agreements, to swear oaths to the new nation (or any other), or to take up arms, even in defense. Pennsylvania patriots believed their actions (or nonactions) favored the British and arrested a group of wealthy Quaker leaders, including Henry Drinker, Elizabeth's husband, and sent them to Winchester, Virginia.

The women were driven to Valley Forge in a coach and four with two black servants riding postilion. They passed quickly through outlying picket lines and were given a pass for headquarters. As Elizabeth Drinker recorded in her diary: "We arriv'd at about ½ past one; requested an audience with the General—set with his Wife, (a sociable pretty kind of Woman) until he came in."

A number of friendly officers were present, including one of Washington's favorite aides, Tench Tilghman, a Philadelphia merchant who knew the Drinkers well. Much of the Revolution's bitterness arose from pitting brother against brother, sister against sister.

The general "discoursd with us freely, but not so long as we could have wish'd, as dinner was serv'd, to which he had invited us, there was 15 of the Officers besides the General and his Wife, Gen. Green, and G[en]. Lee," who had just returned from British captivity. After dinner, "we went out with the General's Wife up to her Chamber [bedroom], and saw no more of him." Washington had given the ladies a pass for Lancaster, the state capital, but he had no power over the State of Pennsylvania. The Quaker prisoners were freed soon afterward, however, and returned to Philadelphia.

On May 10, 1778, wonderful, long-awaited news arrived at Valley Forge. France had recognized the infant United States and become her ally; the treaty had been signed in February. From now on, the war would be different. The euphoric commander in chief ordered a grand celebration for the following day. At nine o'clock on May 11, a cannon shot summoned the soldiers to line up for addresses by their chaplains, including a reading of a summary of the treaty and praise for the king of France. Another booming cannon at about eleven-thirty ordered them to retrieve their weapons from the huts. They fell in for a military parade and drill before Washington, showing off all they had learned from Steuben, before marching back to their encampments for dinner, a good deal of rum, and noisy merriment.

In front of the artillery park, the cleared space where cannons and mortars rested on their caissons, an amphitheater had been improvised out of officers' marquees. In an open space at the center, His Excellency and Lady Washington received the officers as they approached in columns, thirteen abreast, the arms of each rank linked together to signify "most perfect confederation."

Afterward, they all enjoyed a cold dinner—sneered at by a European officer as "a profusion of fat meat, strong wine and other liquors" but heartily relished by almost everybody else. The presence of the generals' wives, the music from an army band—all were enjoyable, but the warmth and affability with which Washington greeted his officers was the supreme pleasure.

"I was never present," wrote an officer, "where there was such unfeigned and perfect joy as we discovered in every countenance. The entertainment concluded with a number of patriotic toasts attended with huzzas. When the general took his leave, there was a universal clap, with loud huzzas, which continued till he had proceeded a quarter of a mile, during which time there were a thousand hats tossed in the air. His Excellency turned round with his retinue and huzzaed several times."

The British response to the news of the French alliance couldn't have been more gratifying: gnashing of imperial teeth, impotent waving of imperial sabers, and the decision to withdraw from Philadelphia. With the French fleet now in the mix, the British decided to pull their army back to New York. Defense of the immensely valuable Caribbean sugar islands became a priority, besides defense of the home islands and targets in the Mediterranean and the Indian Ocean. A last minute attempt to make peace with their former colonists, while retaining them within the empire, was doomed from the outset. General Sir William Howe's resignation was accepted, and he sailed away home, leaving Sir Henry Clinton as British commander, the third so far in the three years of the war.

After six months at Valley Forge, a very new American army was astir, ready to take to the field again. Martha went back to Virginia on June 9 as they prepared to break camp. On June 18, the British abandoned Philadelphia early in the day. Elizabeth Drinker reported that on that day, "when we arose, there was not one Red-Coat to be seen in Town." Many of the staunchest Tories left with them, as they had at Boston. A quarter of an hour later, the American light horse entered the city. "[They] had drawn Swords in their Hands, Gallop'd about the Streets in a great hurry, many were much frightn'd at their appearance." Within a week, order and new policies were in place; Congress returned to the city on July 2 in time to celebrate the anniversary of independence with skyrockets, gunfire, and crowds in the streets. Philadelphia remained under American control for the rest of the war.

The retreating British were harried by Washington's army and state militiamen every mile they marched across New Jersey. On June 28, the American forces attacked their rear guard at Monmouth Courthouse. For a while, it seemed that this might be the great American victory, until Charles Lee managed to turn victory to retreat. Lee was blasphemous, rude, and unbearably slovenly in a day when cleanliness wasn't one of the cardinal virtues, followed everywhere by a pack of snapping dogs, but all those faults had previously been justified by his presumed bravery and military skill. When Washington came up, he rallied the fleeing soldiers and loosed one of his titanic blasts of rage at Lee. More or less a draw, Monmouth was nevertheless heartening to the American public. The British suffered far greater casualties than the Americans and slipped away in the night. Lee was court-martialed and suspended from command; he left the army, along with the dogs—all equally unregretted.

Washington coped with the increasingly less able members of Congress, fighting for the men and arms to win the war, warding off their ill-advised efforts at directing campaign strategy. The plunging value of the continental dollar, compared with the solid worth of the British pound, threatened to bring the Revolution to a screeching halt. The dream that helped keep him going was a massive, coordinated French-American land-sea attack on the main British army ensconced at New York City, but it never happened. The remainder of 1778 and early 1779 brought instead bloody fighting on the western frontiers between Indian allies of Great Britain and territorial militias, leaving hundreds of dead men, women, and children on both sides; a failed American attempt to retake Newport with the aid of a French fleet; a southern initiative by a British force that captured Savannah and Augusta, Georgia; and the capture of British forts along the Mississippi by the Spanish. Washington was frustrated and angry, his temper frequently slipping out of his ironclad control.

Back home, Martha found her granddaughters more charming than ever. Although still longing for a son, Jack was delighted with his little girls. At nearly two, "Ms. Bet has grown very much, and is very saucy and entertaining. She can say any word but Washington." Just a few months old, baby Patty "has grown the finest Girl I ever saw and the most Good natured Quiet little Creature in the World."

Jack had been elected to the General Assembly that spring as the representative for Fairfax County. Never very confident of his own abilities separate from the power of his fortune, he had worried that he might not win. Letting his mother know the election date, he asked her to help bring him luck: "You must remember to set cross leg'd that day for me."

Martha and George settled into what would become their routine for the remaining five years of a war that seemed to stretch out forever. She continued to go home every summer to see to home and family, while he remained with the army, fearing that it would disintegrate if he left. Every fall was a waiting game. Would the British pull out so that he could make at least a flying visit home? Every fall, the answer was the same: no. Martha then climbed into the carriage, journeying for many weary days to join George in whatever hellhole served as winter camp that year. Each year, she re-created a home for her husband that helped him endure delay, anxiety, and homesickness.

Some summers she managed to go south to New Kent and visit her family. Often she was too tired. Those weeks of jolting over bad roads in an aging carriage had started to exhaust her as she neared fifty. In November 1778, she sounded the same note that would continue for years. She—everyone—hoped that this would be the year the British would admit that their American colonies were lost for good and sail away. Delayed and intercepted mail aggravated her uncertainty—"my letters doe not come regularly to hand." So she hoped and doubted: "I am very uneasy at this time. I have some reason to expect that I shall take another trip to the northward. The pore General is not likely to come to see us from what I can hear."

Despite worn-out coach springs, she left as soon as she got word.

When she reached Philadelphia in mid-December, she received George's instructions to wait there for him. A week later, he arrived to talk Congress out of backing a foolhardy plan to attack Canada. Once they had their commander in town, congressmen had quite a lot to discuss with him, as he grew increasingly restless. Because of short supplies, Washington had ordered his men into several small winter encampments along the western bank of the Hudson. Head-quarters, convenient to all the camps, would be Middlebrook, New Jersey.

The contrast between the riches of Philadelphia and the poverty of the army was painful to the Washingtons. Congress had no direct taxing powers, and the states were loath to contribute their share. Lafayette returned to France to make the strongest possible case to the king for money, munitions, and an army to defeat the British. But despite Washington's bitter indictment—"Speculation, pecula-tion, and an insatiable thirst for riches seem to have got the better of every other consideration"—he couldn't avoid the entertainments and balls offered by the wealthy Philadelphians whose support he needed.

By this time, Martha no longer danced, but she never interfered with her husband's vigorous enjoyment of the exercise, even when he danced three hours straight with Kitty Greene at camp. He was always requested to lead out the dance with the most distinguished lady present, and all the women wanted to dance with the hero. Among the powerful elite of the city, Samuel and Eliza Willing Powel, Robert and Mary White Morris, and the rakish bachelor Gouverneur Morris (no relation to Robert) became their friends. Between them, the two Morrises helped contrive to keep an army in the field in its most desperate hours.

Sarah Franklin Bache wrote to her father, Benjamin, in Paris: "I have lately been several times invited abroad with the General and Mrs. Washington. He always inquires after you in the most affec-tionate manner, and speaks of you highly. We danced at Mrs. Pow-ell's on your birthday [January 6], or night I should say, in company together, and he told me it was the anniversary of his marriage; it was just twenty years that night." Certainly an evening together in the elegant second-floor ballroom of the Powel house was preferable to the previous two anniversaries, when they had been separated by warfare.

Delightful as these evenings were, they gave Washington "infinitely more pain than pleasure," according to Nathanael Greene. The commander's sense of urgency drove him to get back to the army before it crumbled. Finally, he was given permission to leave, and he and Martha left the city on February 2. The *Pennsylvania Packet* reported: "During the course of his short stay (the only relief he has enjoyed from service since he first entered into it), he has been honored with every mark of esteem which his exalted qualities as a gentleman and a citizen entitle him to. His Excellency's stay was rendered the more agreeable by the company of his lady, and the domestic retirement which he enjoyed at the house of the Honorable Henry Laurens, Esquire [the president of Congress], with whom he resided."

The weather was mild, with none of the suffering of the previous winters, though food was sparse and poor. There was little snow or frost, and spring came early. The Washingtons lived in the brand-new, two-story Wallace house, a large white frame house in Middlebrook, New Jersey. For the first time since Cambridge, Martha and the aides had room to turn around without tripping over one another.

Having dinner at the commander's house was an honor prized by both officers and civilians. It certainly wasn't the food—described by George jocularly, but probably accurately, as ham and roast beef with a dab of greens or beans, finished up by an apple pie if the cook felt like obliging. Also as usual, Martha enchanted all their guests with her ageless charm. As army surgeon James Thatcher recorded, "Mrs. Washington combines in an uncommon degree, great dignity of manner with the most pleasing affability."

A lot was happening at home in Virginia, and Martha felt out of touch when Jack and Nelly failed to write. Jack had finally bought his own home after five years of marriage, but he and Nelly hadn't quite decided when to move in. They were pleased with Abingdon, a fine house and nine hundred acres outside Alexandria, even though Washington considered it a bad bargain. Nelly was also expecting a new baby at any moment. Martha didn't know where they were or what was happening to them, and she didn't like it. In fact, Jack and Nelly had returned to Mount Airy, where Nelly gave birth to a third daughter on March 21—Eleanor Parke Custis, another Nelly, now that both grandmothers had a namesake.

Although the first attempt at a combined Franco-American attack had failed, the French were still committed to using their fleet in aid of the American rebels. In early May, their minister arrived at camp in company with an unofficial Spanish representative. France had declared war on Great Britain the previous summer, and Spain would follow her lead a few months later. By now, pomp and ceremony were second nature to Washington's army—cannons boomed, muskets fired in unison, infantry paraded and maneuvered, the troop of light horse pranced. The foreign gentlemen stood on an improvised stage with Martha and the other ladies, soon joined by Washington.

That spring and summer, the British tried different strategies. A raiding expedition on Virginia towns bordering the Chesapeake Bay was short-lived, but then a large British force from New York moved up the Hudson, and Martha went home. Having Jack and Nelly settled within easy riding distance of Mount Vernon with their three little girls was a delight. Lund Washington had been courting his cousin Elizabeth Foote. When they married that year, he brought her to Mount Vernon to live. Martha found her a compatible housemate, and they became good friends.

The fall of 1779 was bloody as loyalists and patriots attacked and counterattacked one another in many states, neighbor against neighbor, and frontier violence between Indians and militias worsened, with no quarter given to women or children. An American attempt to retake Savannah was a debacle. The only bright spot was the success of American privateers against British merchantmen and John Paul Jones's capture of a British frigate.

Washington went into winter camp early, settling into Morristown for the second time. That year was even worse than Valley Forge—heavy snow, unpaid troops, and food in short supply, although the men did get their barracks built just before a massive blizzard blew in, the worst in recorded history. When Martha arrived in Morristown just before Christmas, she found the space allotted to the commander too small, cold, and ill equipped. The army had rented an eight-room house from Theodosia Ford, but the upstairs was unfinished, and the landlady still lived in two of the downstairs rooms. All the servants—theirs and Mrs. Ford's—were crammed together into one kitchen room. Most annoying, Nathanael Greene had scooped up the best house, though the allotments usually followed rank.

In the three years since Alexander Hamilton had joined Washington's staff, he had made himself indispensable, so much so that the general refused to give him a field command. Lafayette was the man whom Washington treated as a surrogate son, but Hamilton was also like a son—one of those rebellious, competitive sons who have tense, turbulent relationships with their fathers. Hamilton appreciated Washington's status as an American icon, his lofty spirit, and his ability to keep the army intact. But he desperately resented his own dependence on Washington and yearned for a chance to succeed as a fighting officer, out of the great man's shadow.

For all its discomforts, the village of Morristown was very sociable that winter, and Hamilton had a lively time in both high company and low. Like most of the young aides, he indulged himself with sexual adventures, but he also flirted with proper young ladies at the winter dances. In an almost certainly apocryphal (but too good to leave out) story, Martha called the camp's prowling tomcat "Hamilton."

Hamilton had started to think of marriage, coolly enumerating the attributes he expected in a bride. Then Elizabeth Schuyler arrived in town in February 1780 to stay with her aunt and uncle, and he was lost. Betsy was twenty-two, a small (Hamilton was short and slight), brown-eyed brunette with considerable strength of character. She was the second daughter of the wealthy Philip Schuyler, retired from the army but still active in the patriot cause. Schuyler was one of Washington's greatest admirers, and Betsy came promptly to pay her respects at headquarters.

The young woman made the commander's wife a pair of cuffs, easily basted on to protect sleeves from soil and as easily removed for washing. In a warm note, Martha thanked her for the cuffs, which she found very pretty. She sent her a small present in return—"some rice powder, which she hopes will be acceptable."

Martha liked the company of young people and enjoyed watching romances unfold. It was no doubt especially satisfying to watch the rakish Hamilton become enthralled. Within a month, Alexander and Betsy were engaged, and he wrote asking her parents' permission. Not only was their approval given, the Schuylers came to Morristown and rented a house, where they entertained the young suitor. Over the years, Hamilton's enemies sneered at his illegitimate birth and youthful poverty, but not Philip and Catherine van Rensselaer Schuyler. Although they were both members of the old New York landed elite, they put aside their class prejudices, approving of the brilliant and charming young officer and welcoming him into their family.

That spring, unpaid troops mutinied and were put down by loyal units; leaders of the mutinous soldiers were hanged as an example, and the commander feared that the mutiny might spread. Washington was forced to stay in the New York area to control his own troops and to contain the British troops in the city, while the action of the war moved south, where Clinton was besieging the port of Charleston.

The fall of Charleston in May 1780 was the single biggest American defeat of the war; not only was the major southern port lost, but ships, an arsenal, and the entire southern American army fell into enemy hands, while the victors suffered few casualties. Under the leadership of General Cornwallis, the British proceeded with their southern campaign. The northern colonies might be lost, but surely the southern colonies could be regained for Great Britain by war's end.

Just in time to boost the patriots' sagging morale, Lafayette returned from France in May with the news that his mission on behalf of the American cause had been completely successful. The fleet would return again, money would flow, troops would be paid, arms would be shipped, and a French army under the experienced general Comte de Rochambeau would follow Lafayette within two months. To Washington's further pleasure, Spanish troops under Bernardo de Gálvez had taken Mobile, distracting the British in the Gulf of Mexico even though there was no formal Spanish alliance.

When Martha left camp in the middle of June, she was bone weary and determined to stay home until it was time to go north again. She swore that "I suffered so much last winter by going late that I have determined to go early in the fall before the Frost sets in." In the meantime, she asked relatives to visit her rather than undertake the journey to New Kent—"I find myself so much fatigued with my ride that I shall not be able to come down to see you this summer." She was also worried about George's spirits. She wrote Burwell Bassett about "the distress of the army and other difficultys tho I did not know the cause, the pore General was so unhappy that it distressed me exceedingly." Apparently she was being discreet, since she certainly knew about the financial shortfalls, defeats, and mutinies that weighed so heavily on her husband.

Esther DeBerdt Reed, Joseph Reed's wife, decided that it was time for the women of America to act on behalf of their poorly supplied soldiers. In June 1780, she suggested that money should be raised for the troops as "the offering of the ladies." The movement caught on in other states as these well-connected women wrote to their friends, inviting their involvement; newspapers reported approvingly.

Naturally, Martha Washington became part of the effort. She contributed money herself and wrote to Governor Thomas Jefferson's wife, another Martha, who announced a collection in the churches of mostly rural Virginia. Although the original plan was for Martha Washington to distribute the more than $300,000 collected nationwide, she was far away at Mount Vernon, so George was a poor second choice. At his suggestion for the ladies of Philadelphia, linen was purchased with the money and a large group of women led by Sarah Bache made 2,200 shirts for the soldiers.

An American army was again in the field to oppose the British in the south, commanded by Horatio Gates at Congress's behest. But the victor of Saratoga suffered a mortifying defeat at Camden, South Carolina, resulting in the loss of his command. Nathanael Greene later took over the leadership of an army in terrible disarray and began rebuilding it and attracting popular support while avoiding annihilation by Cornwallis.

Bedeviled as he was, Washington suffered another blow in September on a routine visit to the Hudson River fortress at West Point, commanded by Benedict Arnold. Washington, who admired and respected Arnold as a fighting general, had secured the command for him at his request. When the commander and his party of officers and aides arrived at Arnold's quarters, they found him mysteriously absent and his young wife, abed with their baby, hysterical and seemingly out of her mind. A day's investigation revealed that Arnold had fled downriver to a British warship because he was about to be exposed as a traitor. The British had paid him for information, including the whereabouts of Washington when he was vulnerable to capture; Arnold had been on the verge of turning West Point over to the enemy.

Although he took swift action to defend against any British move, Washington had time to sympathize and worry about Peggy Shippen Arnold, the traitor's much younger wife. A winsome blonde, Peggy was a member of a prominent Philadelphia family, the cousin of Martha and George's friend Eliza Powel, and well-known to them both. Washington, Lafayette, Hamilton, and the other officers were unanimous in their pity for Arnold's innocent wife. They were unaware that she had been a full participant in Arnold's plans, even an instigator, and that her hysterics were staged to trick and confuse them.

Martha rejoined George in early December 1780 at the new headquarters in New Windsor, New York, where they stayed through June. With the turn of the year, there was fresh trouble with the troops. Although the men were now fed and clothed, the length of the war was telling on them. There was another mutiny in January, followed by desertions, and still another mutiny two weeks later.

Safely married into the wealthy Schuyler family, Alexander

Hamilton forced a quarrel on "the great man" over some hasty words, refused to accept Washington's attempt to make amends, and resigned his position. The smooth functioning of headquarters was interrupted (Martha made a fair copy in her best hand of at least one letter for her husband, contrary to her usual habit), and social relations were strained as well. Martha had planned to accompany Betsy Hamilton to Albany for a visit with the Schuylers; the trip was canceled with a weak excuse. Despite Hamilton's bitter complaints against his benefactor, he continued to trust in his sense of justice. After many requests, Washington did provide Hamilton with an opportunity to fight at Yorktown.

The tide was turning in the south. Daniel Morgan won a conclusive, though small, victory at Cowpens, South Carolina, in January, followed by Greene's drawn battle at Guilford Courthouse, North Carolina, in March. Cornwallis won in the field but withdrew before any further encounter could take place; he couldn't afford another such costly victory. Guilford was devastating to the British; their casualties were twice as heavy as the Americans', including several officers, and reinforcements were far away. For the Americans, the news was all good. The smallest victory gave them new hope and encouraged them to hold on. Cornwallis began his march into Virginia toward Yorktown. With an enemy that melted away only to form up again, the old cliché expressed it all: The British were winning the battles but slowly losing the war.

Rochambeau had finally agreed to a joint attack on New York, and Washington was poised for action. Martha planned to go home in May, but she fell ill with a gallbladder attack and spent five weeks in bed. Martha Mortier, the widow of a British army paymaster (whose Manhattan house the Washingtons had lived in during their brief stay in 1776), sent a note under a flag of truce, saying that she had heard of Mrs. Washington's indisposition through intercepted letters; accompanying the note were some invalids' comforts, including lemons, oranges, limes, and two dozen pineapples. George feared that acceptance of these expensive gifts would appear to be consorting with the enemy and returned them with a stiff note. He was still aggrieved that Lund had negotiated with a British vessel to prevent the destruction of Mount Vernon. Without a taste of citrus fruit, the recovered Martha left camp in mid-June.

That summer, Jack and Nelly joined her at home as they often did, although they had finally moved to Abingdon. Mount Vernon rang with the voices of Betsy and Patty, five and almost four. Because of her delicate health from several pregnancies and difficult births, Nelly frequently left little Nelly, two years old, and the new baby—a boy at last, to his papa's relief—to be cared for at Mount Vernon by their grandmother and Eliza Foote Washington. The baby boy, born on April 30, had been christened George Washington Parke Custis, called Wash or Washy.

Wild for joint action and be damned to the budget, Washington had the French officers for dinner several days a week. Thirty guests a day gathered at the commander's table and missed having his wife there to oversee the meal. The camaraderie—not to speak of the beer, rum, and Madeira—boded well for future cooperation, but the French naturally criticized the cuisine. The coffee was too weak, the salad was vinegary, and the food ran together in their single plates. Surely war wasn't a valid excuse for a one-course dinner.

In mid-August, the news arrived: The French fleet under the command of Admiral de Grasse was on the way to the Chesapeake, with three thousand soldiers on board. Between the fleet and Lafayette's forces, reinforced by these French troops, Cornwallis would be trapped at Yorktown. Giving up the dream of New York, Washington and Rochambeau and their armies set off for Virginia, some by boat, the others marching.

On September 9, accompanied by two aides, George galloped sixty miles out of the way to arrive at Mount Vernon late on a golden autumn afternoon. The first sight of his cherished home in more than six years must have filled his heart with joy, as he examined the ongoing construction and noted time's effects on frame buildings. For the first time, he set eyes on the four grandchildren, including his latest little namesake.

He spent three nights at home, dictating letters to militia, state, and county officials to repair the road to be used by the army, to shore up the fords for the use of the wagons, and to rush supplies to the new front. He himself wrote to Lafayette of their imminent arrival with a gleeful postscript: "I hope you will keep Lord Cornwallis safe, without Provisions or Forage untill we arrive. Adieu."

The French generals and their suites followed close behind. They spent their days plotting, planning, and trying to foresee enemy action. Martha was in her element, seeing that the house servants made up sufficient beds, put out soap and towels, warmed water to clean off the dust of the road, and prepared meals that more than made up for the skimpy rations at New Windsor. Washington's aide Jonathan Trumbull recorded, "An elegant seat and situation: great appearance of opulence and real exhibitions of hospitality and princely entertainment."

When the generals rejoined their troops on the march, Jack Custis decided to go along. Family lore and nineteenth-century romanticism to the contrary, Jack doesn't seem to have been appointed as an aide. Rather, he was an observer without duties, free to visit family and friends in the neighborhood. He spent a night at Pamocra, visiting his uncle Bat Dandridge and his grandmother Fanny Jones Dandridge, who lived with the family; she had started to show "her great Age [seventy-one]." He also looked in on his aunt Betsy Dandridge Henley and inquired after runaway slaves from Mount Vernon, many of whom had died of want in the Williamsburg neighborhood. His sole comment on the siege of Yorktown, begun on September 28, was that "the General tho in constant Fatigue looks very well."

Washington may have been cheated of the attack on New York, but Yorktown turned out to be a fine replacement. For once, fortune smiled: the French fleet and both American and French troops arrived at the same time at the same place, and they besieged Yorktown, where Cornwallis and his army were securely trapped. This time, the British navy wasn't able to come to the rescue. On October 17, after less than three weeks of bloody bombardments, attacks, sorties, scant rations, and lack of reinforcements, an enraged Cornwallis signaled for terms to end a hopeless situation. Two days of negotiation ensued, with the British attempting to dictate terms while Washington put them firmly in their place.

On October 19, Cornwallis and his eight thousand men marched out—the officers to be sent home in exchange for captured American officers, the soldiers to be imprisoned in camps in Virginia and Maryland. A treasure trove of weapons, ammunition, artillery, equipment, boats, and Cornwallis's literal war chest filled with hard money fell into American hands. Yorktown was the culminating moment of the American Revolution. After that, it was all over but the shouting—but not anytime soon.

Disposition of American brigades, British and German prisoners, the wounded of both sides, and all the booty; reports to Congress, far-flung military officers, and state officials; inspection of all the work in progress; plans for the future—Washington didn't stop for days on end. That summer, Congress had sent peace commissioners Benjamin Franklin, Thomas Jefferson, John Jay, and Henry Laurens to join John Adams in France. Besides sending a copy of the capitulation and "a summary return of prisoners and cannons" to Congress, Washington sent another copy directly to Franklin in Paris on a French frigate dispatched by de Grasse to avoid delay. As he wrote, "Recent intelligence of Milit[ar]y Transactions must be important to our Ministers in Europe at the present period of Affairs."

Sometime during the siege, Jack Custis contracted a "camp fever," probably typhus, which was endemic in the crowding and filth of army camps. Washington had him taken to nearby Eltham to be nursed by the Bassetts. Typhus was nowhere near as dangerous as smallpox, and his stepfather probably wasn't particularly worried as he continued preparations to return north. Far from recovering, however, Jack sank deeper into illness and fever. A messenger was sent to Mount Vernon to fetch Martha and Nelly, who rushed to his bedside.

Washington finished off his many tasks and left for Eltham to visit Burwell Bassett on November 5. To his surprise, his wife and daughter-in-law were there. He barely had time to see Jack Custis one last time before the young man died, three weeks short of his twenty-seventh birthday. Jack hadn't achieved much in his short life. He hadn't done well at his studies or farming and had never considered a profession or the military. In the years since he had taken over his great estate, it had fallen considerably in value through his own inept management and through the dishonesty of a trusted friend. His three years' service in the General Assembly had been undistinguished.

But he was a loving and lovable son and husband, and his mother and wife grieved deeply for him. Although frequently exasperated by his fecklessness, George also cared for Jack, and his sorrow was intensified by worry for Martha, who was stunned at the loss of her last child. To outlive all four of her children was a terrible burden for such a loving mother.

There was no question of Washington's leaving for Philadelphia until he had taken care of his wife. Congress would have to wait. Jack was buried in the private cemetery at Eltham, with the family in attendance. Martha's brother Bat agreed to administer the estate for Nelly; George couldn't take on that responsibility during wartime. The sad cortege returned to Mount Vernon while George took a side trip to Fredericksburg to call on his mother, whom he hadn't seen since before the war.

When he discovered that Mary Washington was out of town on a visit, he left five guineas for her and went on home. Although she publicly complained of her poverty with the most embarrassing regularity, George was always generous with his mother, and she was very comfortably fixed in her town house. While she finally thanked her son for the money, the letter was otherwise a model of selfishness. Without a mention of Yorktown, she begged him to build her a cabin over the mountains. She did send her love to Martha, adding, "I would have wrote to her but my reason has jis left me." She didn't mention Jack's death.

George stayed at Mount Vernon for a week before leaving for Philadelphia, where he planned to meet with congressmen and other politicians. As he wrote Nathanael Greene, "I shall attempt to stimulate Congress to the best Improvement of our late Success." Otherwise, he feared that they might "fall into a State of Langour and Relaxation." Despite the great victory, George III might prove as obstinate as ever. The war wouldn't be over until a treaty was signed.

Yorktown was on every American's lips. Rather than stay at home in her sorrow, Martha decided to go with her husband for the comfort of his presence. This trip was a reprise of 1775, with escorts, addresses, and cheering crowds. Philadelphia, as usual, outdid every place in its welcome. In addition to the usual celebratory illumination of lanterns and candles placed on windowsills, large transparent paintings, lit from behind, covered many windows like glowing shades. Patriotic and allegorical themes ran riot.

Washington's meetings with Congress were generally successful, as they heeded at least some of his advice about improved military and civilian organization. They agreed to keep and supply an army in the field for the immediate future. The British still held two of the new nation's largest ports—New York and Charleston. Everyone wanted to entertain the hero. Martha also attended some functions, but without her usual zest. George described these "parties of pleasure" as "nearly of a sameness" and "too unimportant for description." He was there to prevent any congressional backsliding before peace was actually achieved.

Business finally accomplished, the Washingtons and their escort left Philadelphia on March 22, 1782, stopping at several encampments before arriving at headquarters a week later. Their new home was a sturdy Dutch farmhouse, a one-story building of stone, at Newburgh, New York, on a hill with a beautiful view of the Hudson River. The largest room in the house was a dining room. To a French visitor, a smoking fireplace and the oddity of the room—seven doors and only one window—were worthy of comment. During the day, a small room was used as a parlor; with the addition of a cot, it became a guest room.

Martha went home in midsummer to look after her grandchildren and widowed daughter-in-law. George hoped to join her there later in the year but found the temper of the army too sullen to allow him to leave. Guests stopped for a visit at Mount Vernon as freely as ever.

Washington's hoped-for summer campaign came to nothing in 1782. He had too few troops, and the French fleet was defeated by the British, with de Grasse taken prisoner. The British Parliament voted against further war, opening peace negotiations with the American commissioners and withdrawing troops from the inland south. Only on the frontier did the violence continue. In November, a preliminary peace treaty was signed; and in December, the British evacuated Charleston. But they still had an army in New York.

During 1782 and 1783, negotiations for the final treaty dragged on endlessly in Paris, with both British enemies and French allies attempting to hobble the new nation and her potential for full independence and growth. Washington would not abandon his post until a treaty was officially signed and ratified. Frustrated and bored, he sent for Martha to keep him company; in December 1782, she came back to the same Dutch farmhouse in Newburgh. All was anticlimax and tedium. One by one, the aides resigned and returned to their own affairs. As Washington wrote, "Time passed heavily on in this dreary mansion in which we are fast locked by frost and snow." A month or two could easily pass without news from Paris. Their mission accomplished, the French troops went home after emotional farewells.

Neither Congress nor the states had done well by their soldiers and officers. Accepting the sacrifice of years of their lives, civilian authorities hesitated to take unpopular measures to raise money to pay the military back wages (sometimes very far in arrears), assure promised pensions, or care for the disabled. There had been several mutinies or near mutinies by enlisted men in the last couple of years, but now even some officers were starting to murmur about asserting themselves while they were still armed and had troops under their command. On March 10, 1783, an unsigned address was circulated among the officers, calling for a meeting to assert their right to fair treatment. A pamphlet was also distributed that was a virtual call to use military force against Congress.

Washington's general orders the next day were firm, expressing his "disapprobation of such disorderly proceedings" and requesting an official meeting on March 15. The temper of that meeting was rebellious even after their commander walked in and made some introductory comments. But when he started to read his prepared remarks, he had to put on his glasses, and as he did so he said, "Gentlemen, you will permit me to put on my spectacles, for I have not only grown gray, but almost blind, in the service of my country." The right words at the right time broke the possible mutiny; loyal officers took over and worked out a compromise with Congress.

Martha was with him during this stressful time, supporting him as he mediated the estrangement between the army that had been treated so shabbily and the Congress (and civil authority) to which he had committed his loyalty. In the next months, he granted furloughs generously, particularly to disaffected troops, keeping them out of trouble and anticipating that they would be demobilized at home. In April 1783, news of an armistice and a provisional peace agreement arrived at camp.

That summer, Congress left Philadelphia when unpaid troops marched in the streets. They reconvened at Princeton, New Jersey, and summoned Washington there. He postponed their departure until late August 1784 because he still had military affairs to wind up in New York and because Martha was again "exceedingly unwell." He had no intention of moving until her health allowed her to make the journey with him. He finally left Knox in command on the Hudson River and moved his headquarters to Rocky Hills, New Jersey, four miles north of Princeton. He and Martha moved into the home of Judge Berrien, a two-story frame building with piazzas on a hill a short distance from the Millstone River.

The only soldiers there were Washington's aides and his guards, whose tents dotted the lawn before the house, along with their captain's marquee. A young painter enjoyed visiting the house, where he made a crayon drawing of the general. He wrote, "I was quite at home in every respect at head-quarters; to breakfast and dine day after day with the general and Mrs. Washington, and members of congress, and noticed as the young painter, was delicious."

Martha finally went back to Mount Vernon in early October,

"before the weather and roads shou'd get bad," to prepare for their homecoming. The Revolutionary years of crowded accommodations and jolting coaches would be over very soon, she hoped, and she and her "Old Man" could resume their peaceful life.

At last, at long last, in November, the final treaty arrived and Washington could go home. Congress had adjourned on November 4, to reconvene at Annapolis on November 26. Washington disbanded the bulk of the army and made plans to reoccupy New York City when the British finally left. Washington and Clinton rode at the head of a small force into the city on November 25. New York was a shambles, much worse than Boston had been. In more than seven years' occupation, trees and bushes had been chopped down, fences and small buildings torn to pieces—all consumed as fuel for British fires.

After a poignant farewell to his officers, Washington set off for Annapolis with his three remaining aides, progress slow because every town on the way wanted to celebrate the end of war with him. It wasn't until December 18 that Congress had a quorum. On December 23, Washington read his formal Farewell Address, trembling with emotion, returned his commission, and became a private citizen once more—he intended to remain one for the rest of his life.

Throughout the weary years, Washington hadn't won many battles, but the ones he won were important to the outcome of the Revolution. To most Americans, he represented the sacrifices, ideals, and final success of independence. Duty and vision kept him in the field for most of eight and a half years. It was his steadfastness that inspired the army and kept both soldiers and officers there year after year.

George Washington was the indispensable man to the success of the American Revolution, and Martha Washington was the indispensable woman to him. He could bear all those years away from home, creating a national army, because she spent part of every year with him, no matter how awful the conditions in camp might be. Their mutual love, confidence, and support helped keep him going in the face of every disappointment, setback, and defeat. Every year she made a home for him, where he could rest and refresh his spirits until it was time to go back in the field another time, for however long it took to win the war. Out of those eight and a half years that he spent in command of the army, she was with him for nearly five, more than half the war, in stays ranging from three to ten months. Martha was truly the secret weapon of the American Revolution.

Washington's own assessment of her importance can be seen in his military expense account. Since he had volunteered to serve without pay, only his expenses were paid. But should Martha's trips to and from Mount Vernon be included? He had hesitated at the beginning of the war to include her trips because they seemed to be private expenses. However, since he had been forced over time "to postpone the visit I every year contemplated to make my family between the close of one campaign and the opening of another, and, as this expense was incidental thereto, and consequent of my self-denial," he considered that her trips were therefore necessary to the performance of his military duties and justified repayment. The total cost had been £1,064.1.0—and a bargain at the price, considering her importance to the American cause.

Unlike Napoleon and scores of other revolutionary heroes who have become dictators since, Washington voluntarily gave up power to the civilian authorities. Accompanied by his aides, he galloped away on the long road home. Hard riding brought them to Mount Vernon on Christmas Eve, to the delight of his eager wife and a new family.

CHAPTER EIGHT

Mount Vernon and a New Family

George's baggage arrived home long before he did. Six teams of horses pulling wagons laden with all his camp paraphernalia, tents, marquee, furniture, clothing, and papers arrived sometime in mid-November. For Martha, the two months after she left New Jersey were marked by both busyness and boredom. No journey to winter camp to anticipate, no need to assemble the coachload of supplies she brought with her each year. Domestic and plantation affairs filled some of her time, but she was really just waiting for her husband's return.

Meanwhile, Martha and her daughter-in-law had agreed on plans for a change in all their lives. Since Jack Custis's death, Martha and George had doubtless discussed rearing one of her grandchildren when they returned permanently to Mount Vernon at war's end. To this most maternal of women, a childless home was sadly empty even when long visits from nieces and nephews helped fill the gap.

Martha had even broached the idea of fostering a grandchild while her son was still living. His heart set on a son, Jack had written a bitterly disappointed letter to his mother when Nelly gave birth to a second daughter, named for his mother. Martha promptly offered to bring up the unwanted baby girl at Mount Vernon. Perhaps at Nelly's behest, he declined: "You took the advantage of Me to ask for her just after my Disappointment. I do not know how to comply for I could not have loved It better if It had been a Boy."

Now, Jack's beautiful widow had remarried and was again pregnant. Martha and George liked and respected her second husband, David Stuart, a physician who practiced in Alexandria. The Stuarts continued to live at Abingdon but frequently came for long visits at Mount Vernon. That pleasant pattern would be maintained—with a change. The two oldest children, Betsy and Patty, would remain with their mother and stepfather. Granting Martha's wish, however, Nelly agreed that the two youngest, little Nelly and Washington Custis, could live at Mount Vernon as the adopted children of the Washingtons. Complicated, distant estates to manage for her son were as daunting to Nelly as the wish to please her beloved mother-in-law was strong.

Adoptions within a family were commonplace in the eighteenth and nineteenth centuries. Childless aunts, uncles, and cousins or lonely grandparents often reared relatives' children, especially those from large families. With or without legal action or a change of surname, these children lived with and were publicly accepted as heirs of their adoptive family without giving up a loving relationship with their birth parents.

With George's arrival at home, Nelly and Washy remained permanently at Mount Vernon. Martha adored the children and devoted herself to them, nursing them through the measles they broke out with in January. Her lost children were replaced by this second generation. Nelly was a sparkling brunette beauty who favored her mother and her aunt Patsy, while enjoying robust health. Two-year-old Washy Custis was a cheerful, friendly little soul with fair hair and blue eyes, so chubby as a toddler that he was called Tub.

History repeated itself as Martha spoiled and favored the lazy little boy while George preferred the winsome, talented girl. Martha put her adoration of Washy clearly: "My pritty little Dear Boy complains of a pain his stomach. . . . I cannot say but it makes me miserable if ever he complains let the cause be ever so trifling. I hope the almighty will spare him to me." There was nothing that pleased her more than having her "little family . . . prattling about me."

The end of the war brought other changes to the inhabitants of Mount Vernon. Elizabeth and Lund Washington moved to their newly built house, Hayfield, five miles away on land that George deeded to his cousin in payment of a debt. They were close enough, though, for frequent visits and dinners.

Martha's niece Frances Bassett, just turned sixteen, was visiting at Mount Vernon during this time. When Fanny's mother died in 1777, Martha had written to her brother-in-law Burwell Bassett: "My dear sister [Nancy Bassett] in her life time often mentioned my taking my dear Fanny if she should be taken away before she grew up. If you will lett her come to live with me, I will with greatest pleasure take her and be a parent and mother to her as long as I live." This was meant to be not an adoption, but rather an opportunity for a young girl to learn all the accomplishments of a lady, including the chance to find a good husband. Williamsburg was no longer the center of social life (Richmond had become the capital in 1780), and northern Virginia had grown in importance. The Revolution had dragged on, and only now was Fanny able to join her aunt.

A willowy brunette with large eyes, she had a pensive, ethereal air. Almost at once, she found just the husband she wanted, and the feeling was quite mutual. Close on the general's heels, his favorite nephew, the son of his youngest brother, Charles, had arrived at Mount Vernon. A few years older than Fanny, George Augustine Washington had fought throughout the Revolution, serving as Lafayette's aide at Yorktown.

With the family connection, no doubt they had met throughout the years, but now Fanny had grown up. The gallant soldier was a romantic figure himself, handsome and heroic. By April, their romance had progressed to the point that a family friend referred to him as "her Major." But marriage had to wait for his health to improve; he suffered badly from chest pains, weight loss, fatigue, and overall debility. His uncle George, despite his own straitened finances, gave him £140 to go to the West Indies. George Augustine sailed away in May, leaving Fanny behind at Mount Vernon.

Later in the summer, Fanny went home for a visit before returning to live permanently at Mount Vernon. Even though the house was filled with company, Martha missed her badly, and so did the children. She was a very compatible girl. On Christmas Eve, shortly after her seventeenth birthday, her father, Burwell Bassett, brought his daughter back to live with her aunt and uncle while she awaited the return of her fiancé. Burwell stayed with the gay family party until New Year's Day. Nelly and David Stuart were there with Betsy, Patty, and their new baby daughter, Nancy.

Fanny attended weddings and parties in Alexandria and Dumfries, staying a couple of weeks at a time, as she made friends with the Craiks, Blackburns, Washingtons, and other neighborhood young people who gathered at these celebrations. Of course, she spent a good deal of time with Martha as well, talking, sewing, and playing with the children. She also liked to ride with her uncle on his plantation rounds.

After a year spent traveling in search of health in Barbados, the Leeward Islands, Bermuda, and South Carolina, George Augustine returned to Mount Vernon on a beautiful Saturday in May 1785 while the wood honeysuckle was in full bloom. The reports he had sent during his travels had not been encouraging. His uncle, at least, didn't hold very high hopes for this treatment, although he had paid for it. He wrote a friend about George Augustine, "Poor young fellow! his pursuit after health is, I fear, altogether fruitless." Everyone seemed to realize that he was consumptive—that is, that he had tuberculosis. Yet somehow, no one thought it unwise that he should become George's plantation manager or marry Martha's young niece.

In July 1785, the household was further increased by the arrival of William Shaw, a British Canadian. The young man came highly recommended by friends for the position of "Clerk or Secretary" that George needed to write letters, keep the plantation books, organize his military papers, represent him in business matters, "& occasionally to devote a small portion of time to initiate two little children (a Girl of six, & a boy of four years of age) . . . in the first rudiments of Education." Shaw remained a little over a year but spent too much time gadding about on pleasure jaunts; his departure in 1786 was overdue, but he remained on good terms with the family.

In April 1785, Martha's mother died at the age of seventy-five, followed nine days later by Bat Dandridge, her only surviving brother (her brother William had drowned during the Revolution). His son John, an attorney and planter, took over the support of his mother and the six other children, becoming one of those reliable nephews who helped keep the family going. Of her seven siblings, only Martha's youngest sister, Betsy, was still living, unhappily married to an alcoholic who swilled brandy all day. He managed one of the Custis estates for a time—another act of family charity.

George's brother Samuel, five times married and deeply in debt, had died during the Revolution, leaving his three children by his fourth wife virtually penniless, with neither their stepmother nor their grown half-brothers able to care for them. George found himself responsible for Sam's wild youngsters. Because of their chaotic family life, none of them had received much supervision, and their rudeness, disobedience, and frequent slovenliness made them a trial to everybody. He eventually put the boys, George Steptoe and Lawrence Augustine Washington, into the Alexandria Academy. Harriot, three years older than Nelly, had been living with relatives but came to Mount Vernon in 1786, where her messiness was beyond even Martha's ability to correct. In 1787, George's favorite brother, Jack, died at the age of fifty-one.

After George Augustine's return, Burrell Bassett sent his written consent for the marriage of his underage daughter. Her older brother brought the letter and stayed for the wedding. On October 14, 1785, a clear, fine Friday with the temperature in the upper sixties, the young couple were married at Mount Vernon just after the candles were lit. Friends from Alexandria helped them celebrate. Later that year, George Augustine took over management of the estate. He and Fanny took Lund and Eliza Washington's place in the household, living there as family members and congenial friends.

Shaw's replacement as secretary/tutor was a Harvard graduate and New Hampshire native, Tobias Lear. After their unsatisfactory experience with Shaw, he was hired only for a year's trial, coming to Mount Vernon in May 1786. There could hardly have been a greater contrast; he devoted himself to the Washingtons' interests and became an indispensable part of their family and social life—intelligent, responsible, a good conversationalist, and a better writer. With the children, he was firm and well organized but also kind and appreciative of their efforts. Martha soon came to love the young man who had been recommended as having "the character of a Gentleman & a schooler." And he returned that love. He described her as "everything that is benevolent & good—I honor her as a second mother & receive from her all those attentions which I should look for from her who bore me."

During these years, a great number of visitors came to stay—and stay. The general's celebrity was a magnet drawing guests. Washington had become an international hero, the object of intense admiration at home and abroad. A pilgrimage to pay their respects to the hero of the American Revolution was de rigueur for many—Europeans taking a look at the colonies that had cast off their king, former colleagues in arms, mere acquaintances, and strangers who could scrape up the shadow of an introduction or even none at all.

His celebrity attracted the visitors, but Martha took care of them. The Washingtons' social code called for gracious entertainment; they felt duty-bound to put up with impertinent strangers who wanted to question Washington closely about his career. Martha often found herself consulting with the house servants about adding extra dishes for dinner or making up beds in the hallways. Often, too, in the evenings George would retire to his library to read or answer correspondence while she and the invaluable Lear kept their guests occupied and entertained. George knew he could depend on Martha's incomparable conversational skills as she talked with guests about politics, the war, the founding of the American nation, or whatever subject they desired.

On one occasion, George left an English traveler, John Hunter, to the company of Fanny and Martha, and the talk soon turned to military matters. Hunter wrote later, "It's astonishing with what raptures Mrs. Washington spoke about the discipline of the army, the excellent order they were in, superior to any troops she said upon the face of the earth towards the close of the war; even the English acknowledged it, she said. What pleasure she took in the sound of the fifes and drums, preferring it to any music that was ever heard; and then to see them reviewed a week or two before the men disbanded, when they were all well clothed was she said a most heavenly sight; almost every soldier shed tears at parting with the General when the army was disbanded: Mrs. Washington said it was a most melancholy sight." His astonishment was no doubt based on the novelty of hearing a woman talk knowledgeably and passionately about war and patriotism—considered by the English to be men's business.

She had settled on a style of dress that pleased her. Following the general modes of the day, she had her gowns made of very fine fabrics. One of her dresses remains intact at Mount Vernon: the tailored lines of its lustrous brown silk would have flattered her now stocky shape; the bodice's square neckline and three-quarter-length sleeves would have been accented by a lace fichu and trim. Pieces of fabric cut from her dresses and passed down through the family as mementos are a beautiful assortment of lampas and damask silks—white with red and pink roses, pale ivory with narrow ivory stripes and delicate bouquets, very pale green with dark and pale pink grosgrain-pattern stripes and more pink bouquets. A visiting Frenchman bestowed his approval on her "simple dignity . . . she possesses that amenity, and manifests that attention to strangers, which render hospitality so charming."

Among their more illustrious guests was one of Great Britain's leading literary figures, Catherine Macaulay. Author of the liberal *History of England*, she had been savaged in England both for her openly pro-American views and her marriage to the very much younger, socially inferior William Graham. Her friend and long-time correspondent Mercy Otis Warren made a classic comment on her marriage at forty-seven to a man of twenty-one: "Doubtless, that lady's independency of spirit led her to suppose she might associate for the remainder of her life with an inoffensive, obliging youth with the same impunity a gentleman of threescore and ten might marry a damsel of fifteen."

Armed with introductory letters from the Warrens, Macaulay, now Macaulay Graham, and her husband arrived for a ten-day visit at Mount Vernon in June 1785. Martha welcomed them warmly, although the author was chiefly interested in looking over George's military correspondence and discussing republican government. Writing to Mercy in fond remembrance of their wartime friendship, Martha thanked her for "introducing a Lady so well known in the literary world as Mrs. Macaulay Graham, whose agreeable company we have had the pleasure of a few days."

But though Washington enjoyed the company of intellectual women, it was his own beloved wife's conversation he relished. Martha had no pretensions of being intellectual, but she was intelligent, observant, and vitally interested in all the experiences that had come her way in life. Now in her late fifties, she was comfortably plump, gray-haired, and grandmotherly in appearance. Most people were still attracted by the flashing smile, friendly eyes, unwrinkled skin, and interest in everyone she met.

George had grown only more contented in nearly thirty years of marriage. He revealed his feelings about the joys of a happy marriage in a letter to his old friend from the Revolution, the Marquis de Chastellux, who had finally married after many years of amorous liaisons. George wrote: "I was, as you may well suppose, not less delighted than surprised to come across that plain American word—'my wife.' A wife!—Well, my dear Marquis, I can hardly refrain from smiling to find you are caught at last. I saw, by the eulogium you often made on the happiness of domestic life in America, that you had swallowed the bait. . . . Now you are well served for coming to fight in favor of the American Rebels, all the way across the Atlantic Ocean, by catching the terrible contagion—domestic felicity—which like the smallpox or the plague, a man can have only once in his life; because it commonly lasts him—(at least with us in America—I don't know how you manage these matters in France) for his whole lifetime." He wished for the newlyweds the enjoyment of their "domestic felicity—during the entire course of your mortal existence."

There were very few people who truly loved farming as George did. He started to get his acreage back in good heart again, to repair the deterioration of the mansion house, and to complete the additions and improvements that had lagged during the Revolution. The enlarged house gave the extended family much needed space and privacy, particularly his study and his and Martha's large second-floor bedroom, separated from the main body of the house by private passageways to be entered only by invitation. At the end of the war, the grand dining room on the north end of the house was still incomplete. The embellishment of that great room continued apace; it was nearly two stories high, with its own outside door, grand Palladian window, bright mint green paint, marble mantelpiece, and delicate white plasterwork on ceiling and walls.

A spacious portico with columns soaring to the second story on the riverside and flagstones underfoot provided the perfect setting to enjoy their dramatic view of the Potomac; it became one of the signature elements of the mansion. The finishing touches were provided on the west front by a pediment, cupola topped by a dove-shaped weather vane, and open arcades tying the mansion to the adjoining outbuildings while allowing glimpses of the river, creating what is essentially today's Mount Vernon.

Much as he enjoyed agricultural retirement, Washington hadn't given up his keen interest in the development of the western frontier or his belief that a strong federal government was needed for the economic and political well-being of the nation he had done so much to form. Beginning in 1784, he and James Madison drew the states of Virginia and Maryland into a series of conventions to work together on issues involving the Potomac River and the Chesapeake Bay; some of the meetings were held at Mount Vernon. Finally, in 1786, Virginia invited all the states to a convention at Annapolis to discuss trade and commercial problems; representatives from the five states present issued a call for a convention of all the states to meet the following May in Philadelphia.

In 1787, Fanny Washington gave birth to a boy, who died four days later. For Martha, it must have been like losing a grandson. But Fanny didn't recover completely from her confinement; instead, she remained weak and started to cough persistently, a worrisome echo of George Augustine. The younger Washingtons went to try the effects of Warm Springs, and Fanny returned in somewhat better health, "but not perfectly recovered" in her aunt's eyes. She was also five months pregnant and feeling superstitious about the loss of her first baby at Mount Vernon.

Early the next year, George Augustine took her down to Eltham for her lying-in, stopping to enjoy her brother's wedding on the way before he returned to take up his duties. Martha lamented her niece's absence greatly and worried about the survival of the expected child. She wrote wistfully, "She is a child to me, and I am very lonesome when she is absent." Fanny delivered a healthy girl, named Anna Maria for her grandmother but called Maria instead of Nancy; they returned to Mount Vernon late the following spring.

That year, the rich and well-connected Powels, wartime acquaintances from Philadelphia, stopped for a while on their way back from a visit to her sister at Westover. The women obviously talked at length about family problems, and Eliza Powel appreciated Martha's "Civilities & attention to me while I was under your hospitable Roof." Although the three little Custis girls ranged in age from eight to eleven, Martha was already worried about their posture. At her request, Eliza bought posture collars, disguised with ribbons, so that her granddaughters would hold up their heads, stand erect, and throw back their shoulders. These devices trained young girls to avoid "those ridiculous Distortions of the Face & Eyes which girls, at a certain age, frequently fall into from a foolish Bashfulness."

Eliza had talked frankly and tearfully with Martha about the plight of her sister Mary Willing Byrd, left a widow with ten children by the suicide of her monstrously indebted husband. Eliza hoped that Martha's "own good heart will plead my apology" for pouring out her troubles. Martha responded promptly and kindly:

"I do most truly sympathize with you on your sister's disappoint-ments in life. These [disappointments] now come, in a greater or less degree, are what all of us experience."

To Martha's serious disquiet, 1787 was starting to sound like 1775 at Mount Vernon. Political discussions were roiling about them, and her husband was mentioned constantly as a leader in the new nation, floundering under the weak government set up by the Articles of Confederation. George was happy in retirement, and so was she. Farming, building, gardening, spending time with Tobias Lear and George Augustine Washington, soon to be joined by David Humphreys, the general was well amused by his interests and the company of these intelligent, compatible young men so like his military family of aides-de-camp.

A life spent on housekeeping, decorating, sewing, looking after Fanny and the little children, and enjoying frequent visits from Nelly Stuart and the other grandchildren seemed just right to Martha. Then there were the scores of visitors, assorted nieces and nephews to help on their way in the world, and their own financial interests to look after. The Washingtons looked much richer on pa-per than they actually were. George had hundreds of acres that went untilled because he could find no tenants—or if he did, they neglected to pay the rent. They also were owed large debts, but since many of the loans had been made to their own siblings and friends, they were largely uncollectible.

Very much against her will, he agreed to lead Virginia's repre-sentatives at the new convention to be held in Philadelphia in May. He believed not only that the work of the convention was crucial, but that his presence was important. Just before he set off, he was summoned to Fredericksburg to visit his mother, who was dying slowly of breast cancer, and his sister, Betty, who was worn to the bone caring for her. Since he was making a galloping visit, Martha didn't come with him. Both women were somewhat improved, and he spent three days with them before going back home.

On May 9, 1787, he left for Philadelphia. This time, Martha didn't accompany him. At first he hadn't wanted to take part, but he had been persuaded that it was his duty. Martha wasn't the only one who realized that he was sacrificing his (their) private interests or that he was putting his hard-won reputation on the line by entering politics. Both James Madison and Henry Knox wrote admiringly of his commitment to the public good. As Knox put it: "Secure as he was in his fame, he has again committed it to the mercy of events."

Their old friend Robert Morris had invited the Washingtons to stay with his family throughout the convention. George declined because he thought the sessions might drag on too long and because he was coming alone. As usual, he would have preferred to have his wife's company. He wrote rather sadly and perhaps a shade defensively: "Mrs. Washington is become too Domestick, and too attentive to two little Grand Children to leave home, and I can assure you, Sir, that it was not until after a long struggle I could obtain my own consent to appear again in a public theatre. My first remaining wish being to glide gently down the stream of life in tranquil retirement."

In Philadelphia, the meeting charged with merely revising the Articles of Confederation scrapped the whole document and started over, creating the United States Constitution. George Washington was unanimously elected president of the convention. As such, he acted with studied impartiality as major issues were debated—representation for large states versus small states, free states versus slaveholding states, the slave trade, the form and extent of executive power. Even though he did not join in the official discussions, no one could doubt that he was in favor of a strong government with a strong executive. Long, long days of discussion, speechmaking, and debate and further long evenings of politicking, negotiating, and compromise finally ended on September 17 with the Constitution that today governs the United States.

Letters to and from Mount Vernon helped him bear those long months away from home when Martha refused to join him. Just as he had during the war, he wrote weekly letters to his manager, now George Augustine rather than Lund, and to Martha, and they responded just as regularly. To miss the height of the planting season and all his family at home was a cruel deprivation for him. As he wrote to his nephew in early September when adjournment was at last in sight: "God grant I may not be disappointed in this expectation, as I am quite homesick."

After George returned home in the fall, the household was enlarged by a new and very welcome semipermanent resident. He had continued to take an interest in the career of one of his favorite wartime aides, David Humphreys, who had a certain literary reputation. Washington had issued a standing invitation: "The only stipulations I shall contend for are, that in all things you shall do as you please." With his pleasing manners and entertaining conversation, Humphreys was a welcome addition to the family circle.

The political task before supporters of the new Constitution was to persuade nine out of the thirteen states of the Confederation to ratify the document. Its opponents were many and fierce; they feared a new, strongly centralized government, especially the power that would be put in the hands of the president. Washington actively used his tremendous prestige in a letter-writing campaign to assist his friends James Madison and Alexander Hamilton in support of ratification.

Martha could clearly see her husband's involvement wouldn't end with ratification. As the national debate continued over the next year, the Constitution's adherents (becoming known as Federalists) defended the creation of a single executive, a president who would be elected every four years, by implying or even stating that George Washington would fill that role. His looming shadow reassured doubters because they knew he had once renounced power and could be trusted to do so again. Not that Martha lacked confidence in George's ability and integrity, but she thought it was time for someone else to do his share. Her husband had given all the time out of their mutual lives that anyone could expect.

But his supporters were adamant. He received a barrage of letters, visits, and weekly piles of newspapers that assumed he was the only man for the job. At least one member of the household was a strong advocate. David Humphreys argued that his acceptance was a duty to a nation that might fail without his presence. Martha was so exasperated that she pretended to have no more interest in the national debate, writing to Fanny, "We have not a single article of news but politicks which I do not concern myself about."

Washington continued to resist the idea of becoming president, resolving at first to decline the honor if it was offered to him. For one thing, he was very happy tending to Mount Vernon. For another, he dreaded that he might seem to have supported the Constitution just to gain the office for himself, a form of self-interest that he despised. Little by little, though, he came to agree that he would accept election but would in no way seek the office.

As the ninth state ratified the Constitution in the summer of 1788 (eventually only North Carolina and Rhode Island held out), the states began selecting their electors for the first presidential election in November. After the turn of the year, Mount Vernon began receiving reports of the returns, overwhelmingly in Washington's favor. But there were still formalities to go through. Although the returns were in, the congressmen weren't. At last, on April 6, 1789, a quorum was reached and the returns were officially counted. George Washington had been elected the first president of the new nation; John Adams would be his vice president.

He was officially notified of his election on April 14, 1789, and set off within two days for New York City, the temporary capital of the United States. That day, he noted in his diary, "About ten o'clock I bade adieu to Mount Vernon, to private life, and to domestic felicity." Alas for Martha, who had dreamed that they would "grow old in solitude and tranquility together."

CHAPTER NINE

The President's Lady

George Washington was inaugurated first president of the United States on April 30, 1789, in New York City. Knowing that every single move set a precedent made a cautious man even more careful, a man who ruled by consensus even more likely to consult others. The president also found that every detail of the day-to-day business of the new government had to be invented. The Constitution created the general framework for this unique form of government, but the rest of the edifice had to be built brick by brick, decision by decision.

The departments of the executive branch were set up in separate bills by Congress that summer and fall, and Washington appointed strong patriots, men he knew and trusted, as department heads. Henry Knox was carried over from the earlier government as secretary of war, Edmund Randolph of Virginia was named attorney general (a part-time consultative position), and Alexander Hamilton became secretary of the Treasury. John Jay refused the position of secretary of state, becoming chief justice of the Supreme Court instead. At James Madison's suggestion, Washington then offered the State Department to Madison's friend Thomas Jefferson, who was in France representing the nation.

Initially, the burden of the presidency was made much heavier by two facts of political life. The new federal government would have jobs to bestow, and a large number of Americans at every social level thought they or their relatives or their friends would be just the men for those jobs, the more lucrative the better. Second, staunch republicans believed that they had the right to speak to their president face-to-face whenever they had something to say, whether it concerned those desirable federal jobs, advice on how to run the new government, or anything else that came to mind.

Especially for the first year of the presidency, Washington was bombarded by letters and visits from job hunters as well as admirers and the merely curious. The brash American propensity for knocking on the door of the rented presidential mansion on Cherry Street and barging in made it almost impossible for Washington to do the actual work of government. In writing to David Stuart, the president explained his dilemma: "I was unable to attend to any business whatsoever; for Gentlemen, consulting their own convenience rather than mine, were calling from the time I rose from breakfast—often before—until I sat down to dinner."

After consultation with Adams, Hamilton, Madison, and Jay, the president announced a formal schedule of presidential access, published in the *Gazette of the United States*. Except for those with government business, he would receive visitors only from two to three on Tuesdays and Fridays. On Tuesdays from three to four, he hosted a presidential levee, or reception, at his house. There he received callers without appointment; any respectable-looking (read: decently dressed) man would be admitted to meet the president. The hourlong levees were very formal: Washington, hair powdered properly white and confined in a queue bag, wearing a black velvet suit and dress sword, nodded to each visitor as he was announced by the aides; everyone remained standing while the rest of the guests gathered; the president then walked around the circle, chatting briefly with each man before they took their leave. These appointed hours and levees were the sum of all visits of compliment—that is, social calls without invitation, just to have a look at the new president. Such calls "on other days, and particularly on Sunday, will not be agreeable to [the president]," the *Gazette* concluded.

At least when Washington arrived in New York, he found the house clean, furnished, and comfortable, thanks to the inimitable Tobias Lear. In advance of his chief, Lear had come up on the stagecoach from Virginia about the end of March. He found everything in disarray and busied himself setting it all to rights. Lear's mission was setting up the household, hiring staff, handling the money, and keeping an itemized account of expenses. He brought Martha's list of necessary household goods, which their landlady bought, and arranged for the tuning and reconditioning of the family spinet, which had been sent up by ship.

Land rich and cash poor, Washington was forced to borrow £600 from a neighbor to cover the costs of the journey and the first weeks in New York. That £600 was expended for the household and official entertainments while Congress debated whether or not to fix a salary or to pay expenses, eventually deciding on the former. The steward hired to run the presidential house was Samuel Fraunces, "Black Sam" of Fraunces Tavern fame, and other servants were hired in the city. Fraunces's cooking was superb: "He tosses up such a number of fine dishes that we are distracted in our choice. . . . Oysters & Lobsters make a very conspicuous figure upon the table."

But George missed Martha, even with Tobias Lear and David Humphreys for company: a bachelors' hall was not his idea of home. He hated for her to be angry with him, and there was no secret about her annoyance at having to leave Mount Vernon again. She had refused to accompany him to Philadelphia for the convention that produced the Constitution. When he left for New York, she tarried at home, volubly regretting his decision to reenter public life. No doubt he wrote asking her to speed up her departure, but none of those letters survive.

Tobias wrote to George Augustine Washington ten days after the president arrived in the city. He asked his friend to pass along the information about the delicious seafood to "Madam Washington . . . (as she is remarkably fond of these fish) [to] hasten her advancing toward New York." He ended on a more serious note: "We are extremely desirous of seeing her here."

Even when joking, Tobias's loving affection for Martha shone through. In the same letter to George Augustine, he asked for a report about local opinion of the arrangements made so far and of the government in general, suggesting that discreet inquiries might be made. Lapsing into whimsy, he wrote, "The Ladies are very expert at this business—suppose Mrs Washington should do it? I know of no person better qualified—her very serious & benevolent countenance would not suffer a person to hide a thing from her. . . . Now I would give a great deal to be present when you inform Mrs Washington of this—or read it to her. If she ever put on a frown it would be on this occasion. . . . What does he mean! she will exclaim! Does he wish to make a spy of me?"

Martha, Nelly and Wash Custis, Bob Lewis, and six slaves, including her maids, Oney Judge and Molly, arrived in New York City on May 27. Billy Lee (now usually called Will), the personal servant and slave who had been with Washington throughout the Revolution, arrived a month later. Will was considerably crippled in both legs; he had been left in Philadelphia for medical treatment before coming on to New York in mid-June. Although he wasn't able to do much in a house with steep stairs, he wanted to come to the city. As Tobias noted, Washington wished "to gratify him in every reasonable wish." Among the four other slaves brought to New York—Giles, Austin, Paris, and Christopher Sheels—young Christopher assisted Will, learning the job and taking over when Will retired. There were already fourteen hired white servants at work.

Martha found the house quite acceptable, thanking God that George and the rest of the household were well: "The House he is in is a very good one and is handsomely furnished all new for the General." On the corner of Cherry and Dover, the three-story brick house faced St. George's Square. It had most of the modern conveniences—seven fireplaces and a pump and cistern in the yard. Several alterations had been made: enlarging the drawing room for presidential entertaining and providing a larger stable and a wash house. With the size of their household, they probably also bought water from the water men, who daily delivered huge hogsheads in their carts to customers.

Only three blocks from the East River, Cherry Street was a noisy main thoroughfare serving the bustling wharves along the river. The sounds and smells of the neighborhood came through the open windows—ships' bells, rumbling ironclad wheels of wagons on the way to nearby Peck's market, stray dogs, horses, carriages, street vendors, hogs grunting and rooting in the open gutters, stevedores unloading ships on the riverfront. In the country, noises and voices were familiar, and the arrival of a carriage represented the height of excitement; in New York, everything was new, and strangers thronged the streets. The children were entranced, especially Nelly. Martha wrote home that she "spends her time at the window looking at carriages &c passing by which is new to her and very common for children to do."

From the moment Martha arrived, callers swept into the presidential mansion with the force of a spring flood. The ladies and gentlemen of the city were delighted to have the president's consort as a focal point for the city's elite social life. She complained to Fanny after two weeks in New York, "I have been so much engaged since I came here . . . but shall soon have time as most of the visits are at an end. I have not had one half hour to myself since the day of my arrival."

Martha had discovered the tedium of constant public attention. Contrary to her usual habit at home, her hair had to be set and dressed every day by a visiting hairdresser, and she attended much more to her clothes, putting on white muslin for the summer. As she reported to her niece: "You would I fear think me a good deal in the fashion if you could but see me," clearly not implying enjoyment.

The boundaries set for the president's lady by her husband and his male advisers were not at all to her liking. Being the nation's hostess has been an onerous task for many First Ladies. As the first president's wife, however, Martha had no way of knowing how radically her life would be curtailed. President Washington had already announced in the newspapers that he and his wife would not attend or host private gatherings, to avoid any appearance of favoritism. How different from the Revolution, where the informal gatherings of officers and their wives at headquarters had been such a delight. Martha was considerably disgruntled to find herself fettered by political considerations.

She was expected to be the hostess of two weekly social gatherings, both quite official—a reception and a dinner party. She arrived in New York on Wednesday and found that "her" reception for that Friday had already been publicly announced. Every Friday while Congress was in session, she received both women and men in the drawing room without invitation, as long as they were formally attired. Then there were the Thursday dinner parties. The official guest list was carefully chosen to avoid any appearance of favoritism—usually balanced both geographically and politically. Cabinet members, senators, congressmen, and foreign ministers were invited regularly without much consideration given to friendships or social graces. Her role as the commander's wife during the Revolution had been a walk in the park compared with that of First Lady.

One symbol of the new formality was "The President's March," composed by a Hessian soldier/musician who had stayed behind after the war. Written in honor of the inauguration, it was usually played whenever Washington entered a theater, concert hall, or ballroom, and it became the presidential anthem. A decade later, the melody was renamed "Hail, Columbia" when lyrics were added.

Martha had barely begun these entertainments when they came to an abrupt halt. Only three weeks after her arrival, George began complaining of fever and pain. A large carbuncle (a hard, solid mass) had appeared on his left thigh, and it grew larger and more painful every day. His doctors diagnosed anthrax, presumably of the cutaneous variety; no anesthesia was available as the father-and-son team of doctors operated on the mass June 17, the son cutting, the father urging, "Cut deeper, cut deeper." George's phenomenal strength brought him through, but afterward he groaned with pain, complaining that any noise hurt his head. Tobias Lear bought fifteen pounds of rope, directing the servants to tie off Cherry Street to keep traffic from passing and to spread the sidewalks with straw to muffle the footsteps of passersby. A week later, he repeated the process after the first rope was stolen.

Martha was terribly shaken by her husband's condition. The doctors thought he might die, and his convalescence took the rest of the summer. He spent six weeks "being confined to a lying posture on one side." Although George returned to work, the incision was still draining in September, as "the wound given by the incision is not yet closed." Acquaintances continued to call on Martha regularly that summer to inquire after the president's health. Without his leadership, it was feared that the nation might splinter into small, weak confederations.

One of the callers became an unexpected new friend, given the differences in their personal styles—the tartly outspoken New Englander Abigail Adams. She had been at home in Massachusetts but returned to the capital in June. The Adamses had rented a large manor house out in the countryside along the Greenwich Road. With beautiful views in all directions, Richmond Hill was about a mile and a half from the city—a pleasant ride or drive for guests to drop in for breakfast or tea. The morning after her arrival, David Humphreys called to pay his respects and take breakfast with the vice president's wife.

Later that morning, Abigail rode in her carriage to Cherry Street, accompanied by her married daughter Nabby Smith. They were greeted by Humphreys and Lear, witnesses to the first meeting between these formidable women. Generally more inclined to critical observation than admiration, the vice president's wife described Martha as easy and polite, plain in her dress—"but that plainness is the best of every article. . . . Her hair is white, beautifull teeth, rather shorter than otherways." She went on, "Her manners are modest and unassuming, dignified and feminine, not the Tincture of ha'ture about her. His Majesty was ill & confined to his Room. I had not the pleasure of a presentation to him, but the satisfaction of hearing that he regreted it equally with myself."

On a second visit to the presidential mansion in July, Abigail was invited upstairs to Washington's chamber, where he lay on a sofa. She found him both dignified and affable—"a singular example of modesty and diffidence." Her positive impression of Martha was only increased by this call: "Mrs. Washington is one of those unassuming characters which create Love & Esteem. A most becoming pleasantness sits upon her countenance & an unaffected deportment which renders her the object of veneration and Respect." Both the Washingtons struck her as just right for a republican government: "With all these feelings and Sensations I found myself much more deeply impressd than I ever did before their Majesties of Britain."

During George's convalescence, the carriage was altered by putting in some sort of bed so that he could lie on his side and be driven about the city. It took four attendants to get him comfortably arranged in the coach. Martha rode with him on these expeditions, doubtless entertaining him with conversation.

As he regained his strength, they went back to fashioning the presidential lifestyle. Although choreographed, Martha's Friday evenings were relaxed and enjoyable compared with the president's levees. Starting at eight o'clock, guests were directed by servants up to the large second-floor drawing room, blazing with candles in the chandelier and candelabra, supplemented by spermaceti-oil lamps; Humphreys or Lear escorted them to the sofa where Martha was seated. After curtseying or bowing to her and being greeted by the president, they moved about the room, chatting with other callers. Even in his diary, George maintained the fiction that he was merely another guest at his wife's entertainment, noting the size and quality of the crowd. Refreshments were light, varying with the seasons— wine, tea, lemonade, cake, fruits (sometimes including delicacies like pineapple and coconut), ice cream. The table was decorated with gilt ornaments. As the guests left, they were escorted to their carriages by Bob Lewis.

Abigail enjoyed her position as second lady of the land. She wrote to her sister, "My station is always at the right hand of Mrs. W.; through want of knowing what is right I find it sometimes occupied, but on such an occasion the President never fails of seeing that it is relinquished for me, and having removed Ladies several times, they have now learnt to rise & give it me, but this between our selves, as <u>all distinction</u> you know is unpopular."

Dinner parties were more of an uphill slog. Lear had cards printed for the dinners; once the guest's name and the date were filled in by hand, they were delivered personally by one of the aides. At first, many of the guests were strangers, both to the Washingtons and to one another. Men predominated at most of these dinners when Congress was in session. In fact, sometimes no women were invited at all, since most congressmen had left their wives back home while they lived in lodging houses. Of the twenty-four senators (Rhode Island didn't join the Union until the following year), only six had brought their wives to New York.

Martha was perfectly comfortable with groups of men unleavened by female company. Her years of experience entertaining the male guests who stayed for dinner at White House or Mount Vernon after completing their business (on average outnumbering female guests four or five to one) and the fifteen, twenty, or thirty men at the commander's table during winter encampments paid off in the new world of presidential dinner parties.

Beginning promptly at four on Thursdays (Washington never held back dinner for a tardy guest, no matter his rank), government officials, members of Congress, and foreign dignitaries were invited in rotation, assembling in the large first-floor dining room. The guests didn't necessarily know or like one another, agree on general principles, or have any idea of pleasant table conversation. Some scorned all social graces as demeaning to honest men and held back on principle (and shyness) from chatting amiably on general topics, bantering, or returning complimentary toasts. Even Martha found conversation trying under the circumstances.

She sat at the head of the table, George halfway down on her left, when all the guests were men. With ladies present, she sat across the table from her husband. The secretaries served as deputy hosts at a table elegantly decorated with china ornaments and artificial flowers. Sam Fraunces, formally attired down to wig and gloves, directed the servants. Dinner was the usual two courses. At one dinner, a guest noted that the first course included soup, fish roasted and boiled, meats, gammon, fowls, "etc." (the "etc." probably including fresh and pickled vegetables). For the second course, there were apple pies and puddings, iced creams, jellies, and more "etc."; and the meal ended with watermelons, muskmelons, apples, peaches, and nuts.

Beer, cider, and wine were offered with dinner, and toasts were drunk in Madeira at the end. After a while spent conversing, Martha took the ladies, if any, upstairs for coffee. George usually joined them as soon as possible. He heartily enjoyed the company and conversation of women. Although some of the ruder men departed without going upstairs, most of them joined their host and hostess in the drawing room. One senator from North Carolina enjoyed dinner with the other senators at the Washingtons' and added, "After it, I had the honour of drinking coffee with his lady, a most amiable woman. If I live much longer I believe that I shall at last be reconciled to the company of old women [she was fifty-nine; he was fifty-six] for her sake, a circumstance I once thought impossible."

No one who attended Martha's receptions or the presidential dinners could have detected her dissatisfaction. Although Washington was sometimes criticized for stiff ceremoniousness, his lady was always praised for her easy friendliness. The president was a man of natural dignity and aloofness, never one for back-slapping camaraderie. As his national stature increased, so did his reserve. Both from inclination and policy, he had created a commanding public presence. But his wife's first thought was for her guests. In putting them at their ease, she softened and humanized her overpowering husband, allowing him to relax a bit and show something of the private family man.

When Martha went out shopping or paying calls, Bob Lewis usually went in the carriage with her. A dozen and a half kid gloves, leather galoshes to fit over her shoes (ordered from Philadelphia), an umbrella, a large Bible weighing in at a whopping nine pounds, seed pearl pins and earrings, fur cloaks for herself and her husband— shopping in a city could provide some interesting finds. As for the formal calls or calls of ceremony, callers often hoped the hostess wouldn't be at home; merely leaving a card sufficed for most social obligations. But Martha wasn't satisfied with that cold comfort; when she really wanted a good visit, she sent a note in the morning to inquire if her friends would be available that day.

Thank goodness for the wives of Washington's closest advisers in the social desert of that year. Besides Abigail Adams, both Betsy Hamilton and Lucy Knox were old friends and companions from the Revolution. The women had formed unbreakable bonds during those years and loved spending time together. Martha had also been on friendly terms with Sarah Jay for years.

These friendships among the women helped smooth the working relationship among the men. Washington and Adams didn't care for each other, but they became more tolerant and accustomed to each other's personalities and styles through the social activities they shared with their wives. Hamilton sought power and influence under Washington's sponsorship, and the president respected the younger man's national vision and financial acumen. But they hadn't been personally close for nearly a decade. The friendship between Martha and Betsy made their political and professional relationship easier.

Nelly and Washington Custis, ten and eight years old, respectively, were always their grandmother's concern and delight. When she arrived in New York, her "first care" had been to arrange for their education, even though they didn't begin lessons until later in the summer. Lear would be much too busy about the president's business to continue their tutelage. Nelly loved school for the opportunity to learn and make friends with the other little girls. Wash, however, didn't like to study and was very easily distracted. For the first few months, he worked with a private tutor, a graduate of Trinity College, Dublin, who was assistant to a Columbia University professor. In addition to their school friends, Nelly and Wash played with the children of members of government. Part of the attic was given over to the children as a play area, where they sometimes put on theatrical performances.

Certain purchases marked the differences in age and interests between Nelly and Wash. Nelly received books, music books, a palette, and a fancy hat, while Wash got a ball and marbles, a small cannon, and a set of watercolors. The old spinet was traded in for a fashionable new instrument. Nelly studied with Alexander Reinagle, a first-rate Austrian composer and performer. Even after he went to Philadelphia in the fall, he continued to send bundles of sheet music for her to play. She also learned painting with William Dunlap, the young man who had painted Washington at the end of the Revolution. At ten, Nelly was beginning what would be a lifetime avocation with her carefully rendered vases of flowers. Forcing Wash to study the basics was a full-time occupation; there were no extra lessons for him.

Late in the fall, Martha made new school arrangements. Wash had failed to learn much from his tutor, so he was transferred to a small school with seven other boys. Nelly also was moved to a fashionable new boarding school, just opened in September, where she was a day student. Among the subjects covered at Mrs. Graham's on Maiden's Lane and then on Broadway were spelling and grammar, arithmetic, geography, embroidery, dancing, and French.

The city offered far more amusements than the sights from their windows or formal elite entertainments. Americans were fascinated with the new, the strange, the bizarre. And New York was full of the new, the strange, the bizarre—frequently on public display at the cost of a few shillings for admission. Such exhibits were considered to fall under the broad rubric of education or natural history, although some of them were closer to freak or raree shows, zoos or carnivals. Martha and George were interested in seeing anything unusual; hardly a thing was displayed that year that they didn't see.

Entrepreneurs gathered collections of "natural curiosities," both living and dead. Almost as soon as they came to town, the children were taken to Wall Street to see Dr. King's exhibition of orangutans, sloths, baboons, monkeys, and porcupines. They all enjoyed the "speaking image," a large doll suspended from a ribbon in "a beautiful Temple" that answered questions put to it by the audience. Then there were the waxworks on Water Street, not far from their house. Mr. Bowen's wax likenesses included the British royal family, George Washington in military uniform being crowned with laurels, and biblical scenes.

Concerts, lectures, and dancing assemblies were opportunities for enjoyment, but the best of all entertainments in New York for the Washingtons was the theater. George had first seen a professional performance in Barbados as a teenager and fallen under the spell of the theater. He had drawn Martha into his intense appreciation of both comedy and drama. *Cato* represented serious republican theater to them both, but they loved bawdy comedies like Sheridan's *School for Scandal*, which they saw many times throughout their lives. One of the president's more puritanical guests found the play, with its glittering dialogue, attempted seductions, and ill-natured gossip, "an indecent representation before ladies of character and virtue." That one remark says everything about the cultural differences between northern Presbyterians and southern Episcopalians.

The only theater in New York was on John Street between Broadway and Nassau, a red wooden building entered through a roofed passageway. Those who came in coaches were requested to "order their Servants to take up and let down with their horses' heads to the East River, to avoid confusion." The president's box, where he invited numerous guests, was painted with the arms of the United States. His and Martha's attendance was advertised in advance to drum up business, their arrival greeted with "The President's March" and a standing ovation.

Weekends were family times. Every Saturday, George ordered out the coach. He and Martha, often with the children, rode around the town and out into the countryside for an hour or two, amusing themselves observing whatever was going on. They left at about eleven a.m., the forenoon, and returned home in good time to change for dinner. Occasionally they followed the "fourteen mile round," a popular carriage ride that made a circuit of lower Manhattan Island; an extended version took in the village of Greenwich. Sometimes they invited the Adams or Knox families for an informal dinner.

Attending church had always been part of the Washingtons' life. Trinity Church on Broadway, burned during the British occupa-

tion, was still being rebuilt in 1789, so they joined other Episcopalians at St. Paul's Chapel farther up the street; a canopied pew
was provided for the president. Washington was present the following March when Trinity was reconsecrated, its gothic spire reaching
two hundred feet into the heavens, counting the lightning rods. For
the rest of the year, the Washingtons could be found in the presidential pew at Trinity on Sunday mornings. Occasionally they attended churches of other denominations for special celebrations.
When he was traveling, Washington attended whatever local church
was available. Their charity was almost daily—cash to old soldiers,
wood to poor widows, large numbers of tickets purchased for
charity concerts, fifty guineas for the relief of imprisoned debtors.

After church on Sunday, they stayed quietly at home, reading,
sewing, talking, studying, writing letters. George usually devoted
himself to making plans for Mount Vernon and writing long, detailed letters to George Augustine about those plans. Nor did Martha
let her attention wander far from Mount Vernon and family affairs
in Virginia, writing her own letters of inquiry and instruction.
Nieces needed looking after—Harriot Washington given permission to visit a cousin, special attention for Patsy Dandridge requested
from New Kent relatives, Fanny Washington reassured of her aunt's
love. She sent special messages for her grandniece: "Give sweet little
Maria a thousand kisses for me. I often think of the dear little engaging child and wish her with me to hear her little prattle."

For her dear Fanny, she bought a watch "of the newest fashion,
if that has any influence on your taste," with a chain like those worn
by Mrs. Adams and "those in the polite circles." Her commonsense
attitude toward pretension surfaced: "[The watch] will last as long
as the fashion—and by that time you can get another of a fashionable kind."

While George sent home instructions about planting, she sent
them about sewing and housekeeping. She organized the sewing
for Charlotte and other house slaves as piecework—fabric and
thread for each item bundled together—and sent special items like
Wash's shirt ruffles to be hemmed at home. She clearly didn't think
everything would be properly cleaned without her oversight, often

sending detailed orders about having the kitchen scrubbed and whitewashed, all the bedding aired, or the bedsteads, so prone to harbor bugs, scalded and disinfected.

The fall brought sad news from Virginia—expected, but sad nonetheless. On September 1, George learned that his mother had died of breast cancer. He and the menservants wore mourning armbands and cockades in her honor. Although their relationship had never been easy or truly congenial, he respected and loved Mary Washington.

Soon afterward, Jack Custis's poor bargain for Abingdon had to be dealt with. Both Martha and George formally agreed by letter with David Stuart's decision to let the property go, returning it to the original owner with the payment of a fair rent. Financially it made perfect sense, but emotionally it was hard. The Stuarts moved with Betsy and Patty Custis to Hope Park, a plantation near Fairfax Courthouse "in the windings of a forest obscured," as Nelly put it. It was much too far from Alexandria, Mount Vernon, and an active social life for girls just entering adolescence.

Besides their dinners, concerts, and theater evenings, the Washingtons and the Adamses made occasional pleasure jaunts together. At a Thursday dinner, the president proposed that both families take the barge on an excursion to visit Prince's Garden, a well-known nursery and orchard at Flushing on Long Island. But the plans needed a readjustment for Martha's benefit. Abigail remarked that, as she "does not Love the water we agreed that the Gentlemen should go by water and the Ladies should meet them at a half way House and dine together." On October 10, the men were rowed to the island early in the morning, where Washington found that "the shrubs were trifling." Martha and Nelly, Abigail, and the pregnant Nabby Smith (for the third time in three years) waited until eleven to set out in the Washingtons' coach on "a most Beautifull day." In the countryside far up Manhattan Island overlooking the Harlem River, the two parties met at Mariner's tavern, where they all dined.

Washington wanted to visit all the states of the Union while president, listening to public opinion everywhere. After Congress adjourned, he set off on a tour of the northern states on October 15. As he was a southerner, he felt it important to go north first, emphasizing his national, rather than regional, allegiance. This was very much public business. His itinerary was published so that all citizens who desired it could arrange to see him. He traveled in his chariot and six, accompanied by two aides and six servants. This month-long tour (he returned November 13) was an important affirmation that he was president of a united nation.

Everyone knew that Martha would be lonely without her husband. In his absence, she and Abigail planned to spend a great deal of time together "on terms of much sociability." Martha invited the Adams family to dinner and to a concert by Alexander Reinagle, and Abigail invited her to dine at Richmond Hill with the Knoxes and several other friends. She also continued her usual activities.

Nevertheless, with George gone, she was unhappy so far from home and family, among strangers, no matter how friendly. Martha was bored and lonely without her husband and the female relatives who had surrounded her throughout her life. In a letter to Fanny, she had wondered about a friend's marriage to a northerner: "It would be hard to her to leave all her friends. . . . What could be her inducements to marry a stranger?" That summed up her attitude.

Although she made many friends, none of them became truly intimate. For her, family was the center of life's pleasures, not just for the occasional visit, but living together under one roof. With painful intensity, she missed Nelly Stuart and Fanny Washington, who had provided her with day in, day out companionship and the intimacy that she craved. They could discuss friends and relatives with their infinite variety of interests, illnesses, marriages happy or not, childbirths, deaths, and the whole range of human existence. In New York, she sorely missed the women of her family.

During the dreary month that George toured New England, she sank into a depression. Comings and goings at the house slowed to a trickle in the president's absence. She repined and often stayed at home: "I live a very dull life hear and know nothing that passes in the town. I never goe to the publick place—indeed I think I am more like a state prisoner than anything else, there is certain bounds set for me which I must not depart from—and as I can not doe as I like I am obstinate and stay at home a great deal." With some exaggeration, she enlarged on this theme later: "I have been so long accustomed to conform to events which are governed by the public voice that I hardly dare indulge any personal wishes which cannot yield to that."

George came back in a good mood, buoyed by his reception on the tour and the generally positive attitude he observed among the people. Despite certain disappointments and disagreements with other leaders, the new government was up and running, most important federal positions filled, courts in place, many precedents set, some taxes collected. Better than anyone, Martha understood how unwillingly her husband had become president and how he dreaded being thought self-interested. She observed of his reaction to the tour: "I am persuaded that he has experienced nothing to make him repent his having acted from what he conceived to be alone a sense of indispensable duty."

Once he was at home and happy, Martha largely overcame her depression. But she was still debating with herself, and no doubt with him, about the sacrifice of years of their lives to public service, particularly since they were growing old. She wrote to Mercy Warren in December: "As my grand children and domestic connections made a great portion of the felicity which I looked for in this world. I shall hardly be able to find any substitute that would indemnify me for the Loss of a part of such endearing society. . . . I have [seen] too much of the vanity of human affairs to expect felicity from the splendid scenes of public life."

In their late fifties, they were definitely considered elderly by eighteenth-century standards. They fell prey much more easily to illness and recovered more slowly. Their hair was white and thinning, hearing fading, sight dimming, teeth giving out. Both needed strong glasses for reading, writing, or (in Martha's case) sewing. Martha wore weaker spectacles around the house, keeping her two pairs of glasses in a double spectacle case. George's teeth had begun to go bad when he was young, and one by one they had been extracted. Martha had always had beautiful teeth, but finally she must have lost a few of them because she began to wear some sort of bridge. False teeth of the day were made up of human teeth and/or carved from the ivory tusks of animals such as hippos. They were held in the mouth with wires and metalwork. Wooden teeth are myths concocted by later writers.

Both Martha and George were worried about George Augustine's health because they loved him and Fanny and also counted on him to keep their financial affairs at Mount Vernon in order. His tuberculosis seemed to be getting worse. When he wrote in mid-December, George Augustine complained of the "disorderd state of my Head" and weakness and inflammation in the eyes.

Christmas 1789 was a quiet family affair, but New Year's Day was a major holiday in New York—traditionally celebrated by the Dutch with a cake called "New Year's cookie" and cherry bounce, rum or brandy sweetened and flavored with cherries. All the members of the government, foreign "public characters," and "all the respectable Citizens" came "to pay the compliments of the season" to the president. Since New Year's fell on Friday, Martha's drawing room, according to Abigail, "was as much crowded as a Birth Night at St. James, and with company as Brilliantly drest, diamonds & great hoops excepted."

Congress reconvened January 4, 1790, and Washington delivered his first address on the state of the nation. Thomas Jefferson had returned from France and would take up the post of secretary of state in the spring, after taking care of long neglected personal business in Virginia. In the meantime, John Jay took care of the day-to-day business of foreign affairs. Alexander Hamilton began working on a plan to put the nation on a sound financial footing. The president expected another productive political year. In three years, at the end of this term, he would be able to hand over the position to a younger man.

In the meantime, something had to be done about their house. Living arrangements on Cherry Street were makeshift at best, since the house was not only their residence, but the working office of the president and his staff. As the government developed, he needed more secretaries. Five young men were now living at the house, bunking together in overcrowded bedrooms on the third floor. The live-in slaves and servants also shared rooms on the third floor, the attic, and the outbuildings. Martha was concerned by this over-crowding, believing that it caused illness to spread. As she wrote about a nephew with an unhealthy family: "Living in small Houses and being crowded many in a room is a very great cause of thair being so sickly."

The neighborhood was definitely less than fashionable, close as it was to the East River docks and the shanties of German and Irish immigrants. Government and society had moved to the west side of the island, close to the Hudson River. Federal Hall, where Congress met, was on Wall Street facing Broad. The majority of government officials lived in that neighborhood. The Spanish and French ministers lived on Broadway, as did Jay, Knox, and several senators and congressmen. Hamilton, Morris, and the powerful Livingston family lived on Wall Street. But these weren't upper-class residential enclaves. Residential and commercial buildings were intermingled with shops, boardinghouses, taverns, hairdressers, schools, and a dry nurse—all to be found on the same streets with fine houses.

The French minister, the Comte de Moustier, was returning to France with the sister-in-law who lived with him; her many eccentricities included keeping a pet monkey to coo over. The Marquise de Brehan was a talented artist, widely believed to be Moustier's mistress. They occupied the largest and best house in town, on Broadway just below Trinity Church, the new four-story Macomb mansion with drawing rooms perfect for presidential entertaining. Washington quickly sought to rent the house when Moustier announced his departure; he also bought two large mirrors, various partitions, table ornaments, and furniture that the minister didn't care to ship home. The house boasted a wide hall with large, high-ceilinged rooms on either side; these public rooms had French doors opening onto a balcony with a view of the Hudson River.

On February 23, the Washingtons moved in. They thoroughly enjoyed their spacious new home, where they could even keep two cows in the stable area to provide milk for household cookery. The milk in New York, brought over from Long Island farms, had a strong taste because of the wild garlic growing in the island's pastures and turned sour quickly.

The family had to do without Tobias Lear for a few weeks when he went home to Portsmouth, New Hampshire, to marry his sweetheart. Mary Long, the daughter of a colonel, had just turned twenty when they married on April 18, 1790. After a few weeks' leave, Tobias and Polly (the usual nickname for Mary) returned to New York to live at the president's house. It was convenient for them, but it was probably also George's partial solution to Martha's loneliness when he was forced to be away. To a great extent, Polly Lear took Fanny Washington's place: she was a pretty, sociable young woman who became Martha's closest female companion during the first term, at home or out and about, helping plan her official functions.

The Washingtons were delighted with the arrival of Thomas Jefferson, a southern planter of similar background to themselves, albeit a decade younger; if not a close friend, he was someone George had felt an affinity for during the years since the Revolution, writing to him frequently for advice. The tall, lanky redhead rented lodgings on Maiden Lane, close to the other members of the government, and called on the president on Sunday afternoon, March 21. One of Jefferson's like-minded friends in New York was the Virginian James Madison, so wizened that he looked elderly at forty. Madison was a brilliant parliamentary and political strategist who had been Washington's closest adviser and confidant in the early days of the presidency, helping design the machinery of government and guiding measures through the House, where he served as a representative. Another of Madison's friends had been Alexander Hamilton, with whom he had worked so valiantly on *The Federalist Papers*.

But the two had become estranged over the question of the national debt. As secretary of the Treasury, Hamilton was charged with devising a plan to place the nation's credit on a solid basis at home and abroad. When Hamilton presented his *Report on the Public Credit* to Congress in January, there was an instant split, roughly geographic, north vs. south. His report called for the assumption of state debts by the nation, the sale of government securities to fund this debt, and the creation of a national bank. Washington had become convinced that Hamilton's plan would provide a strong economic foundation for the nation, particularly when he thought of the weak, impoverished Congress during the war, many times unable to pay or supply its troops.

Madison led the opposition, incensed because he believed that dishonest financiers and city slickers would be the only ones to benefit from the proposal, while poor veterans and farmers would lose out. Throughout the spring, the debate continued. Virtually no other government business got done as Hamilton and his supporters lobbied fiercely for the plan's passage and Madison and his followers outfoxed them time and again in Congress. Although pretending to be neutral, Jefferson was philosophically and personally in sympathy with Madison.

By April, Hamilton's plan was voted down and seemed to be dead, just as a new debate broke out over the placement of the national capital. Power, prestige, and a huge economic boost would come to the city named as capital. Hamilton and the bulk of New Yorkers and New Englanders wanted the capital to continue in New York City; the city government had already begun building a grand presidential residence at the tip of the island in hopes that it would sway votes. One large group was in favor of Philadelphia, the nation's leading city, and a third group (which included Jefferson and Madison) was in favor of a new city altogether, to be built somewhere in the upper South.

Washington had never imagined the level of hostility that the debates of 1790 would reach. He wrote that the matters before Congress had been "agitated with a warmth & intemperance; with prolixity & threats; which it is to be feared has lessened the dignity of that body." Political parties, to his mind, were the plague of effete, tyrannical European kingdoms. He assumed that intelligent, patriotic Americans could work together, making compromises for the good of the new Republic. Despite these initial rumblings, he still believed it possible.

Washington and Lafayette at Valley Forge in 1777–78, by John Ward Dunsmore. *(Library of Congress)*

Washington and his troops entering New York City, 1783. *(Private collection)*

George Washington Parke Custis, by
Robert Edge Pine, 1785.
(Washington and Lee University)

Martha Parke Custis, by Robert Edge
Pine, 1785.
(Mount Vernon Ladies' Association)

Eleanor Parke Custis, by
Robert Edge Pine, 1785.
(Mount Vernon Ladies' Association)

Elizabeth Parke Custis, by
Robert Edge Pine, 1785.
(Washington and Lee University)

Frances Bassett Washington, by
Robert Edge Pine, 1785.
(Mount Vernon Ladies' Association)

Macomb residence, Wall Street, the second presidential mansion in New York City. *(New-York Historical Society)*

Morris residence, High Street, the presidential mansion in Philadelphia. *(American Philosophical Society)*

Arch Street ferry, Philadelphia, by William Birch, 1800. *(American Philosophical Society)*

The Washington family, by Edward Savage, ca. 1789–98.
(National Portrait Gallery, Smithsonian Institution)

Mount Vernon with the Washington family on the portico, by Benjamin Henry
Latrobe, 1796. *(Courtesy of Louise and Brad Mentzer)*

West front of Mount Vernon, attributed to Edward Savage, ca. 1792.
(Mount Vernon Ladies' Association)

Eleanor Parke Custis Lewis, by
Samuel Trumbull, after Gilbert Stuart,
ca. 1805–10.
*(Woodlawn/National Trust for Historic
Preservation)*

The Washingtons'
bedroom.
*(Mount Vernon Ladies'
Association)*

George Washington's funeral procession in Philadelphia, by William Birch, 1800.
(American Philosophical Society)

Martha Washington's
third-floor bedroom at Mount
Vernon.
(Mount Vernon Ladies' Association)

Martha Washington,
by Gilbert Stuart, 1796.
*(National Portrait Gallery,
Smithsonian Institution)*

On Sunday, May 9, Washington noted in his diary that he stayed at home all day, suffering from a bad cold. The next day, he didn't write in the diary; he was seriously ill, having developed pneumonia. Each day he sank deeper, burning with fever and becoming delirious. His physicians feared that he would die. The house was thronged with company, expressing their sympathy to Martha and asking for the latest news. The future of the nation depended on him just as much in 1790 as it had in 1789. One senator wrote of the scene: "Every eye full of tears. His life despaired of."

On May 15, the doctors believed he was dying. But around four or five in the afternoon, his illness reached a crisis. He broke into a very heavy sweat, which continued through the night, his fever dropped, and he began speaking intelligibly again. Jefferson wrote: "From total despair we are now in good hopes of him." At his age, Washington didn't bounce right back but was "in a convalescent state for several weeks after the violence of it [the pneumonia] had passed," he wrote, with no inclination to do more than the barest minimum of his duties.

Martha herself was limp with relief at George's second miraculous survival. She wrote to Mercy Warren: "During the President's sickness, the kindness which everybody manifested, and the interest which was universally taken in his fate, were really very affecting to me. . . . Happily he is now perfectly recovered and I am restored to my ordinary state of tranquility, and usual good flow of spirits. For my part I continue to be as hap[p]y hear as I could be at any place except Mount Vernon." Depression was a fleeting condition for her when her husband needed attention.

To see his wife happy and contented always made George happy as well, because he depended so much on her to keep up his own spirits. Whenever she was unhappy or depressed, he became "uneasy," which translated to worried sick in his lexicon. They were always attuned to each other's health and feelings. Martha wrote about her happiness at returning to Mount Vernon for a visit, primarily because she believed "the exercise, relaxation and amusement . . . will tend very much to confirm the President's health."

By June 6, he felt well enough to continue his efforts at bringing his advisers into harmony, and he went on a three-day fishing trip with a party that included Jefferson and Hamilton. Martha was obviously aware of George's concern about the tensions in the administration and with his old ally James Madison. Personality conflicts—and this one was becoming quite personal—were the sort of matter on which he valued her opinion. Since Jefferson was a widower and Madison a lifelong bachelor, who hadn't yet met Dolley Todd, she was unable to form the friendships with their wives that might have at least tempered some of the acrimony.

Jefferson's opinion of Martha was never very high. He gave her credit for being unspoiled by the flattery that was lavished on her. But he thought her "a rather weak woman" who admired her husband far too deeply. His taste ran to flirtatious married women like Angelica Schuyler Church, Hamilton's beautiful sister-in-law. He didn't recognize either Martha's intelligence or the strength of her principles. Instead, he attributed her lack of pride and affectation to "the goodness of her heart, not to the strength of her mind."

Besides the strong political factors that encouraged Jefferson and Madison to compromise with Hamilton on finance, the president's illness and his desire for their cooperation may have played at least a small part. Toward the end of June, the three men dined at Jefferson's lodgings and agreed to a complex trade of votes that led to the adoption of Hamilton's financial plan and the agreement that the capital would be moved to Philadelphia for ten years. A site would be chosen by the president somewhere on the Potomac River, where a new capital city would be built. The government would move south in 1800.

The previous year, Washington had been too ill to celebrate the anniversary of independence. This year, he and Martha had a lot to celebrate—his health restored, a financial program in place, and a new capital to be planned in the area he had always favored. July 4 was a Sunday, so the celebration took place the following day. To the firing of cannons and small arms and the beating of drums, all the congressmen, senators, public officers, foreign representatives, members of the Order of the Cincinnati, and militia officers went to the president's house for wine, punch, and cakes. The Washingtons then went with the crowd to St. Paul's to hear an oration on independence.

While Congress was still in session, the Washingtons continued inviting government members and their wives on excursions. In June, Martha and Abigail took "a very agreeable Tour" to the falls of the Passaic River in New Jersey. This was the first big waterfall that Martha had ever seen. Spray from the falls rose like smoke high in the air. White water dropped a hundred feet into a cleft; far below, the semigloom was colored by "a beautiful rainbow in miniature."

On July 10, they put together a group in several coaches—John and Abigail Adams, Henry and Lucy Knox, Alexander and Betsy Hamilton, Thomas Jefferson, Tobias and Polly Lear, the aides, and everybody's children. They all drove up to visit old Fort Washington at the northern end of Manhattan Island, the scene of a Revolutionary War battle, before enjoying a catered dinner at a house that had once been Washington's headquarters.

Although he had fought native Americans fiercely on the frontier during the French and Indian War, Washington's views on the proper relationship with the Indian nations to the west and south had evolved. He stood against the plans of states like Georgia to despoil the Indians of their land, sending David Humphreys to meet with the Creeks to discover their opinions of the American nation. Basically, his government treated the Indian confederations as foreign powers and attempted to win them over to the American side, despite the influence of British and Spanish agents. During his presidency, several groups of Indians came to the capital to meet with the president and were entertained with great ceremony. Warfare was never his goal, although within two years he appointed Anthony Wayne commander of the army with the express mission of defeating the tribes of the Northwest to quiet the frontier.

The southern Creeks, wooed by the British and the Spanish, not to speak of the Georgians, were diplomatically very important; a major faction was led by Alexander McGillivray. Although his father was a Scot and his grandfather French, he inherited leadership through the maternal line. Arriving in New York in late July, McGillivray led a large entourage of Creek leaders; Abigail Adams was fascinated by them, describing them as "very fine looking Men, placid countenances & fine shape." They stayed for about three weeks at an inn near Richmond Hill, where they visited often. She admired McGillivray, remarking with unconscious irony that he "speaks English like a Native." The Creeks were entertained at formal dinners by the Washingtons, the Adamses, and many other political leaders. After a treaty was signed on August 7, they had a great bonfire outside their inn, "dancing round it like so many spirits hooping, singing, yelling," before attending an official celebration and returning to the South.

Congress adjourned soon afterward, and Washington took the opportunity for a quick visit to Rhode Island, which he had deliberately avoided on his northern tour of the year before. It had not then ratified the Constitution. Finally, a bare majority of the state's leaders realized the futility of going it alone and had joined the other twelve states of the United States.

As they prepared to leave New York, the Washingtons gave a farewell dinner at the mansion for the governor, mayor, and city aldermen. Despite pleading that they be allowed to leave without ceremony, all the city and state notables and militia turned up early on the morning of August 30, 1790, to escort them in procession from the house to the river. At the wharf, their escorts moved to right and left, and the Washingtons, their family, aides, and servants marched through cheering lines and onto the presidential barge to the accompaniment of a thirteen-gun salute. According to the *Gazette*, "Mrs. Washington appeared greatly affected on this occasion." On the New Jersey side, Washington dismissed the barge and sent it back to the gentlemen who had built it for his use.

Tobias and Polly Lear stayed behind in New York, winding up housekeeping, overseeing the thorough scouring of the Macomb house, the packing of furniture in hay and china and ornaments in bran, and the sale of extra furniture, the cows, and the old chariot. It was a slow business. The Lears didn't leave the city until fall, taking a stagecoach to Philadelphia. Two sloops were rented to carry furniture and the servants. In the new capital, they moved into rented lodgings until work on the mansion was far enough along for them to move in.

Traveling south toward home, the presidential party stopped in Philadelphia to see about the house they would occupy. Delightfully enough, the large Morris mansion on High Street had been rented for them. Both Martha and George had been guests there; the Morrises obligingly moved to another house at the corner of the same block to make the house available for them.

Safely settled in at Mount Vernon, George regained his health as he rode over his land and tended to farming. He amused himself with a longer excursion to select a site for the new capital. For many solid geographic and economic reasons, he chose an area of Maryland at the southern end of the Potomac. That it was close to Mount Vernon meant he could look over the work as it progressed.

Martha too was in her element, reunited with Fanny Washington, surrounded by children. Nelly Stuart would have come over for a long visit as soon as her former mother-in-law arrived; they corresponded often, and Martha always let her know when they were returning to Mount Vernon. By this time, Betsy and Patty Custis were in their teens, as was Harriot Washington. Nelly and Wash were eleven and nine. The Stuarts' three little girls were stair steps from one to six. Fanny and George Augustine's Maria was a little over a year old, lately joined by another Washington namesake, the baby George Fayette. It must have been bedlam with ten children around the house, but it was just the sort of happy uproar that Martha loved.

That fall, a young Philadelphian visited Mount Vernon and wrote home to his father, "Hospitality indeed seems to have spread over the whole place its happiest, kindest influence. . . . Mrs. Washington is the very essence of kindness. Her soul seems to overflow with it like the most abundant fountain, and her happiness is in exact proportion to the number of objects upon which she can dispense her benefits."

During their three-month stay at home, Martha finally convinced George that he had made a mistake in restricting their social life so severely. He had bowed to his advisers' opinions to avoid criticism. But, as she probably pointed out to him, they had been criticized all the same, accomplishing nothing but making her unhappy. Considering how attentive George was to his wife's feelings, it was amazing that it took her a year to convince him to relax his strictures. The formal presidential entertainments would continue in Philadelphia, basically unchanged, but she would be free to accept private invitations and to entertain her own friends as she liked.

On November 28, 1790, Martha and George arrived in Philadelphia, children and servants in tow. Of course, renovations and additions to the Morris house had taken longer than expected and still weren't finished—to George's great irritation. Punctuality was one of his watchwords, and he complained mightily and often when others failed to value it as highly as he did. Making Philadelphia the capital was a bonanza for the building trade, not to speak of landlords and merchants. The town rang with hammer blows as builders tried to get all the rental houses and lodgings in shape for the fall influx of government officials and legislators.

Bush Hill, a country house rented by the Adamses, was also in disarray. Abigail had gotten to Philadelphia in October, and Polly Lear called on her in the midst of her lumber and boxes. According to the exasperated Abigail, Polly assured her "that I am much better off than Mrs. Washington will be when she arrives." The Lears had been arranging things at the Morris house, overseeing "58 loads of furniture delivered . . . 2 days work with carts."

To the three-story brick house flanked by brick walls, they had added a wing for a servants' hall and bedrooms, as well as the inevitable enlargement of the stables. Behind the walls, there was a good-size garden with large trees, ending at a coach house and stables that opened to an alley. Servants lived in the new ell, over the stables, and in outbuildings. Some white servants, including the household steward, had come from New York; others were hired in town. Among the Mount Vernon slaves, Molly and Oney had accompanied the Washingtons; the cook, Hercules, his son Richmond, Christopher, and Austin, a man of all work, came shortly afterward by stage or boat.

The two large "public" rooms on the first and second floors had been enlarged for presidential entertainments by throwing out bow windows overlooking the garden. Bow windows were the height of fashion, making rooms lighter and airier. Extra crimson fabric had to be purchased to extend the drapes in the dining room. On the second floor, the family had two drawing rooms, their bedrooms, and dressing rooms (Martha's warmed by a new cast-iron stove). The Lears occupied a large room on the third floor, along with two rooms for the aides, who had to accept the bachelor's lot of shared rooms. The president's office was also on that floor; those calling on government business had to climb two steep flights of stairs to reach it.

Philadelphia had become larger and more elegant with each passing year. A French observer claimed that "Philadelphia may be considered the metropolis of the United States. It is certainly the most beautiful and best-built city in the nation, and also the wealthiest, though not the most ostentatious."

Not only was Philadelphia much larger than New York (42,520 to 32,305, according to the 1790 census), it boasted many more civic amenities. Its broad paved streets had oil lamps, sturdy posts to prevent carriages from running up on the sidewalks, and convenient public water pumps. It was much cleaner than New York as well, though it did have hogs running loose and rooting in the gutters. But Philadelphians had a logical explanation: the swine were part of the city's street-cleaning efforts.

High Street, where the Washingtons lived, was becoming known as Market Street. The two names were used interchangeably for a while until Market finally won out. On three blocks of this very wide street, a couple of blocks from their house, market arcades had been built down the middle of the roadway, with stalls rented between the pillars to meat and produce sellers. Traffic passed on the outsides of the buildings, and the inner aisles became a covered promenade.

In Philadelphia, there were many old friends and some engaging new ones. Through Morris, Willing, Powel, Allen, Chew, and Shippen family connections, the Washingtons met many other wealthy, well-educated, and sophisticated people, to the voluble disgust of republican critics. Probably the most glamorous of their new friends were William and Anne Willing Bingham. Their three-story brick house with its Palladian windows and fanlights on Third Street, set within carefully designed formal gardens, seemed palatial to Americans—especially those who visited and saw the freestanding marble staircase in the front hall and the mirrored drawing rooms hung with paintings. Equally impressive were Landsdowne, the country estate of John Penn, the last proprietary governor of Pennsylvania, and his wife, Anne Allen Penn, and Judge Richard Peters's Belmont, with its famous gardens, approached down a grand avenue of hemlocks. Martha and George frequently rode or drove out to visit these estates and enjoy the country air.

The Washingtons again took up their schedule of official entertainments, but Martha could now call informally on her friends and invite them for tea and conversation. Together, she and George occasionally attended the city's dancing assemblies and concerts, as well as dinners and balls in private homes. Martha bought yards of black velvet for a ball gown and several fans to flourish at these formal occasions, as well as lottery tickets and other presents for relatives back home.

Martha and George attended services at the nearby St. Peter's Church at Third and Pine, only a few blocks down from their house toward the river. The rector there, as well as at Christ Church, was Bishop William White, Mary Morris's brother. They continued their charitable gifts from small amounts for old soldiers or needy widows to larger sums for church building funds and other civic activities.

It was Martha's lifelong habit to spend an hour in the morning over her devotions, praying and reading from the New Testament and the Anglican Book of Common Prayer (1662). In late 1789, as the old Church of England in America was reorganized into the Episcopal Church, the prayer book was revised and published in a new American version. Martha bought a copy for herself as well as others she sent home to the women of the family in September.

Despite Quaker opposition, the stage was thriving in Philadelphia at the South Street Theater. The Old American Company, which the Washingtons had enjoyed in New York, presented a performance of *The School for Scandal* at the president's request. Washington bought eleven tickets for the evening. A stage box was reserved for the president, his lady, and their guests, complete with red draperies, cushioned seats, and the United States coat of arms draped over the front of the box. They went often during the season, also sending Nelly and Wash, the Washington boys, and Austin, Hercules, Christopher, and Oney on various occasions.

The greatest of all "rational amusements" in Philadelphia was Peale's museum. Charles Willson Peale had achieved considerable success as a portraitist of the American elite; beginning twenty years before, he had painted the Washingtons several times. Settling in Philadelphia and fathering a number of children—Raphaelle, Titian, Rembrandt, Rubens, and Van Dyke, among others—he was struck with the idea of setting up a museum of natural history.

First advertised in 1786, his museum at Third and Lombard consisted of two skylighted galleries added to his house. A neighboring shed housed live animals; the exhibits varied as these natural curiosities died and were replaced. The museum featured his own paintings of national heroes, the bones of an unidentified gigantic animal from the Ohio frontier, mammoth teeth, mineral specimens, insects and butterflies, a marine room with mounted fish and sharks, and Indian and South Seas artifacts. Most striking were the preserved specimens of birds and beasts, mounted in natural poses with watercolor backgrounds to lend realism. A conspicuous sign in the gallery read: "Do not touch the birds. They are covered with arsnic [*sic*] poison." Not that most people paid attention, but the preservative coating wasn't enough to kill them. Martha was known for her tiny feet; she must have been astonished at the model of a Chinese lady's bound foot and her four-inch-long shoe. The Washington family visited several times, paying the admission price of twenty-five cents, before the president became a sponsoring member.

Expeditions to the botanical gardens and nursery on the banks of the Schuylkill River, established by Quaker botanist John Bartram, made a pleasant drive out of town. The gardens and greenhouses displayed familiar and exotic American plants, collected on botanical expeditions as far away as Spanish Florida; Bartram's sons sold roots, seeds, and even live plants. Among the other entertainments enjoyed by Martha and her family in the metropolis were wax-works, a sea leopard (seal) on display, French musicians who played at the door for tips, and street jugglers. Later there were balloon ascensions, a panorama, and the first elephant ever exhibited in Philadelphia, a sad-eyed beast kept penned in an alley off the market shed and given rum and brandy for the amusement of the spectators.

The children were settled in school and arrangements made for their music, language, and art lessons. By January 25, 1791, a dancing teacher began coming to the house Mondays, Wednesdays, and Fridays at five p.m. It was desirable to have lots of children at the lessons to form sets for the popular country dances; even Abigail's six-year-old niece was invited to join them. Doubtless the Washington boys and the children's friends also danced at the president's house.

Washington had just brought George Steptoe and Lawrence Washington, his rapscallion orphaned nephews, to study at the University of Pennsylvania. Fortunately, they had settled down and acquitted themselves well at school. Balanced on the cusp between childhood and adolescence, Nelly wore a dancing dress trimmed with silver thread and spangles but had just gotten a new doll. She had made fast friends with the daughters of Washington's friends—Maria Morris, Susan Randolph, and Elizabeth Bordley. Elizabeth's elderly father shared the president's devotion to experimental agriculture. Wash had so many friends at school that Washington feared there was more playing than studying going on.

The spring and early summer of 1791 brought changes to the Washington household. Polly gave birth to Benjamin Lincoln Lear on March 11; the boy was named for Tobias's mentor and patron, a leading general in the Revolution, with Washington as his godfather. Martha and George were always happy to welcome a new child to their home.

David Humphreys went to Portugal as American minister; his place was taken by Martha's nephew Bat Dandridge. Between them, the Washingtons never ran out of helpful nephews. She told Fanny that Bat was "as yellow as a mulato"; he was probably suffering a relapse of Virginia's endemic malaria. Bat also had to be inoculated immediately against smallpox.

When the current steward proved unsatisfactory, Sam Fraunces was summoned from New York to take over. Then, on April 5, Edmund Randolph called on Martha to warn her that some of his household slaves, brought from Virginia, had claimed their freedom. They had cited the Pennsylvania law that declared adult slaves free after a residence of six months in the state. When she relayed the information to her husband, George was concerned about the financial consequences. If any of the Custis dower slaves became free, he would have to reimburse the estate. Neither George nor Martha seemed disturbed by the moral dilemma of keeping slaves in a free state.

Only Hercules, Austin, and Molly were of age. They decided to send the two men back to Mount Vernon from time to time on trumped-up excuses to circumvent the six-month residency requirement; Martha had already promised Austin's wife to send him home for a visit. They apparently didn't fear Molly's leaving. Lear was acutely troubled by this trickery and could excuse himself only by thinking of how well these people were treated by the Washingtons; the slaves themselves doubtless saw through the charade.

After Congress adjourned in early March, Washington waited for the roads to improve before setting out on March 21 for his southern tour, the other half of his trip the previous year. Rumor suggested that his national policy was unpopular in the South, and he intended to find out. This trip of some two thousand miles completed his intention of visiting all the states of the Union. On his way south, the president spent four days at Georgetown talking sense to the local landowners, whose political animosities and greed were endangering the future of the new capital. Both going and returning, he stopped at Mount Vernon to check on things.

In his absence, Martha avoided a repetition of the past year's depression. She had a new miniature painted by Peale and took Nelly and Wash on several jaunts, including a visit with friends at a great estate in New Jersey, capped off with a stop at the Bristol Fair in Bucks County. Tobias Lear's mother came for a long visit, at Martha's invitation, to admire her new grandson.

That summer, everyone was sickly except Nelly. They decided not to make their usual trip to Mount Vernon, uprooting the entire household, but to stay quietly in Philadelphia. George Augustine Washington had spent some time on doctor's orders at one of the mountain spas in another futile attempt to improve his health, and Fanny had just given birth to a third child, Charles Augustine.

By August, George Augustine was so much worse that he was unable to sit a horse, much less manage a large plantation. Suddenly, all was action as Martha and George packed up children, servants, and aides and set off for Mount Vernon in September. Bob Lewis took over temporary management of the estate, and Washington asked Bob's brother Howell to join the presidential household. The whole caravan was back in Philadelphia by the time Congress convened on October 24, 1791.

The first year of the presidency had seen an encouraging display of cooperation in nation building. The next years were filled with rising controversy over just how the government was to operate. And as the president coped with dissensions among the men he trusted, the sad drama of his favorite nephew played itself out. It wasn't just the loss of someone he and Martha loved; both of them worried about how Mount Vernon could continue to operate without an experienced farmer in charge.

A plantation manager was hired at last, and the Washingtons went home annually during congressional recesses while George Augustine died slowly of tuberculosis. Sent away again to the mountains as his health spiraled downward, he was constantly spitting up blood, sometimes floods of it when his lungs hemorrhaged, and was at times unable to speak. In August and September 1792, he was bedridden and unable to walk—"a shadow of what he was." Finally, he, Fanny, and their three children moved to her family home in New Kent County, hoping the warmer climate might be helpful. It wasn't. George Augustine died on February 5, 1793. He was buried in the family burial ground at Eltham, joining Martha's son, Jack, and her sister Nancy Bassett. George took this death especially hard, since George Augustine was his favorite of many nephews and the heir apparent to Mount Vernon.

It was clear as well that Fanny had contracted tuberculosis from her husband. Martha worried about her niece, urging: "I hope you will now look forward and consider how necessary it is for you to attend to your own health for the sake of your dear little Babes."

Whatever the general public might have thought in 1791 and subsequently, Thomas Jefferson and James Madison had decided that the nation was in jeopardy from the machinations of Alexander Hamilton. All his financial measures were leading down the gilded road to monarchy and damnation. Washington, in their developing view, was merely his dupe. Jefferson couldn't imagine that Washington seriously found Hamilton's plans better than his own for the nation—although at this point, Jefferson had few concrete plans other than opposing Hamilton. Jefferson took an extreme states' rights position, combating every attempt to strengthen the federal government, while the president was committed to creating a strongly united nation.

Foreign affairs, too, were a crucial factor in the development of political parties. Hamilton had fought the British bravely in the Revolution, but he still admired and wanted to emulate many British institutions. Jefferson had been in Paris when the Bastille fell in 1789 and was filled with enthusiasm and admiration for the French Revolution. Even as new rulers came and went and the shadow of the guillotine loomed, he stood fast in his love for France and hatred for Great Britain. To Hamilton, all this was violence and anarchy that might engulf the United States.

Alexander Hamilton was a brilliant man but a terrible politician. Neurotic impulses often ruled his behavior, and he suffered from the fatal delusion that he was a master manipulator, causing needless distrust and dislike. Thomas Jefferson actually *was* a master manipulator, especially in combination with the detail-oriented James Madison. As Hamilton and Jefferson came to stand for coalescing political parties, they fought over matters of substance, but there was an underlying personal hostility as well. They hated each other, each considering the other a hypocrite with secret plans who was trying to use the president for his own ends. And they were both right.

Agreeing to block Hamilton in Congress, Jefferson and Madison decided that they needed their own newspaper to combat the pro-government *Gazette of the United States*. Their friend Philip Freneau, a bad poet but an exceptional polemicist, shared their politics. In August 1791, Jefferson hired him as a translator for the State Department with the understanding that his official workload wouldn't interfere with the newspaper he agreed to publish.

In October, Freneau came out with the first issue of the *National Gazette*; by February, he had launched an unremitting barrage of criticism against Hamilton and all his plans, indirectly disparaging the president as well. Jefferson was aware that Washington "was extremely affected by the attacks ... I think he feels those things more than any person I ever yet met with." But although he claimed to be "sincerely sorry" for the injury to the president, such attacks were essential to his political aims. When Washington inquired about the coincidence of a government employee imported to publish a newspaper attacking that government, Jefferson equivocated. Technically, he told the truth while asserting a lie. Such specious defenses didn't impress Martha; she came to abhor the sly politician who used her husband so badly.

Hamilton leapt to arms, publishing articles in his own defense in the other paper and skewering Jefferson. To Washington, this "spirit of party" was terribly upsetting. To try to bring the opponents together, he began holding formal cabinet meetings. Surely, talking face-to-face, they could get over their difficulties. He saw the issue as northern vs. southern interests. He didn't yet realize that political parties had become a reality in the United States, with partisans committed to destroying the careers of their opponents. There would be no going back.

Washington had had enough of refereeing a progressively nastier game. Early in 1792, he informed Jefferson, Hamilton, Knox, and Madison that he would retire at the end of the term. The government was in working order, and he and his wife wanted to go home to enjoy the remainder of their lives.

When both Hamilton and Jefferson, as well as most other leaders, begged Washington to accept a second term, his sense of duty overcame his own desire for retirement. Martha was bitterly opposed to this decision and begged him to decline. She genuinely feared that her aging husband would not survive the presidency: his two close encounters with death and the partisan savagery among his cabinet members seemed reason enough for his retirement to a sensible woman. She was convinced that long hours, worry, emotional turmoil, and lack of regular country exercise were undermining his health. As far as she was concerned, her sixty-year-old husband had done all that could be expected for his country.

It was almost unbearably disappointing to Martha when George again bowed to duty. He agreed to accept a second term if the vote was unanimous. After a simple inauguration in the Senate chamber on March 4, 1793, the torments of the second term began, far crueler than anything she could have anticipated.

CHAPTER TEN

The Torments of the Second Term

*L*ess than a week after Washington's second inauguration, dramatic news arrived from France. Louis XVI and Marie-Antoinette had been guillotined; Lafayette had barely escaped his country alive, only to be thrown into an Austrian prison. Many of the aristocratic French officers who had fought in the American Revolution, as well as their families, were imprisoned and later executed. Pro-French radicals toasted the death of the king and celebrated in the streets of Philadelphia and other American cities. Naturally, there was a strong conservative reaction against France among other Americans, particularly the wealthy, who tended to favor Great Britain. Washington was deeply skeptical about the future course of the French republic but had no inclination to support the British.

With Congress in recess, Washington went to Mount Vernon in April because his farm manager was dying—and soon learned that the France of Robespierre and the Jacobins was at war with England, the Netherlands, Prussia, and Russia. He rushed back to Philadelphia. By the terms of the treaty of 1784, the United States was obligated to support her French ally. But the France of Louis XVI had disappeared with his beheading. Was the treaty still binding? Jefferson said yes, Hamilton no. Washington stood firm in his belief that the young nation should avoid foreign entanglements and conflicts. The United States had everything to lose by plunging into war with neither an army nor a navy worth mentioning. At his urging, the Neutrality Proclamation was declared on April 22, 1793.

Every time the French government changed, a new minister with fresh instructions and objectives was sent to America. Edmond Charles Genêt, a particularly aggressive and undiplomatic envoy, had landed at Charleston on April 8. He acted as a free agent, not bothering to present his credentials to the government right away. For some weeks, he appealed directly to American citizens, commissioning privateers and talking of forming an army to attack the Spanish colonies. Republican newspapers supported this charismatic Frenchman and his government, demanding an end to neutrality and an alliance against France's enemies. On May 18, Genêt finally called on the president and then continued his gadfly activities in Philadelphia, vocally opposing the actions of Washington and his government—some thought fomenting a violent new revolution in the United States.

While trying to balance foreign and domestic affairs with the hostility among his cabinet members, Washington was also called on to advise Fanny Washington about her finances and future, as well as attend to the management of Mount Vernon. With a tenuous calm reigning in Philadelphia, he went home again in July for a week or so, celebrating the Fourth of July in Alexandria and installing his nephew Howell Lewis as temporary manager. Martha stayed in Philadelphia, where she invited friends and their children to view the fireworks on Market Street from the roof of her kitchen. She devoted herself to looking after the family and providing comfort for her sorely beset husband as he dashed back and forth from Virginia to Pennsylvania.

The deadly yellow fever epidemic that struck Philadelphia in July was an ominous note in keeping with the rest of Washington's second term. Yellow fever first broke out in North American port cities in the mid–eighteenth century. The virulent fever, carried by the *Aedes egypti* mosquito, required three factors to become epidemic. Philadelphia provided them all—the arrival of infected human victims, breeding grounds for clouds of mosquitoes, and thousands of people without immunity living crowded together.

Ships from the West Indies, where the disease was raging that summer, arrived regularly at the Delaware River wharves, and the city's cisterns, wells, and swampy areas provided an ideal environment for mosquitoes. The streets around the docks were chock-full of immigrants, living cheek by jowl in decrepit buildings. They lacked immunity because they had never been exposed to the disease.

The outbreak started down on Water Street in July, a slum lodging-house tenant here, a sailor there, then a sharp increase in deaths throughout the neighborhood. City authorities tried to convince themselves that it wasn't the beginning of an epidemic, just the usual summer fevers among the poor. To Martha's great sadness, Polly Lear contracted a fever and died on July 26 after a week's illness, probably not yellow fever to judge by the absence of the typical symptoms. Tobias bore his loss "like a philosopher." The Washingtons attended the funeral of the "pretty spritely woman," and Hamilton and Jefferson overcame their differences long enough to join the other pallbearers.

By August, the raging fever, black vomit, bleeding orifices, delirium, and jaundice—all symptoms of the disease—had spread to sufferers in more privileged neighborhoods, and every day fatalities were doubling, tripling, quadrupling. Barrels of tar were burned in the streets and gunshots rang out, both well-known antidotes against the fever. To avoid panic, church bells were no longer rung for the dead, and the doors of victims' houses were marked to warn off visitors.

In the face of this monstrous onslaught of yellow fever, people with means and some without began leaving Philadelphia for the countryside, first a trickle, then a stream, and at last a flood, until nearly 40 percent of the population had gone. Still the death toll mounted, gravediggers driving wagons through the deserted streets, crying, "Bring out your dead." Bodies were thrown over cemetery walls, ready-made coffins were piled up near the State House, and trenches were dug in potter's field to bury the poor in mass graves.

George decided to send the family to Mount Vernon in early August for their safety. As a matter of pride, he felt obligated not to leave town earlier than his announced departure date, but Martha flatly refused to leave without him. If he wanted to put his life in danger, so would she. Since Jefferson, Knox, and Randolph had all evacuated, the work of the government had come to a standstill. As he wrote to Tobias Lear, who was abroad on business: "Mrs. Washington was unwilling to leave me surrounded by the malignant fever wch. prevailed, I could not think of hazarding her and the Children any longer by <u>my</u> continuance in the City . . . [it] was becoming every day more and more fatal." The entire family left on September 10.

Both Alexander and Betsy Hamilton had come down with the disease in early September, he seriously, she lightly. Martha sent good wishes and several bottles of good wine, one of the sovereign remedies of the eighteenth century. The enmity between Jefferson and Hamilton was so fierce that in a letter to Madison, Jefferson characterized his opponent's illness as imaginary, brought on by Hamilton's "excessive alarm." Mocking his supposed timidity on water and horseback, Jefferson expressed his doubt that Hamilton's "courage of which he has the reputation in military occasions were genuine." This from a man who hadn't fired a shot in the Revolution and had abandoned Richmond in the face of approaching British troops when he was governor of Virginia.

George and Martha spent the fall at Mount Vernon, devoting themselves to their own affairs. Fanny Washington and her three little children joined them. Although she had inherited property from her husband, Fanny had no idea how to handle it. She clung to her aunt, enjoying the pleasure of her company at Mount Vernon "to soften the sorrows I must feel on going there."

Cold weather at last put a stop to the epidemic. The final death toll was about five thousand—nearly 12 percent of Philadelphia's entire population, leaving behind empty houses, failed businesses, and overcrowded graveyards. One of the victims was Samuel Powel, the city's mayor and the Washingtons' friend. Martha wrote a little later about Philadelphians: "They have suffered so much that it can not be got over soon by those that was in the city. Almost every family has lost some of thair friends—and black seems to be the general dress of the city."

Congress declined to reconvene in a city where their lives might still be in danger. Along with hundreds of Philadelphians, its members gathered in the suburban village of Germantown, a hilly little place of summer houses. The Washingtons arrived there on November 1, renting a partially furnished house from Isaac Franks. They had two wagonloads of furniture sent out from Philadelphia to fill in the gaps. The two-story house sat smack on the main Germantown road, opposite Market Square.

Genêt's recall had been demanded, but the envoy didn't care to risk his life with the latest turn of the revolutionary wheel of government in France. He remained in New York, where he married one of Governor Clinton's daughters. The wild fervor of the Philadelphia street mob had been dampened by the epidemic, and Freneau had gone bankrupt, which removed one aggravation. Then Jefferson resigned from the government, to the president's true regret. Despite their differing opinions, Washington respected his secretary of state's manifest abilities, little realizing that Jefferson was already hard at work building an opposition party. It would take its name from its major tenet—the Republican party.

That winter was cold, with the Delaware River "so full of Ice that noe vessel can pass." The theater and the dancing assemblies had been canceled during the epidemic and remained so for months. Martha wrote in February: "We have been very dull hear all winter, thare has been two assemblys—and it is said that the players are to be hear soon. If they come and open the new theater I suppose it will make a very great change. . . . Something of that sort seems to be necessary as a great number of the people in this town is very much at a loss how to spend their time agreeably. The gay are always fond of some new [scene] let it be what it may. I daresay a very little time will ware off the gloom if gay amusements are permitted hear."

Martha liked the theater, balls, and assemblies but amused herself just as easily at home—talking with her husband, family, and friends, enjoying her needlework and books. She had always read the Bible and the Anglican prayer book, but during these years, she greatly expanded her reading tastes. Especially in Philadelphia, the publishing capital of the nation with numerous printing presses, gazettes, and well-stocked bookstores, she found pleasure in the variety of books available.

The evangelical preachers who proselytized in Virginia—Baptists, Presbyterians, and Methodists—had never attracted Martha, nor had the austere Quakers. She remained loyal all her life to the Anglican (by then American Episcopal) Church and its doctrines. Within its doors were a wide range of religious opinions and practices. Very few hellfire-and-damnation sermons were preached in her church, and she took comfort from its familiar litany. Unlike more puritanical denominations, Episcopalians didn't declare life's pleasures sinful unless carried to excess—dancing, drinking wine, playing cards for small stakes, wearing pretty clothes, and traveling or entertaining on Sunday after church.

Martha explored her religion in more depth through several books; most of them emphasized the importance of good works and tolerance for the beliefs of others, in addition to Christian faith. From Bishop George Horne's *Commentary on the Book of Psalms* to John Berridge's *The Christian World Unmasked*, they were thoughtful and inspirational books for the general public by popular Anglican clerics.

More interesting was her choice of the *Works of Josephus*. One of the most reprinted histories in the world, it is a firsthand account by a first-century Jew of the Jewish rebellion against Rome, the destruction of the temple at Jerusalem, and Jesus in the flesh. It provides a clear exposition of Jewish history and beliefs.

Martha also read literary miscellanies put together more for the expanding reading public than for scholars. They were often entitled *The Beauties of . . .* and included an introduction and biographical information on the authors of the selected poetry or prose pieces. One of the most popular of these collections was *The Beauties of Milton, Thomson, and Young.* Her library included *The Beauties of Nature* as well as a copy of Mercy Warren's *Poems, Dramatic and Miscellaneous.*

Novels weren't readily available to her as a girl and young woman, but she took happily to them in her sixties. She read Oliver Goldsmith's *Vicar of Wakefield*, Regina Roche's thriller, *Children of the Abbey*, Samuel Johnson's bit of satirical exotica *The Prince of Abyssinia (Rasselas)*, and Elizabeth Inchbald's *A Simple Story*. All their plots incorporate sexual attraction, the search for happiness, and loads of double dealing. Even though the virtuous are rewarded in the end, the characters are put in morally hazardous situations on their treks to the last page.

Inchbald was a famous British actress and playwright whose novel became a transatlantic best-seller. The first half of *A Simple Story* recounts the love story of a feckless and self-willed young socialite, a Protestant, and her guardian, a Jesuit priest. The sexual tension between them is so palpable that he asks to be released from his vows when he inherits an earldom; they marry, but she eventually strays. To offset such racy material, the second half of the book deals as tepidly as possible with the reconciliation between the priest/earl and their daughter.

Martha was religious, but not a prude. She fully understood sexual attraction and was uninhibited in her enjoyment of plays and books whose plots revolved around its effects. She was tolerant in real life as well. Even as a married woman, Kitty Greene and her flirtations had been gossiped about; after Nathanael's death, people accused her of having affairs with married men. For years, she lived with her children's much younger tutor until she finally married him. Martha gave dinners and went to the theater with her when she was in the capital and always wrote to Kitty with loving kindness.

George subscribed to stacks of newspapers that she also read. She subscribed to magazines, several of which started up in this period but seldom lasted long. Among them were *The New York Magazine, or Literary Repository*; *Oswald's Gazetteer*; and the *Lady's Magazine and Musical Repository*.

Having lots of books and newspapers around the house encouraged the teenage Nelly in her lifelong habit of reading. She now studied both French and Italian, sometimes getting up at a quarter to five in the morning to do her lessons. Her grandmother was very strict about her music. The poor girl practiced for hours on the harpsichord, playing and crying, crying and playing, but she became a fine musician. She and her friends giggled and gossiped about the boys in their social set. George found them delightful, but Martha was sometimes a bit aggravated by their silliness: "I hope when Nelly has a little more Gravatie she will be a good girl—at present she is I fear half crasey."

Wash hated the educational part of school (playtime was fine)— studying, writing, reading, and doing homework. Even when his grandparents tried to force him to do his lessons, he was down the stairs and out the door as soon as they turned their backs. Martha had no doubt the schools were to blame: "In this city everyone complains of the difficulty to get their children educated—my dear little Washington is not doing half so well as I could wish . . . and we are mortified that we cannot do better for him."

In early February 1794, Elizabeth Scott Peter, the wife of a wealthy Georgetown merchant, Robert Peter, came to visit for about six weeks, bringing letters from home along with Betsy and Patty Custis. Barely turned seventeen, Patty was engaged to the Peters' son Thomas. It seems to have been a love match, but financial agreements still had to be made. As Martha noted approvingly: "The old gentleman [Robert Peter] will comply with Doctor Stuart's bargain." She went on: "Patty has given him leave to visit her as a lover. I suppose by that he is agreeable to all parties—if it is so I shall be very happy to see her settled with a prospect of being happy." She believed in good financial settlements, but she also believed in marrying for love, as she had.

A week after Congress adjourned in June, George took one of his quick trips home. On Sunday, June 22, he went for a ride to the falls of the Potomac. His horse stumbled on the rocks, and he wrenched his back severely while preventing it from falling and throwing him. In his weekly letter, he told Martha about the accident but reassured her that he was better. Since she already believed that the presidency was killing him, she was beside herself with anxiety.

No doubt she wrote to her husband, but her letter to Fanny Washington demanded full details: "I have been so unhappy about the Presid[en]t that I did not know what to do with myself." Martha feared that he had underplayed his injury: "Don't let me be deceived. . . . I beseech you to let me know how he is soon as you can and often." If he was to be detained there any longer, she would "get into the stage or get stage horses" and come down to care for him herself. Their coach was in Virginia. No matter how awful stagecoach travel was, with its backless seats, smelly passengers, baggage crammed into every spare inch, and poorly sprung vehicles, Martha was ready to brave it all for him.

But George returned to Philadelphia on time, so she didn't have to take the stage. This was a landmark accident in the life of a horseman famous for his strength and agility. In the eighteenth century, people in their sixties were definitely elderly. The first term had aged them both; the second finished the job. Still thin and muscular, George rode or walked most days for exercise, but he was becoming noticeably stooped, deaf, and dependent on his glasses for reading.

At five feet tall, Martha put on weight easily; she no longer rode horseback and frequently indulged her fondness for candy and desserts. The pleasing plumpness of her middle age had become grandmotherly stoutness, complete with double chin. She often suffered from colic and severe stomach pains. Both of them were prone to colds and general aches and pains.

Fanny Washington had decided to move into the president's house in Alexandria so her children could go to school in town. She was in easy visiting distance from either the Federal City or Georgetown. Her old friend from the early days at Mount Vernon, Tobias Lear, started riding over from Georgetown, where he was in business. By early August, they were married. He knew she was tubercular, but consumption had romantic overtones at that time, as its victims grew thin and languid, with luminous skin. They had a few happy months, but the following March both Fanny and her daughter fell desperately ill with some passing fever. Maria recovered, but it was too much for Fanny's weakened state of health. Within a week, she was dead. Although they had been prepared for her loss by Lear's despairing letters, George wrote, in a letter signed by Martha also: "It has fallen heavily notwithstanding."

Fanny's orphaned children were then seven, six, and five. As their stepfather, Lear was responsible for them. Tobias and his mother kept the boys together, along with his son, Lincoln, and saw to their schooling. But Maria was so rude to Mrs. Lear and so unmanageable in her grief that she was sent to boarding school and then to live with an aunt until she married. Although Martha loved the little girl, she couldn't take another child into the president's house. She wrote Mrs. Lear, "It gives me pain to think that a child as circumstansed as she is should not have a disposition to make herself friends—her youth will plead for her."

The summer of 1794, politics took a turn for the worse. The excise tax on whiskey had been controversial since its imposition; on the frontier, distilling grain into whiskey was the most efficient way of producing a commodity easily portable over trails and terrible roads. Those accused of breaking the law would be tried in district courts far from their homes—an expensive journey whatever the outcome of the trial. In the summer of 1794, farmers/distillers in western Pennsylvania rebelled against the tax and attacked tax collectors in what became known as the Whiskey Insurrection. Although encouraging changes in the law, Washington would not accept any defiance of federal authority. He believed that the nation's stability and future rested on respect for the law.

Rather than going to Virginia, George and Martha and the children moved back out to Germantown, where he could be readily available as the crisis continued. It was cooler there than in Philadelphia, and everyone feared a repetition of the previous year's epidemic—unnecessarily, as it happened.

After negotiations between the rebels and federal representatives broke down, the president called up several state militias in late September, riding along with them in his light buggy as far as Carlisle. In the face of a large army, the rebels gave in without a battle, a number of arrests were made, and two leaders were sentenced to death (later pardoned by Washington).

Republicans were outraged for one or all these reasons: they opposed excise taxes; they opposed an attack against western farmers, their constituents; the hated Alexander Hamilton was at the president's side; and the army raised had been unnecessarily large and overwhelming. Washington believed that the large army had prevented bloodshed; a smaller force would have encouraged the rebels to fight.

Freneau might be gone, but other pro–Republican party newspapers had started up throughout the nation. In Philadelphia, Benjamin Franklin Bache, Franklin's grandson, was a master of invective who made Freneau look mild. Soon to become known as the *Aurora*, his paper was pro-Republican, anti-Federalist, pro-French, anti-British, and the president, who in his view led the opposition, was fair game for vicious attacks. Innuendo, accusation, even the publication of forged letters from the days of the Revolution—he felt justified in using whatever weapon came to hand. Washington had never imagined the lengths to which a free press could go. He was hurt by the barrage but never suggested any action against the papers. Martha's anger and pain on her husband's behalf were no secret; she couldn't brush off attacks on the man who was her hero as well as the nation's.

Washington grimly held on to his mission of establishing the government on firm foundations. First Knox and then Hamilton resigned their positions to attend to their own business affairs. What about his neglected acres? Rather than friends and innovators, his cabinet was composed of second-rate men. His pleasure in life now came largely from close friends and family, planning and sending instructions to Mount Vernon, and dreaming of retirement. The family returned to Philadelphia that fall without making their usual trip home during the congressional recess.

One danger to the nation down, a new one loomed. Great Britain had never evacuated her forts in the Northwest Territory of the United States; agents there encouraged Indian attacks along the frontier. At sea, she refused to accept American neutrality and right to trade with France and seized American sailors to man British ships. John Jay left in the fall to negotiate a treaty and avoid war.

Jay's Treaty was even more divisive than the Whiskey Insurrection. When it was published and, at Washington's insistence, ratified in June 1795, many Americans were outraged. Mobs burned

Jay's effigy in the streets, and the newspapers howled. Even though the treaty avoided war and provided limited trade between the nations, Republicans saw it as treason to France and beneficial only to city merchants.

After the disappointment the previous year, Martha and the children went home in July for a long stay. Nelly Stuart was seriously worried that her namesake daughter, now sixteen, was being spoiled beyond redemption by her grandmother and the high life of Philadelphia. She insisted that the girl should spend the winter with her at Hope Park, and Martha agreed that an entire year apart was too long. Young Nelly was aghast. Not that she didn't love her own mother, but her grandmother had become the mother of her heart. The Washingtons and Washington Custis left for the capital on October 12, leaving Nelly with her mother and stepfather and the Stuart children.

Nelly's hurt feelings quiver in her letter to a friend: "No one believed I should be left behind. However it is so. To part from Grandmama is all I dread. . . . It is impossible to love any one, more than I love her." She adapted to her situation, though, especially when she and her older sister went to stay in town with their married sister, Patty Peter. Betsy, as her grandparents still called her, had restyled herself Eliza, a far more elegant name.

But Nelly wasn't the only one who suffered. Martha's letters were redolent of loneliness. Besides all sorts of gifts from a gold chain to a pincushion, she sent just as much unneeded advice—for Nelly to clean her teeth every day, keep her feet dry when out in the cold, and take good care of her clothes.

Patty had just given birth to her first baby, a girl, Martha's first great-grandchild. When Eliza and her mother went home, Nelly stayed behind "as housekeeper, Nurse—(and a long train of Etcetra's)." The baby was named Martha Eliza Eleanor Peter: "Thus all the names of its nearest relations are taken in at once. . . . I approve very much of this way of getting quit of all the family names."

Soon afterward, Eliza became engaged and got married in a flurry, to her later deep regret. She disliked her stepfather and home situation and envied her married sister. The man she chose was Thomas Law, an Englishman who had made his fortune in India; in the new federal district, he became a land speculator on a grand scale. Twenty years her senior, he had two sons by an unmentioned mother. Martha and George were upset that he was a foreigner who might take Eliza away from the country. Because he was a stranger to them all, although apparently respectable, George strongly advised David Stuart to insist on an ample settlement as a matter of prudence. Eliza assured her grandparents, who were disturbed by the secrecy and swiftness of her engagement, that she did indeed love Thomas Law. Although they were always civil and welcoming to Law, they never felt the same friendship for him that they did for Thomas Peter.

The controversy over Jay's Treaty had not died down over the winter; in fact, it had become worse by spring. France had weighed in, declaring that the treaty broke their former agreement of alliance with the United States. Now they claimed the right to board American ships at sea and began to do so in the West Indies. The new French minister used the pages of Bache's *Aurora* to attack the president as pro-British, an affront for a man who had remained on guard against British machinations since the Revolution.

A related matter deeply troubled both George and Martha. Lafayette's wife, along with their daughters, had joined the imprisoned hero, but she had sent their son George Washington Motier Lafayette to America with his tutor, expecting that he would live with the Washingtons. Although the president had sent money to the Lafayettes and requested that envoys look after their well-being, the explosive relationship with revolutionary France and its American supporters made him fearful of taking the boy in. For some months, young George lived with the Hamiltons in New York. Finally, with the support of Republican political leaders, the boy and his tutor arrived in Philadelphia, joining the president's family in April.

Another June came, and another escape to Mount Vernon. But just before they left, there was an escape of a different sort that shocked Martha to the core. Her maid Oney Judge slipped away from the house to take shelter with free black friends before escaping to Portsmouth, New Hampshire, by ship. To Martha's mind, the young woman had no reason to leave; she was a favorite whose workload was light, and she was always treated with affection. She and George decided that only a man—perhaps a Frenchman?—could have seduced her away. Martha felt a responsibility for the unsophisticated girl under her care, especially since her mother and sister were expecting to see her back at Mount Vernon.

What she could never understand was that there was no seducer, just a simple desire to be free. Ona, as she preferred to call herself, wanted to live where she pleased, do what work she pleased, and learn to read and write. Her flight was precipitated by Martha's telling her she would be left to her granddaughter Eliza Custis, who was capricious and ill-tempered.

Ona Judge professed a great regard for Martha and the way she had been treated, but she couldn't face a future as a slave for herself and her children. Despite attempts by Washington's friends to convince or recapture Ona, she stayed put, living out her life as a free woman. And Martha never understood why she had fled.

At Mount Vernon, Nelly rejoined the family, and there was much visiting among the Washingtons, Stuarts, Peters, and Laws. The house was crowded with all sorts of company, including "the ministers of France, Great Britain, and Portugal, in succession . . . besides other strangers," including a dozen Catawba Indian leaders. As often happened in the Tidewater, both Martha and Nelly had recurrent spells of malaria, suffering bouts of chills and fevers.

George made a trip to Philadelphia in September to consult on foreign affairs and to publish his Farewell Address as president. He wanted to make it clear well in advance that there would be no third term. In the address, drafted by Hamilton, he set out what he saw as the accomplishments of the first presidency, along with his hopes and advice for the future of the nation. He gave the manuscript to a friendly newspaper publisher and then returned to escort the family on their last trip north in October. He wrote to Bob Lewis in advance, "I shall make my last journey, to close my public life the 4th of March; after which no consideration under heaven, that I can foresee, shall again withdraw me from the walks of private life." We can almost hear Martha applauding in the background.

The Farewell Address made for a somewhat more civil political environment, though Ben Bache was intransigent. Knowing that Washington would soon retire allowed some of his critics to remember their former admiration for him. He indicated no preference for his replacement and didn't allow himself to be enticed into any partisanship in the fall election.

The cold was ferocious that winter. By late December, it was possible to walk across the Delaware on the ice. Within a week, thousands of walkers, skaters, horse-drawn sleighs, and booths selling refreshments could be seen on the frozen river. The last year of what Martha had come to think of as their imprisonment—1797—dawned windy, clear, and cold. After church, she and the president received crowds of callers who had come to the presidential mansion "to compliment the season" for the last time. Every event, every assembly, had a melancholy feeling—each was the last time for their many friends and admirers before they withdrew permanently to Virginia.

Martha and George enjoyed themselves more than they had in years. The large and elegant New Theatre was only a couple of blocks from their house. Boasting a talented professional stock company with new scenery and costumes, the theater advertised some performances as "by request" of the president and his family. A historical play, *Columbus; of a World Discovered*, included a storm, an earthquake, a volcano eruption, and a procession of Indians.

The owners of the Pantheon and Rickett's Amphitheatre were similarly inspired to present special performances of acrobatics on horseback and other dangerous equestrian feats. Concerts, exhibitions by artists, lectures, assemblies, teas, and endless addresses from grateful federal, state, and local governmental bodies took up their time. The official entertainments to which Washington had committed them eight years earlier rolled on. The president's levees, his lady's drawing rooms, and the Thursday dinners continued to punctuate their weeks. Everyone in government who should have been invited to dinner was entertained. It took four separate dinners to accommodate a very large delegation of Cherokee chiefs.

And then there was Washington's last birthday celebration—his sixty-fifth, elderly indeed. Congress adjourned early, and most of its members came to pay their respects. Cannons fired the requisite federal salute—now sixteen rounds rather than thirteen, with the addition during his presidency of Vermont, Kentucky, and Tennessee as states. Of all the social activities during the Washington administration, these birthday celebrations were the most detested by his critics. They indicated a reverence for the man rather than the institution and smacked suspiciously of monarchy. Nonetheless, that year's birthnight ball, which had become such a fixture of Philadelphia society, was the grandest ever. The retiring president offered a toast, again his last: "May the members thereof [the dancing assembly] and the <u>Fair</u> who honor it with their presence long continue the enjoyment of an amusement so innocent and agreeable."

The British minister's wife thought Mrs. Washington's heart seemed a little melted, "as she never expects to see Philadelphia again." She was wrong. Just a week before they left forever, Martha wrote about their last season in Philadelphia and her hopes for retirement: "The winter has been very sevear hear ... but is now moderating and drawing to a close, with which the curtain will fall on our public life, and place us in a more tranquil theater."

Beginning during the Revolution, certain letters like this one—to accomplished women like Mercy Warren or Eliza Powel or her official responses to tendered gifts—were drafted for her by Washington and later by Lear. She then copied the drafts and signed them as her own. But the formal correspondence with its consciously literary turns of phrase lacks the charm of her own letters to intimates. Those were affectionate, down-to-earth, and frequently lightened with self-deprecating humor—much like the lady herself. Whatever sentiments she asked her ghostwriters to express, she wasn't a woman to sign anything she didn't mean.

Remaining only long enough to attend the inauguration of John Adams as president on March 4, 1797, the Washingtons bade farewell to their friends in Philadelphia. As he wrote to his wife back home in Massachusetts, Adams understood that Washington was well out of an unpleasant situation and that he, Adams, had gotten himself well into it. Neither of them, however, quite realized that Abigail Adams would also be fair game for partisan criticism.

Aided by Tobias Lear, Bat Dandridge remained behind to see to the cleaning of the mansion for the Adamses, the packing of the furniture and other things they were taking home, and the sale or distribution as gifts of items not wanted for Mount Vernon. George and Martha loaded the children, young Lafayette and his tutor, aides, slaves, Nelly's dog, Frisk, and a parrot, and mountains of baggage into two groaning coaches. The overflow—ninety-seven boxes, fourteen trunks, forty-three casks, thirteen packages, three hampers, and ever so much more—was sent by ship. Despite a very heavy cold and cough, Martha Washington refused to hear of any delay in setting off for Virginia.

One absentee surprised her as much as the earlier flight of Oney Judge. Their chief cook, a slave named Hercules, called by the children "Uncle Harkless," disappeared from the house on the day they were scheduled to leave for Virginia. Although liked and valued by all the family, he apparently had not relished the role of enslaved old retainer. His flight, however, didn't affect Martha in the same way as Oney's; she didn't love him as she did the young woman. Although Washington continued halfheartedly asking his friends to be on the lookout for Hercules for a few months, he was gone forever. A good cook never had to search too far for employment.

It took them a week to get home, and their progress was impeded by the crowds who came out to honor the retiring president. Militia troops escorted them, kicking up clouds of dust, and everywhere people in carriages, on horseback, and on foot appeared along their route, as Nelly observed, "to see, & be seen & Welcome My Dear Grandpapa."

Like many later First Ladies, Martha Washington was exhausted by the calls on her time and angered by the attacks on her husband. After the doubtful pleasures of the presidency, she left for Mount Vernon as though they were departing for the promised land.

CHAPTER ELEVEN

"Under Their Vine and Under Their Fig Tree"

$\mathcal{G}$rape vines and fig trees appear more than twenty times in the Old Testament as emblems of peace, plenty, and contentment. For Martha and George Washington, familiar as they were with the King James version of the Bible, two verses were especially potent symbols for their retirement and often appeared in their correspondence. The book of First Kings described a sort of earthly paradise under the wise and powerful rule of King Solomon: "And Judah and Israel dwelt safely, every man under his vine and under his fig tree" (1 Kings 4:25). The book of Micah prophesied a day when there would be no more war and men would "beat their swords into plowshares." In the next verse, that peace was described: "But they shall sit every man under his vine and under his fig tree; and none shall make them afraid" (Micah 4:3–4).

For a tired old soldier who had just returned from eight years of vicious political warfare, the vision of a place where he could sheathe his sword and turn his hand to the plow was pretty close to heaven. Even more so for Martha. As much as George had suffered from the Republicans' newspaper attacks, Martha had suffered twice as much for her husband because she was helpless to protect him. The second term had been hell.

When they arrived home on March 15, 1797, they found Mount Vernon much as it had been at the end of the Revolution—the absence of its owners had led to deterioration and dilapidation, but this represented a new challenge for the intrepid pair. As Martha exulted: "We once more (and I am very sure never to quit it again) got seated under our own Roof, more like new beginners than old established residenters, as we found every thing in a deranged [state], & all the buildings in a decaying state." George threw himself into a whirlwind of construction, garden plans, and farming—complaining about the neglect while clearly enjoying himself mightily.

Martha reorganized the housekeeping. She had grown accustomed to having a steward in the presidential mansion and at sixty-five no longer wanted to oversee all the housekeeping herself. After she discovered that a steward or housekeeper from Philadelphia would demand outrageous wages to move south, she made do with a local woman, who worked under her direction.

Martha also half-jokingly appointed Nelly, now a sprightly girl of eighteen, as the "deputy housekeeper." Nelly relished her informal household training and helped entertain guests by playing the harpsichord, singing, and conversing amiably. By her own account, she was also "deputy nurse" for ailing members of the family. Her duties weren't so onerous, though, that she couldn't spend weeks at a time with her sisters in the future federal capital, becoming known as Washington City, or with friends in Alexandria, attending dances, parties, and the theater. The purpose of these visits, of course, was to introduce her to society and to help find a suitable husband.

One possibility was close at hand. Depending on the course the French Revolution took, George Washington Lafayette might once again be very eligible indeed. Nelly was furious when she heard that Philadelphia gossip had linked their names. As she wrote a friend, "The opinion of the wise (that <u>friendship</u> alone cannot exist between two young persons of different sexes) is very <u>erroneous &</u> <u>ridiculous</u>. . . . I shall ever feel an interest & sincere regard for <u>my</u> <u>young adopted Brother</u> [he was seventeen to her eighteen]—but as to being <u>in love with him</u> it is entirely out of the question." Martha would never have encouraged a romance that would take her darling adopted daughter across the sea. To a woman who dreaded ferry rides, an ocean voyage would have been impossible.

The care and feeding of nieces was still one of her amusements. With the loss of Fanny Bassett Washington Lear, she invited another Fanny for a long visit. Fanny Henley, her sister Betsy's daughter, was about Nelly's age; she came to stay for several months one year and came back the next year to spend time with Eliza Law and Patty Peter.

As it had been following the Revolution, Mount Vernon was again flooded with guests. When the Washingtons were at home, visitors couldn't be far behind. All of them wrote about their gracious reception by Martha and Nelly. In the winter, the ladies would be found in one of the small parlors. In summer, they were more likely to be sitting in the wide hall, cool and breezy with both outside doors open.

Guests always commented favorably on Martha's looks, even though she was in her mid-sixties. One observed that "she retains strong remains of considerable beauty." As always, though, it was her character and conversation that they found especially attractive. Her account of the family was given "in a good-humored free manner that was extremely pleasant and flattering." She was praised for lacking any "affectation of superiority in the slightest degree" To sum it all up: "Mrs. Washington is a very agreeable, lively, sensible person."

Having lived through the most stirring days of American history, Martha thought of herself almost as a historical resource and was always glad to guide visitors about Mount Vernon. An impressed guest said, "Mrs. Washington is one of the most estimable persons that one could know, good, sweet, and extremely polite. She loves to talk and talks very well about times past." To another guest, she inquired for news, remarking that although she was no politician, she liked to read the newspapers. As she sat knitting, doing needlepoint, and netting, she freed George to go about his business. But no one felt slighted. A lady remarked: "The extensive knowledge she has gained in this general intercourse with persons from all parts of the world has made her a most interesting companion, and having a vastly retentive memory, she presents an entire history of half a century."

With Washington's encouragement, Gouverneur Morris managed to negotiate the release of Lafayette, his wife, and the girls from the prison at Olmutz. The most filial son imaginable, young George demanded to leave for France to be reunited with his family. He and the tutor left for New York in October 1797, where he boarded a ship and safely joined them in exile. Only later were they able to go back to France and recover a portion of their family estates.

Meanwhile, the latest French government, the Directory, waged undeclared war on American ships at sea and treated American representatives disgracefully, demanding bribes from them to see the foreign minister. Despite Republican excuses for this behavior, war was looming. Alexander Hamilton and other Federalists in opposition to John Adams tried to draw Washington into the fray, and he became ever more convinced that France and her American supporters could destroy the constitutional government.

The hostile talk that went on at Mount Vernon about the French is obvious from a letter Nelly wrote at the time: "Were I drowning & a straw only in sight, I would as soon think of trusting to that slender support . . . as place the smallest dependence upon the stability of the French republican government. Neither would I trust the life of a Cat in the hands of a sett of people who hardly know religion, humanity or Justice, even by name."

In July 1798, President Adams named Washington commander of the American army to counter French aggression. His acceptance was reassuring to most of the nation, even though he would take the field only in case of an invasion. Against the president's wishes, he appointed Hamilton as his second in command. Washington made only one six-week trip to Philadelphia (no doubt to Martha's relief) to organize the new army. The threat of war slowly dissipated as Adams sent representatives to treat with France the following year, and it ended completely when a treaty was signed.

To everyone's happiness, Tobias Lear returned as a neighbor and personal secretary. His business had failed, and he now lived at River Farm, the 360 acres of Mount Vernon that Washington had promised to his nephew. It was Lear's rent-free for life, after which it would pass to George Augustine and Fanny's children.

Despite Martha's assistance, George still found that the constant stream of guests interfered with his reading and correspondence. He invited one of his sister Betty's sons, Lawrence Lewis, to live at Mount Vernon and serve as an unpaid deputy host, which allowed him to withdraw into his study in the evenings.

The arrival of Lawrence, a childless widower twelve years Nelly's senior, solved the problem of her marriage. They became engaged in late 1798 and married on Washington's birthday the following year. In a candlelit ceremony, he gave away his adopted daughter, dressed at her request in his Revolutionary uniform. Customs had changed in Virginia, and a sort of honeymoon had become fashionable. A few days after their marriage, the Lewises set off on a round of family visits, stopping by to look at White House while they were in New Kent County.

When they returned to Mount Vernon five months later, Nelly was pregnant, and she and Martha put their heads together. They had missed each other during the separation. Although Lawrence owned land in Frederick County, the Lewises wanted to continue living at Mount Vernon. When George was finally made aware by his wife of this desire, he agreed—ostensibly to please Martha, but he had also missed Nelly. He offered them two thousand acres of the estate, which Lawrence could begin farming at once. Three miles away, there was a lofty hill with a view of Mount Vernon where they could build their own home. No one expected that move to be anytime soon.

Aside from the general infirmities of age, Martha and George were both in good health, now the last survivors of their own large families. His last brother, Charles Washington, died that fall; his sister, Betty Lewis, had died in 1797. Martha's much younger sister Betsy Henley also died in 1799. Yet both of them were full of plans for the future. He was reorganizing Mount Vernon to make it more easily manageable, and the great-grandchildren were very much on her mind, not to speak of Betsy's daughter Fanny Henley.

In late November, Nelly gave birth to Frances Parke Lewis after an extended and painful labor. Like all the women of her time, she had gathered her women: her grandmother, mother, sisters, house servants, and a midwife were with her for the birth. Because her labor had been so difficult, Nelly was ordered to stay in bed for some weeks until she fully recovered. Early in December, her brother and husband rode off to New Kent County to look over Wash's extensive property there. Tobias Lear remained behind to keep the ladies company and assist Washington.

The winter of 1799 was as cold and miserable as 1759, the year Martha and George married. On December 12, George returned from his daily ride around the plantation wet and shivering but refused to change his damp clothes before dinner. The next day, he went out into the snow and sleet to mark trees for cutting despite the very evident beginnings of a cold—he was never deterred by bad weather. That evening, he read the newspapers aloud to Martha and Lear, his throat congested and voice muffled. In the middle of the night, he experienced great trouble breathing. When the terrified Martha wanted to go for help, he refused to let her get up until morning, lest she too should become sick. With the blazing fires of evening down to ashes, the house was freezing cold.

At dawn, she finally got up and sent for a doctor, who was later joined by two more physicians. Lear and Christopher Sheels, George's personal servant, joined her in their bedroom. Other members of the household came and went throughout the day as George lay struggling for every breath. Only Nelly stayed away, still too weak to get out of bed. The doctors tried all the painful weapons in their limited arsenal—bleeding, purging, blistering, vomiting—but to no avail. George had apparently contracted quinsy or epiglottitis, both throat infections that progressively close the windpipe until the patient suffocates.

George's dying was prolonged by his strength. Throughout that long, horrible day, Martha sat in a chair in the room, leaving only to check on Nelly or to fetch two wills, one of which she burned at his request after he had selected the one he wanted. That evening, December 14, 1799, he finally stopped breathing. Lear was holding his hand when he died.

Martha asked quietly, "Is he gone?" When Lear assented, she murmured, " 'Tis well. All is now over. I shall soon follow him. . . . I have no more trials to pass through." Rendered tearless by the depths of her grief, she couldn't yet break down. In the meantime, she sent messengers to the far-flung family, summoning them home. She insisted that Nelly stay tucked in with her newborn daughter, following doctor's orders. She didn't want to take the chance of losing another of her loved ones.

As the family gathered, George Washington's body lay in state in its lead-lined mahogany coffin for three days, according to his deathbed wish. The night he died, Martha moved into a small third-floor bedroom. She closed his study and their bedroom for good, never again to sleep in the large bed they had shared so happily.

CHAPTER TWELVE

The Widow Washington

$\mathcal{B}$one-chilling cold still embraced Mount Vernon that Wednesday morning, December 18. Shocked and grief-stricken when a messenger brought them the news of George Washington's sudden death, family members had gathered over the past three days, met by Tobias Lear when their coaches rattled up the graveled drive to the front door, their voices filling the silent mansion: Nelly and David Stuart with their brood of six from near Fairfax Courthouse; from the new Federal City, Eliza and Thomas Law with two-year-old Eliza, Patty and Thomas Peter with two little girls, Martha and Columbia, and the baby, John Parke. Nelly was still abed with newborn Frances; Lawrence Lewis and Washington Custis were too far away in New Kent County to be recalled in time. Of the Washington family, only nephew Bushrod Washington in Alexandria lived near enough to be summoned.

Everyone was clad in mourning black, including the slave attendants. It was up to the women of the family and the household servants to prepare the light refreshments that would follow the ceremony; lay out serving pieces, glasses, plates, silver, cups, and saucers; buff up whatever needed it; set up and cover tables with cloths; fold napkins; and tend fires throughout the house against the fierce cold. People arrived throughout the late morning and early afternoon—two hundred soldiers in the uniform of the Virginia militia marched down the road from Alexandria, accompanied by a military band. Friends and officials from the neighborhood rode horseback or drove in their carriages. Hostlers would have been kept on the run by the hallooing of each new arrival, hustling to lead all the horses and vehicles down the dirt road to the stables.

And through all the bustle and preparation, Martha sat frozen-faced with misery, too grief-stricken to take part in the funeral procession or talk or even cry. Sorrow had turned this woman, all movement and smiles and lighthearted talk, to stone. She stayed in the house, perhaps even up on the third floor, as they moved the heavy coffin holding her beloved onto the portico overlooking the icy Potomac. She could not force herself to take part. Appearances simply didn't matter to her at this moment.

The procession formed there on the portico, the coffin carried by members of the militia and six honorary pallbearers. The cavalry led, followed by soldiers with arms reversed, the band with its muf-fled drums beating, beating, clergymen, Washington's riderless horse led by black-clad servants. Nelly Stuart, Martha's once and forever daughter-in-law, took her place in the funeral procession, followed by other family members and mourners. The cortege moved slowly, with dignity, to the old brick family vault a hundred yards away on the riverbank, newly cleaned, its wooden door re-paired. After the Episcopal minister read the order of burial, Masonic rites followed. Arrayed in ceremonial aprons and other regalia, the Alexandria Lodge conducted burial rites in a solemn and mov-ing ceremony. On that cold, still day, sounds rang out sharply, and inside the mansion, Martha Washington would have heard it all—the funeral dirge, the marching and shuffling feet, the masons' words, the minister's prayers, the crackling volleys from the sol-diers' muskets after the door of the tomb was closed and sealed.

Following the ceremony, the mourners walked back to the warm house. In the large dining room, they partook of cake, cheese, tea, whiskey, and wine as they shared memories of the hero. Still, Martha stayed apart, mourning dry-eyed.

The nation also mourned. To the tolling of muffled church bells and repeated volleys of the federal salute, a memorial service was held in Philadelphia, still the capital, attended by the government's leaders. Processions, ceremonies, orations, and sermons continued throughout the nation for the next two months. More than four thousand attended the service in Philadelphia, where Henry "Light-Horse Harry" Lee, a loyal Revolutionary comrade, had been chosen by Congress to deliver the eulogy. The first phrase of that tribute is famous in American history: "First in war, first in peace and first in the hearts of his countrymen," but the rest of the line is generally forgotten: "he was second to none in the humble and endearing scenes of private life." Like all his contemporaries, Lee understood that George Washington's partnership with Martha and his home life with her were essential to his public achievements.

Over the next few days, the guests left Mount Vernon and Martha resumed some semblance of her former life. After nearly forty-one years of devoted partnership, she never truly recovered from the pain of Washington's death—and didn't really want to. Her bedroom on the third floor was comfortably warmed by a Franklin stove, where she sometimes gathered the members of the household around her. Wash slept in the room across the hall, and younger slave girls sat with her in her own room, or in the landing hall with its leather sofa and armchair, as she taught them to sew.

As it had been throughout their lives together, George Washington's first concern in his will was for his "dearly beloved wife." Martha was to control and receive the income from the entire estate. After her death, Nelly and Lawrence Lewis would receive two thousand acres of the estate as well as the distillery and grist mill, which they were currently renting, Washington Custis another twelve hundred undeveloped acres north of Alexandria, and George Augustine Washington's sons two thousand acres along the river, including the farm under their stepfather's control. The house and the remainder of the estate would return to the Washington family when Martha died. Since George Augustine's untimely death, George's chosen heir was another nephew, Bushrod Washington, the son of his brother Jack. A graduate of William and Mary, Bushrod was an attorney who was sensitive to the chagrin of the Custises at this disposition of Mount Vernon, but he turned down Wash Custis's urgent offer to buy him out. Throughout the next months, Bushrod consulted frequently with his "beloved Aunt" about the proper means to deal with their intermingled financial interests. Since she had no heart for running the plantation, Martha followed his sensible advice about selling a good deal of the stock and scaling down operations.

Her widowhood was enlivened by the permanent inhabitants of the house over the next two and a half years: Nelly and Lawrence Lewis and their two daughters, Frances Parke, a plain, shy little girl, and Martha Betty, born in 1801, claimed by her mother to be "the most lovely and engaging little Girl I ever saw"; Wash Custis; and Tobias Lear, Fanny Bassett Washington's widower, who remained in his role as a combination relative, friend, secretary, and wise counselor.

Nelly and Lawrence began building a grand red-brick Georgian mansion on their inherited land three miles away from the Mount Vernon mansion, but they planned to remain with Martha as long as she lived. More beautiful than ever now that she was in her twenties, Nelly spent her days as her grandmother's companion, ran the household, and helped charm and entertain their many visitors. Lawrence cooperated with Bushrod in running the plantation, helped desultorily by Wash, whose approaching Custis legacy made it unnecessary for him to work very hard at anything. As he turned twenty, this slight, fair young grandson delighted Martha's heart, although she fretted constantly over his health and well-being.

The Stuarts, Laws, and Peters came regularly for extended visits, and the house was gay with the sound of children's laughter. Besides the little Lewis girls, there were four other great-grandchildren under the age of four, as well as Nelly Stuart's six children from her second marriage, ranging from adolescents down to a toddler the age of her own grandchildren.

In the months following her husband's death, Martha was deluged with letters of condolence and requests for mementos. President and Mrs. Adams sent letters by William Shaw Smith, his secretary and her nephew. At their request, he was to see the widow and deliver their sympathy personally. Although the young man waited two days, Martha was simply unable to bring herself to see a stranger.

Her letter of reply was filled with anguished grief. Lear reported to Smith that after she read the Adamses' letters, she finally found release in a flood of tears.

Lear dealt with much of the correspondence, drafting her replies or simply answering letters himself. Nelly also answered some letters from close family friends. The expense of this barrage of mail grew so heavy that Congressman Henry Lee and Secretary of State Timothy Pickering arranged for Martha Washington to enjoy the privilege of franking—mailing free—letters and packages for her lifetime, a right previously enjoyed only by government officials.

The widow responded generously to requests for mementos of the great man, whose memory she tended so faithfully. For example, Paul Revere's Grand (Masonic) Lodge of Massachusetts wrote in early January 1800 requesting a lock of Washington's hair to be preserved in a gold urn with the jewels and regalia of the lodge. Two weeks later, Lear responded on her behalf with a letter enclosing the requested hair and assuring them that Mrs. Washington "views with gratitude, the tributes of respect and affection paid to the memory of her dear deceased husband, and receives with a feeling heart, the expressions of sympathy contained in your letter."

But a far greater demand was made on her public-spiritedness. Congress requested that Washington's body be removed from the family tomb to be interred in the new capital city, and she agreed. Abigail Adams wrote, "She had the painfull task to perform, to bring her mind to comply with the request of Congress, which she has done in the handsomest manner possible in a Letter to the President which will this day [January 7, 1800] be communicated to congress."

William Thornton enlarged on Martha's views on this matter to John Marshall. "The body of her beloved friend and companion is now requested and she does not refuse the national wish—but if an intimation could be given that she should partake merely of the same place of deposit it would restore to her mind a calm and repose that this acquiescence in the national wish has in a high degree affected. You, who know her, are not unacquainted with her high virtues, and know that her love for the departed would be the only reason why such a wish could be entertained." Despite Martha's assent, however, her husband's body was never moved. Any final decision about the erection of a monument remained mired for years in political wrangling and infighting, while George Washington rested peacefully at Mount Vernon.

Alone among the founding fathers, Washington freed his slaves. During his later years, he had become convinced that holding human beings in bondage was wrong and determined to free his own slaves in his will. Many of the slaves at Mount Vernon, however, were not his to free. Besides those rented from a neighbor, more than half the estate's slaves were included in the Custis dower holdings. Martha was legally entitled to their labor during her lifetime, but she could neither sell nor liberate them, even had she wished to, because they were part of the family estate, which would eventually go to her grandchildren.

During the past forty years, the laborers at Mount Vernon had married or cohabited, and their numbers now included generations of their children as well. The status of these descendants depended entirely on whether their mothers belonged to Washington or to the Custis estate, because a slave's status was derived from her or his mother. Thus, a woman and her children could be freed while their father remained in slavery; conversely, a husband could become free while his wife and children remained enslaved. One family could be freed, while their first cousins were kept in bondage, and so on with grandparents, aunts, and uncles, splitting families apart through the generations. The emotional ramifications of these separations were dreadful to contemplate and could not be effected without considerable pain to all the enslaved residents of Mount Vernon.

To spare his wife, Washington had directed that the emancipation of his slaves take place after her death. But the coming separations hung over everyone's heads, and Martha grew convinced that some of the blacks wished her dead. As her legal adviser, Bushrod Washington suggested she free Washington's 123 slaves promptly, which she did on January 1, 1801. Some of the freed people continued to live at Mount Vernon with their families, others migrated to nearby black settlements, and the rest set off to discover what freedom could offer in other parts. In so much else influenced by her husband's thinking, Martha had never come to believe that slavery was wrong.

The habit of visiting Mount Vernon as a secular shrine did not cease with Washington's death. Visitors continued to flock there to pay their respects, not only to the memory of the first president, but also to his much admired consort. With the assistance of Nelly, Martha received them graciously, often bestowing small mementos of her husband. Visitors usually found Martha and Nelly, and sometimes Nelly Stuart, Eliza Law, or Patty Peter, in the small parlor, reading, knitting, or chatting. Martha offered hospitality to all callers—breakfast, dinner, tea, lodging for the night, a walk around the house and garden, long conversations about the nation's history.

Among the several parrots in cages on the riverside portico was her favorite cockatoo, which she fed, talked to, and caressed every day. Visibly aged by sorrow, she was a short, stout figure dressed in black with a ruffled white cap. Although she was still fair and smiling, age and grief had etched wrinkles on her face. She had seemed almost immortal, and now visitor after visitor seemed shocked to discover that she had aged overnight. As one visitor put it, "The zest of life has departed."

Henrietta Liston, the former British ambassador's wife, wrote that "Mrs. Washington received us with her usual kindness, and not without tears . . . our spirits were much dampened, and I listened with tender interest to a sorrow, which she said was truly breaking her heart; it was really doing so."

But with strangers, she kept up appearances. In the summer of 1801, New York politician John Pintard recorded that "[we] were received very friendly by Mrs. Washington who bears her age remarkably well. She converses without reserve & [with] seeming pleasure on every subject that recalls the memory & virtues of her august consort. . . . Mrs. W. was very attentive at table. . . . The conversation was quite free easy & familiar."

Besides the admirers, Martha also tenaciously remembered those who had hurt her husband. When Thomas Jefferson was elected in 1800, she commented freely and acidly on his presidency. She never forgave the former intimate who had wounded her husband so cruelly for political ends.

As widow of the first president, she was often visited by Federalists, with whom she enjoyed talking about politics. One visitor recorded in 1802: "We were all Federalists, which evidently gave her particular pleasure. Her remarks were frequently pointed, and sometimes very sarcastic, on the new order of things and the present administration. She spoke of the election of Mr. Jefferson, whom she considered as one of the most detestable of mankind, as the greatest misfortune our country had ever experienced."

Martha decided to make her own will nearly a year after George's death. The land and slaves were not hers to leave, but she did own a town lot in Alexandria (her husband's gift), cash, bonds, investments, and the quite valuable contents of Mount Vernon. Attorney General Charles Lee, one of George's appointees, made a testamentary draft and sent it to her in September 1800. Like many people of the time, she tucked it away until she felt her health starting to fail. Month by month throughout the last half of 1801 and early 1802, she passed more and more time in her third-floor retreat, meditating, praying, and resting as she felt the increasing burden of old age. Finally, she had Nelly recopy Lee's draft, perhaps with some revisions. During a visit from Patty and Thomas Peter, she signed her will on March 4. The witness were Patty and Lawrence and two strangers—perhaps visitors—following Lee's advice to select "two or more disinterested Witnesses."

The most valuable furnishings, silver, and her one personal slave went to Washington Custis, with Nelly Lewis receiving only slightly less; she and Lawrence had inherited nearly half the Mount Vernon acreage from George. These grandchildren were, of course, also her adopted children. Eliza Law and Patty Peter came into considerably less. A substantial portion of the house's contents were set aside for sale to fund other legacies, and all the grandchildren bought freely at that sale.

With a number of needy nieces and nephews, Martha looked after the Dandridge clan. Although she was the eldest, she had outlived her seven siblings and felt responsible for their children. Knowing the importance of a dowry, she left five hundred pounds each to her four nieces, all as yet unmarried—the three daughters of Bat Dandridge and the daughter of Betsy Dandridge Henley. Smaller amounts for remembrance were left to Maria Washington, her grandniece; Nelly Stuart; and Elizabeth Washington, Lund's widow and her longtime friend. The junior Bat Dandridge was left the Alexandria lot, and Benjamin Lear, Tobias's son, received a hundred pounds. She also left Pohick Parish a hundred pounds toward the purchase of a glebe, land for the support of the rector.

The primary charge on the estate was paying for the education of her sister Betsy's youngest sons, Bartholomew and Samuel Henley, and her brother Bat's grandson John Dandridge. A hundred pounds also awaited each of them when they began their careers. The residuary legatees were then to be Maria Washington, John Dandridge, and any living great-grandchildren.

In the first week of May, she fell seriously ill with one of her frequent stomach upsets, called bilious fever, and sent to Alexandria for the family doctor and friend, James Craik, himself now seventy-one years old. Feeling the end approaching, she prevailed upon him to remain with her. During this final illness, uninvited visitors continued to arrive. One reported: "The pleasure which we had anticipated in this visit was greatly diminished by the illness of Lady Washington." But the group questioned Dr. Craik very closely indeed on Martha's appearance, way of life, and likelihood of survival. Instead of sending them packing, he satisfied their curiosity with the same sense of duty that the residents of Mount Vernon showed toward other sightseers. He even pointed out her favorite cockatoo, observing that "being neglected since her sickness, he seemed quite lost & dejected."

Martha had at least three weeks to prepare for death—taking communion and bidding her dear ones farewell. The Laws, Peters, and Stuarts joined the Lewises and Wash Custis in attendance, spending most of the month of May at Mount Vernon, seeing her daily. Shortly before her seventy-first birthday, she died of old age, weakened by her illness, at noon on May 22, surrounded by her grandchildren. As Thomas Law described her attitude, "Fortitude & resignation were display'd throughout, she met death as a relief from the infirmities & melancholy of old age."

For three days, her coffin rested in the large dining room, the body clad in a white gown she had chosen "for the last dress." On May 25, in a quiet Episcopal ceremony in marked contrast with her husband's more formal obsequies, her coffin was placed beside his in the family tomb. Nelly Stuart again presided over the rites and the subsequent gathering of family members and a few friends.

Her obituary in the *Alexandria Advertiser and Commercial Intelligencer* summed up her life: "On Saturday the 22nd of May at 12 o'clock P.M. Mrs. Washington terminated her well spent life.... She was the worthy partner of the worthiest of men, and those who witnessed their conduct could not determine which excelled in their different characters, both were so well sustained on every occasion. They lived an honor and a pattern to their country, and are taken from us to receive the rewards—promised to the faithful and the just."

George Washington had passed on the office of the presidency, setting the standard for the peaceful succession of American administrations in the years to come. But no future president could achieve his almost mythical status as *the* founding and first president. Nor could any future First Lady replace Martha Washington as the *first* First Lady, the woman who had stood at Washington's side, supporting him throughout the founding of the American nation.

The Real Martha Washington

*S*earching for the real Martha Washington didn't seem at first to promise much drama, romance, or adventure. Compared to the tart-tongued and opinionated Abigail Adams or that unrivaled political hostess, Dolley Madison, the dignified elderly lady pictured by Gilbert Stuart seemed yawningly dull—her only possible claim to fame being her marriage to George Washington.

By destroying all the letters she and her husband exchanged, she prevented any future generation from knowing them through their own words. Worse yet, only the barest outlines of her childhood, girlhood, and first marriage were known—a document here, a fact or two there, all generously larded with two and a half centuries of speculation, unreliable family lore, and romantic fabrication. Martha Washington was frozen in the American historical imagination, famous as a symbol yet completely unknown as a woman.

Stripping away the myths and falsehoods, reinterpreting what was already known, and discovering bits and pieces of new information, I began to glimpse and then to see clearly the real Martha Washington—a woman whose story I wanted to tell.

In 1758, Martha was twenty-six years old, a mature woman with a fully formed character—and a strong, formidable character it was. On her mother's side, she came from several generations of women who lived in York and New Kent counties in the Virginia Tide-water. They survived all that life offered—from frontier conditions to genteel prosperity, continuous pregnancies, the painful births and frequent deaths of their children, endemic and incurable fevers and dysenteries, feeding and clothing large families in crowded houses. Her mother was orphaned, most of her foremothers were wid-owed. The lives of these colonial women—their experiences, family history, memories, traditions, lore, and attitudes—all shaped Martha Dandridge's character. Virginia was bred in the bone, and however far she traveled in the world, it remained with her.

As the eldest of a large family, she was accustomed to consider-able responsibility from childhood on, and her experiences as an adult made her even stronger and more capable. After Daniel Custis proposed to her, she and her family were publicly attacked by his snobbish father. It must have been deeply mortifying to have John Custis insult them at his favorite tavern and up and down the streets of Williamsburg, but Martha was determined enough for two and brought about the marriage she desired.

By 1758, she had been through tragedies sufficient to make a weaker woman take permanently to her bed. From her eighteenth year on, she suffered a series of devastating losses. Her closest brother died in 1749; in 1754, her eldest son died at two and a half; her father dropped dead in 1756, leaving her mother with a new-born baby and a houseful of children; her eldest daughter died in 1757 just before her fourth birthday; three months later, her re-maining son fell gravely ill, while her husband died a sudden and painful death; and in 1758, her adolescent sister died. Martha Custis kept on coping as she would throughout the losses that lay ahead for her.

When Daniel Custis died, leaving his widow in charge of an enormous estate held in trust for their children, including the dower third that was hers for life, she might have thrown up her hands, hiring someone to oversee her financial affairs or making foolish decisions on her own. But she was both intelligent and shrewd, asking for advice, taking what seemed wise to her, reject-ing the rest, and carefully studying her husband's records. Her financial correspondence is coolly businesslike. She made it clear to all the Custis merchants and lawyers that she would continue business relationships with them as long as she was satisfied with their services but wouldn't hesitate to make changes otherwise. Her orders for the plantation and records of loans are models of efficiency.

What about the marriage to George Washington that eventually made her famous? For biographers, that's a two-part question. Were they in love when they married, and did they love each other later? There's really no room for doubt about the answer to either question in regard to Martha Custis. Very pretty, charming, entertaining, and rich, she could pick and choose among her present suitors or wait for those whom the future would bring. But after George's first call on her, she immediately invited him back. She wanted him from the beginning. Every bit of contemporary evidence shows that she adored him throughout their lives together—he knew it, their friends knew it, and the general public knew it.

What did he feel for her? As nineteenth-century writers reinvented Washington to suit their own ideas, they seized on Washington Custis's description of a chance meeting at a neighbor's house. According to Custis, Washington immediately fell in love with the charming widow and pursued her wholeheartedly. The discovery of two letters that Washington wrote to Sally Cary Fairfax during his engagement to Martha Custis knocked out the story of love at first sight. There's no credible way to read the letters he wrote in the fall of 1758 other than as those of a young man suffering from a forbidden love; they're practically incoherent, the outpouring of a sorely troubled heart. He was infatuated with Sally and distraught at her criticism of his coming marriage to Martha Custis.

Does that mean he married Martha *only* for her money? Just as false as Custis's accidental love tale is the idea that the Washingtons' marriage was affectionate but cool and that George pined for Sally Fairfax until he died. Sally was unattainable by the mores of his class and time—neither of them wanted to run off and live outside society's reach somewhere on the frontier. If Martha, despite her wealth, hadn't been lovely and appealing, George had plenty of time to look around. There were always attractive young ladies with respectable dowries and wealthy widows. Neither George nor Martha had to marry just at this time.

George was given to musing on love and marriage in later life, criticizing coquettes who toyed with men's affections (Sally?) while waxing lyrical about the pleasures of marriage with the right partner. He warned Martha's young granddaughters not to "look for perfect felicity before you consent to wed." He asserted that "more permanent & genuine happiness is to be found in the sequestered walks of connubial life, than in the giddy rounds of promiscuous pleasure."

Martha Dandridge Custis was a lovely and sexually attractive woman. Her first husband defied his terrifying father—something he had never dared to do previously—to marry her. George Washington's rival during their courtship confided to his brother about the happiness he expected to find in her arms. She was a woman confident of her own appeal. Whatever she may have guessed about Sally Fairfax (probably quite a lot), she doesn't seem to have doubted her ability to secure her husband's love.

And she was certainly right. After they married, there is not a sign that George was a bored or unhappy husband. They shared a bed throughout their marriage (no separate bedrooms here), and he desired her companionship as often as possible when he was away from home during the war and the presidency. Washington was concerned, almost obsessed, with his wife's comfort and safety. If money had been the *only* motive for their marriage, he needn't have bothered. Once they were married, he controlled the money, and only their mutual love explains his care for her. All three of his extant letters to Martha begin "My dearest," and there is no reason to doubt that she was indeed his dearest love.

George admired his wife for many reasons besides her looks and sex appeal. Conversation was one of the prized social graces of the eighteenth century, and Martha could talk to anyone about anything, far outstripping her husband's more serious approach. After a conversation with her, guests went away with the pleasant sense of being appreciated and admired. She was all motion, sparkle, and delight, never haughty, greeting visitors with her beautiful smile,

234 · MARTHA WASHINGTON

radiating warmth and welcome. She was kind, concerned for the feelings of others, and charitable to an extreme.

During George Washington's public years, she screened callers for him and joined in their conversations. Martha Washington was her husband's closest confidante, the person he could always trust to consider knotty problems, according to their family, aides, and secretaries. Trust Thomas Jefferson to get their relationship completely wrong. At a dinner at Monticello, he expounded on George Washington's hardness in both public and private life, declaring the most uxorious of men "a hard husband."

No one could argue that Martha had a theoretical bent of mind or that she took the lead in her husband's evolving political views. But she was an intelligent and concerned participant who moved along the path toward revolution and nationhood with him. She read newspapers, magazines, and pamphlets, discussing all the news of the day at dinner and in their evenings together.

Very few of his southern contemporaries followed George Washington in his growing determination to free his slaves. Martha never reached his certainty that slavery was wrong, but she was no more likely to argue with him over the disposition of his human property than she was over his decision to leave Mount Vernon to a Washington. She recognized his property as his own to do with as he wished.

Nor would he have tried to convince her to free the other slaves who labored at Mount Vernon, since she had no legal power to do so. They were part of her dower right to Daniel Custis's estate—the widow's third that she controlled throughout her lifetime. She could not sell, give away, or free the Custis slaves without accounting to the estate. At her death, they automatically became the property of the Custis heirs.

Martha Washington was a brave woman, not the timid creature posited by many of her husband's biographers. She wasn't fearless, but she was brave enough to do things anyway. Boats made her nervous, but she made several hundred ferry crossings in her comings and goings. Smallpox inoculation frightened her. A gob of pus from a smallpox victim was inserted into a cut on her arm; all might be well, or her body might break out in a mass of pustules, leaving her scarred for life. To be with her husband, she didn't hesitate for a moment to have the procedure. Despite the very real dangers of capture by the British during the Revolution, she stayed at Mount Vernon or joined her husband—no hiding in safety for her. Her strongest fears were for others—her husband and children, grandchildren, nieces and nephews.

It's almost impossible to write the biography of a woman before the twentieth century without writing a lot about daily life, especially for a woman as happily domestic as Martha Washington. To write only of high points and great deeds is to ignore most of human life and the things that give the greatest joy—whether riding around the fields to check on the progress of a new strain of barley for George or Martha's knitting stockings and hemming hankies for her grandchildren.

As L. P. Hartley wrote, "The past is another country. They do things differently there." We stand at Mount Vernon and imagine that we are experiencing part of Martha Washington's life. But her world didn't sound the same, smell the same, or look the same. She didn't move in a vacuum, nor did her husband. To understand her, we have to understand the customs of her country—eighteenth-century Virginia.

George Washington was a very great man, essential to the formation of the American nation. But he was not the perfect man of marble, faultless, all wise, and self-controlled. Like everyone, he was a churning mass of contradictions. At times, he could be violently angry, nagging, censorious, insecure, indecisive, depressed, or obsessed with ill health. To ignore Martha's role in the great man's life is to ignore the emotional components of his character. She was essential to his sense of well-being, the one person with whom he could let down his guard and be himself. Both Abigail Adams and Dolley Madison are seen as essential to their husbands' lives and careers because their letters were saved. Martha and George Washington spent as little time apart as possible, but when they were parted, they wrote weekly. By destroying those masses of letters, Martha maintained their privacy but completely obscured her own role in her husband's life.

Once Martha and George Washington married and he became famous, it is difficult to see her clearly. She was completely bound up in his life, and her contributions to American history were made in support of his career. Her constant presence at winter camps allowed him to stay in the field throughout the American Revolution. As the nation's hostess, she resisted all attempts to make her into a queen, as he had refused to become a king. Pulled far from her natural orbit, Martha Washington brought unself-conscious dignity and charm to the new role of First Lady of a new nation.

Not elected and free of official oversight, presidents' wives wield tremendous political and social influence. With their unique access to the nation's leader, they are subject to constant scrutiny by allies and enemies, the press, and the general public. These women are expected to assume national responsibilities, willing or not, and their private lives are routinely examined, discussed, and criticized. There is no guidebook to help a new First Lady; she must look back at her predecessors to decide how to shape her role and to survive in the limelight. Martha Washington's imprint on the position has been decisive. As the first in a long line, she invented the role while confronting with grace its inevitable quandaries, successes, and heartaches. Admired and respected in her lifetime, Martha Washington set the standard for all First Ladies.

Acknowledgments

For anyone interested in Martha Washington, Mount Vernon is the starting point. Preserved by the Mount Vernon Ladies Association for a century and a half, it is both a patriotic shrine and a pathway for understanding the nation's past. Whether touring the mansion, outbuildings, gardens, and exhibition areas, attending a symposium, or doing research in the library and curatorial collections, the Mount Vernon experience is remarkable. I owe heartfelt thanks to James C. Rees, executive director; Linda Ayres, associate director for collections; and Ann Phillips Bay, associate director for education, for ongoing help throughout the years. Barbara McMillan, librarian, and Carol Borchert Cadou, curator, exemplify research assistance at its best. They have helped me unstintingly in ways too numerous to spell out. Other staff members who were very helpful are Dawn Bonner, administrative assistant; John Payne, museum technician; and Melissa Naulin, former assistant curator.

Mary V. Thompson, research specialist, is in a class by herself. She shares her valuable research reports and insights about the Washingtons and their lives at Mount Vernon with great generosity and never hesitates to look in new directions. All her admirers look forward to seeing more of her work in print. Both she and Carol Cadou read and commented on portions of the manuscript.

The research for this book was assisted materially by a Frances Lewis fellowship in women's studies from the Virginia Historical Society. Members of the fine staff were uniformly supportive, and I wish to thank Charles F. Bryan Jr., president and CEO; E. Lee Shepard, director of manuscripts and archives; William M. S. Rasmussen, Lora M. Robins Curator of Art; Nelson D. Lankford, director of publications and scholarship, who first encouraged me to apply for a fellowship; Frances Pollard, director of library services, who always steered me right in working with the collections; and Gregory Stoner, library assistant.

At Colonial Williamsburg, Linda H. Rowe, historian, guided me through early Williamsburg records and offered excellent suggestions on the finished manuscript. Thanks also to Cathleene B. Hellier and Patricia A. Gibbs, historians, and Louise Wrike, secretary, Department of Historical Research. During a Williamsburg symposium, my friend Nancy Carter Crump provided essential information on domestic life. Thanks also to Betty Leviner and Mary Wiseman.

Despite their backbreaking schedule of publication, the staff of the George Washington Papers at the University of Virginia are always willing to help researchers. Thanks to Philander D. Chase, Frank E. Grizzard Jr., Edward G. Lengel, and Beverly H. Runge for making material available and checking unpublished material for me. Both Frank and Ed read portions of the manuscript and made valuable suggestions.

I appreciate the support of Leslie L. Buhler, executive director; Melinda L. Huff, curator of collections; and Jill Sanderson, director of education, at Tudor Place in Georgetown, the home of Martha Custis Peter. Wendy Kail, archivist, was a delight to work with. My interest in the Custis family began with Woodlawn, the home of Nelly Custis Lewis. Once again, thanks to my friends Ross G. Randall, director; Craig S. Tuminaro, former associate director for preservation programs; and former curator Margaret Davis and her husband, Max.

Warren M. Billings gave me a crash course in early Virginia history, life, and legal matters and was an always available resource. Several distinguished Virginia historians read part or all of the manuscript. Many, many thanks to Thad W. Tate; Emory W. Evans; Mark F. Fernandez; Sandra Gioia Treadway, who also delved for information at the Library of Virginia; and Jon Kukla. Several nonhistorian friends read portions of the work to be sure that it would be clear to the general reader: Chris Alderman, Jane Brady, Louise Hoffman, Lynn Adams, Colin Schmit, and Harold Alderman. Of course, all remaining errors and ambiguities are my own.

Sara B. Bearss, senior editor of the *Dictionary of Virginia Biography*, kindly brought the letters concerning Charles Carter's courtship of Martha Custis to my attention. Her fellow editor, Brent Tarter, made the original transcription of Carter's letter and read this manuscript, making essential suggestions. And they extended my deadline for the *DVB*. Thanks all around.

Mary H. Manhein, director of the LSU Faces Lab, arranged for the age regression of Charles Willson Peale's miniature of Martha Washington. N. Eileen Barrow, forensic imaging specialist, did the sensitive and accurate work of going back in time and showing us the youthful Martha Custis. Michael Deas created the beautiful portrait that should have been painted in 1757 but wasn't.

Thanks to Michael Sartisky, president and CEO of the Louisiana Endowment for the Humanities, a great supporter of the literary life of New Orleans, for providing a fine writer's office; to Florence M. Jumonville, chair of the Louisiana and Special Collections Department, Earl K. Long Library, University of New Orleans, for obtaining microfilms of period newspapers; and to David G. Spielman, a photographer who specializes in making writers look good.

Wendy Wolf is an editor whose brief comments and subtle directions improve a manuscript without changing its essential character; she was able to lure a born procrastinator over the finish line. My agent, Jonathan Dolger, knows how to match an author with the right editor. Thanks to the Tennessee Williams/ New Orleans Literary Festival, where I met both these sterling characters.

The people at Viking Penguin worked with consummate professionalism to produce a handsome book on the shortest of deadlines. Paul Buckley art directed a book jacket that I imagine Martha Washington would have admired: I certainly do. He worked closely with artist Michael Deas to ensure that her portrait was both beautiful and true to the subject. The jacket design by Maggie Payette and the interior design by Nancy Resnick are graceful and easy to read. Sona Vogel was the perfect copyeditor, and Susan Groarke very accurately proofed the galleys. Production editor Kate Griggs coordinated everyone's efforts diligently, while Sandra Maffiore saw the book through the press. Clifford J. Corcoran, Wendy Wolf's assistant, was always available to answer questions, take care of snafus, and hold the author's hand when needed.

At the celebration of the bicentennial of the White House in 2000, I decided to write this book. My friends John C. Riley, associate director of the White House Historical Association, who invited me to attend; Clare Edwards, vice regent of Mount Vernon for Connecticut; and Ellen McCallister Clark, library director, Society of the Cincinnati, encouraged me to do it, and then there was no going back. John and Ellen also read portions of the manuscript.

Last, thanks to three terrific women. Chris Wiltz and Susan Larson told me years before I dared that I had to give up my day job and write full-time. When I finally made the leap, they encouraged me every step of the way. My executive assistant, Elizabeth Schmit, besides working on this book and other projects, kept my real life going. I couldn't have done it without them.

Notes

Abbreviations

CWF   Colonial Williamsburg Foundation
DGW   *The Diaries of George Washington*, 6 vols., eds. Donald Jackson and
          Dorothy Twohig (Charlottesville: The University Press of Virginia,
          1976–1979).
MVLA   Mount Vernon Ladies Association
PGWCLS *The Papers of George Washington: Colonial Series*, 10 vols., ed. W. W. Ab-
          bott (Charlottesville: The University Press of Virginia, 1983–1995).
PGWRWS *The Papers of George Washington: Revolutionary War Series*, 13 vols.,
          eds. Philander D. Chase et al. (Charlottesville: The University Press
          of Virginia, 1985–).
PGWCFS *The Papers of George Washington: Confederation Series*, 6 vols., ed.
          W. W. Abbott (Charlottesville: The University Press of Virginia,
          1992–1997).
PGWPS   *The Papers of George Washington: Presidential Series*, 11 vols., eds.
          Dorothy Twohig et al. (Charlottesville: The University Press of
          Virginia, 1987–).
PGWRTS *The Papers of George Washington: Retirement Series*, 4 vols., eds.
          W. W. Abbott et al. (Charlottesville: The University Press of Vir-
          ginia, 1998–1999).
VHS   Virginia Historical Society

PROLOGUE: On the Road to History

1   **"domestic enjoyments":** James T. Flexner, *George Washington*, 4 vols.
    (Boston: Little, Brown, 1965–1972), 1:229.

2 **"I am truly sorry"**: Joseph E. Fields, *"Worthy Partner": The Papers of Martha Washington* (Westport, Conn.: Greenwood Press, 1994), 213.

3 **"for we are extremely desirous"**: *PGWPS*, 2:248.

3 **"all the girls" and all quotes on page 4**: Robert Lewis, "A Journey from Fredericksburg, Virginia, to New York," May 13–20, 1789, MVLA, 2–3.

5 **"All was silent melancholy"**: Ibid., 4.

5 **"the dreaded hour appeared"**: Ibid.

6 **"unimproved" country**: *PGWPS*, 2:205.

6 **"the most dangerous and difficult"**: Ibid., 2:419.

7 **"the children were very well"**: Fields, 215.

7 **"shifted herself"**: Lewis, 6–7.

8 **"the great parade"**: Fields, 215.

9 **"my dear Mrs. Washington"**: *PGWPS*, 1:461.

9 **"scenes of bustle & trouble"**: Ibid., 2:3.

9 **"harass[ing] her with company,"**: Ibid., 2:382.

9 **"any parade that might be intended."**: Lewis, 10.

10 **"an excellent Band of Music"**: J. Thomas Scharf, *Chronicles of Baltimore* (Baltimore: Turnbull Brothers, 1874), 254.

10 **"without the least accident"**: Fields, 215.

12 **"Dear little Washington" and all other quotes on this page**: Ibid.

13 **"The paper will tell you"**: Ibid.

CHAPTER ONE: Little Patsy Dandridge

16 **"howling wilderness" and "foule noise"**: Richard Cullen Rath, *How Early America Sounded* (Ithaca, N.Y.: Cornell University Press, 2003), 147, 151.

16 **"William Woodward, the Indian Interpreter"**: "Biographical and Genealogical Notes and Queries," *William and Mary Quarterly*, 2nd series, 4 (April 1934): 174–79.

20 **"To name generation after generation"**: *DGW*, 1:l.

CHAPTER TWO: Courtship

28 **"an agreeable young Lady"**: Edmund S. Morgan, *Virginians at Home: Family Life in the Eighteenth Century* (Williamsburg, Va.: CWF, 1952), 31.

28 Daniel Custis recorded his own height as five feet seven in his "Invoice Book" and then struck through it and changed the figure to five feet six. He might have been considering the proper fit of his suit if he added an extra inch to his height. "Invoice Book &a," Lee Family Papers, VHS.

30 **"Fidelia"**: James B. Lynch Jr., *The Custis Chronicles: The Virginia Generations* (Camden, Maine: Picton Press, 1997), 55–56.

30   **"To hell, Madam":** Ibid.

31   **"vile names or give . . . any ill language":** "A Marriage Agreement," *Virginia Magazine of History and Biography* 4 (1897): 64–66.

31   **"young Alice":** York County Records, Deed Book 5, 236–37, York County Project, Department of Historical Research, CWF. Research and data collection done with assistance from the National Endowment for the Humanities under Grants RS-0033-80-1604 and RO-20869.

32   **"This comes at last . . .":** Douglas Southall Freeman, *George Washington*, 7 vols. (Fairfield, N.J.: Augustus M. Kelley, 1981, rep.), 2:294.

32   **John Custis made a will:** He bought a small piece of property for Jack, separate from the Custis and Parke holdings, and left him nine young enslaved boys, as well as the boy's mother, Alice. When Jack came of age, Daniel Custis was to build and furnish a house for him on the property. In the meantime, the land and slaves were held in trust by one of the elder Custis's nephews. York County Records, Will Book, CWF.

CHAPTER THREE: Young Mrs. Custis

34   **Tomb inscription:** Lynch, 87–88.

37   **"for Mrs. Custis's use":** "Invoice Book," VHS.

42   **"called her women together":** Jack Larkin, *The Reshaping of Everyday Life: 1790–1840* (New York: HarperPerennial, 1988), 94.

42   **"so sweet an office":** Sally G. McMillen, *Motherhood in the Old South: Pregnancy, Childbirth, and Infant Rearing* (Baton Rouge: Louisiana State University Press, 1990), 111.

43   **"my son":** "Invoice Book," VHS.

43   **"favourite boy,":** "Diary of John Blair," Lyon G. Tyler, ed, *William and Mary Quarterly*, 1st series, 7 (January 1899), 152.

43   **"black Jack":** York County Records, Will Book 22, 292–93, CWF.

43   **"games and contests":** John W. Reps, *Tidewater Towns: City Planning in Colonial Virginia and Maryland* (Williamsburg, Va.: CWF, 1972), 179.

46   **"Tomb for my son":** "Invoice Book," VHS.

48   **"for Second Mourning,":** Ibid.

50   **"the best three Thread laid Twine," and all other quotes on this page:** Ibid.

CHAPTER FOUR: The Widow Custis and Colonel Washington

53   **"agreeable and lasting to us both":** Fields, 5.

55   **"C.C. is very gay":** Marion Tinling, ed., *The Correspondence of the Three William Byrds of Westover, Virginia, 1684–1776*, 3 vols. (Charlottesville: The University Press of Virginia, 1977), 2:646 and 646n.

55   **"Mrs. C__s is now the object of my wish" and all other quotes on this**

page: Charles Carter to Landon Carter, April 26, 1758, Carter Family Records, Sabine Hall.

56   **His original inheritance:** Part of this property later came to be called Ferry Farm. Operated by George Washington's Fredericksburg Foundation, it is open to the public.

59   **"Towering over most men":** George Washington's great height was remarked on by all observers, but his exact height isn't really known. From his own orders to London merchants, describing himself as six feet tall, to the deathbed measurement of six feet three and a half inches, there is considerable variation. The estimate of six feet two and a half inches was used as an average.

61   **"to be grave":** Fields, 25–26.

62   **"how joyfully I catch":** *PGWCLS*, 6:10–13.

62   **"Do we still misunderstand":** Ibid., 6:41–43.

63   **"Colonel Washington . . . is married":** Ibid., 6:175n.

63   **"I . . . beg leave to present":** Ibid., 6:187–88.

CHAPTER FIVE: Gentry Life at Mount Vernon

67   **"in the best manner you can":** *PGWCLS*, 6:200.

68   **"mirth and gaiety":** Fields, 129.

70   **"Honored Madam" and other quotes:** *PGWCLS*, 1:304–05.

70   **When visiting in Fredericksburg:** After it was sold by the Lewis family, the beautiful Georgian mansion was named Kenmore by nineteenth-century owners. Operated by George Washington's Fredericksburg Foundation, it is open to the public.

71   **"uniformly handsome and genteel":** Ibid., 6:317.

72   **"an excellent table":** Lincoln MacVeagh, ed., *The Journal of Nicholas Cresswell, 1774–1777* (New York: Dial Press, 1924), 253.

72   **"Martha Washington. 1759":** *The Bull-Finch: Being a Choice Collection of the Newest and Most Favourite English Songs* (London: R. Baldwin and John Wilkie), Mount Vernon Library, MVLA.

73   **"I am now I believe fixd":** *PGWCLS*, 6:359.

73   **"I have had a very dark time":** Fields, 146.

73   **"I have not a doubt":** Ibid., 268.

73   **"1 oz seeds":** Patricia Brady Schmit, *Nelly Custis Lewis's Housekeeping Book* (New Orleans: Historic New Orleans Collection, 1982), 107.

74   **"little Patt" and all quotes on the following page:** Fields, 147.

74   **"very fast":** Ibid., 147–48.

74   **"nothing more agreeable" and "Musick Professor":** Judith S. Britt, *Nothing More Agreeable: Music in George Washington's Family* (Mount Vernon, Va.: The Association, 1984), 11, 19.

75 **She may have trilled:** All lyrics from *The Bull-Finch*.

77 **"her Children are as well":** *PGWCLS*, 8:20, 25.

77 **"I deal little in politics":** Ibid., 7:58

79 **Beautiful little Patsy:** Some writers have argued that Patsy first showed signs of epilepsy when she was four because of a letter from Martha (its present location is unknown) that reported, "she has lost her fitts & fevours." However, there is no record of parental concern, unusual doctors' visits, or large quantities of medicine in any of Washington's letters or in his meticulously kept guardian's accounts until January 1768. Most likely, in 1760 Patsy went into convulsions from a high fever but recovered. That illness seems to be unconnected to her later development of epilepsy. Fields, 131; *PGWCLS*, 8 passim, *DGW*, 2 passim.

79 **"The unhappy situation":** *PGWCLS*, 8:496.

81 **"I must confess to you":** Ibid., 8:414.

82 **"having yielded to Importunity":** *DGW*, 3:108–09.

83 **"a Subject . . . of no small embarrassment to me":** *PGWCLS*, 9:209–10.

84 **"inconsiderable" and "Nothing in my power":** Ibid., 9:215–16.

84 **"of exceeding good Character":** Ibid., 9:219–20.

84 **"I shall say nothing":** Ibid.

85 **"in better health and spirits" and all other quotes on this page and the following page:** Ibid., 9:243–44.

88 **"useful knowledge" and all other quotes on this page:** Ibid., 9:406–07.

90 **"We had never seen":** Graham Hood, *The Governor's Palace in Williamsburg: A Cultural Study* (Williamsburg, Va.: CWF, 1991), 178.

91 **"the General Congress at Philadelphia":** *DGW*, 3:254–68.

92 **"I was much pleased":** David John Mays, ed., *The Letters and Papers of Edmund Pendleton, 1734–1803*, 2 vols. (Charlottesville: The University Press of Virginia, 1967), 1:98.

CHAPTER SIX: Lady Washington and the American Revolution

94 **"no pecuniary consideration":** *PGWRWS*, 1:1–3.

94 **"unwillingness to part with you" and all other quotes on this and the following page:** Ibid., 1:3–6.

96 **"as I have no expectations":** Ibid., 1:12–14.

96 **"My great concern":** Ibid., 1:15–16.

96 **"a cutting stroke":** Ibid., 1:19–20.

96 **"a happy Meeting":** Fields, 161.

97 **"the infernal curiosity":** *PGWRWS*, 2:72.

98 **"the Hospitality of the House":** Ibid., 2:432.

98 **"I believe Mrs. Washingtons Charitable disposition":** Ibid., 3:129.

98 **"let her have a barrel":** Fields, 163.

100 "to come to me": *PGWRWS*, 2:162.

100 "I expect her home Imediately": Ibid., 2:256.

100 "I will cheerfully do" and all other quotes on this and the following page: Ibid., 2:376.

102 "a very great somebody": Fields, 164.

102 "I don't doubt": Ibid.

103 "great regard and affection"; "defense of our rights"; "these troubled times"; "not to grace"; "best compliments"; "that their sentiments": Flexner, 2:58–59.

103 "I left [Philadelphia]": Fields, 164.

103 "Mesdames Washington, Custis, and Gates": Flexner, 2:59.

103 "particular instructions and advice": Ibid., 2:409.

104 "This is a beautyfull country": Fields, 164.

104 "I am still determined": Ibid., 224.

104 "Every person seems" and "God knows how long": Ibid., 164.

105 "the distance is long": Ibid., 167.

106 "that Medusa": Charles Lee as quoted in George A. Billias, *George Washington's Generals and Opponents* (New York: Da Capo Press, 1994), 81.

107 "Quaker-preacher": John F. Stegeman and Janet A. Stegeman, *Caty: A Biography of Catherine Littlefield Greene* (Athens: University of Georgia Press, 1977), 22–23.

108 "with that politeness": Lyman H. Butterfield, ed., *Adams Family Correspondence* (Cambridge, Mass.: Belknap Press, 1963), 1:385.

108 "in every point of View": *PGWRWS*, 3:1.

108 "Old Sow": Mark M. Boatner III, *Encyclopedia of the American Revolution* (Mechanicsburg, Pa.: Stackpole Books, 1994), 588.

109 "our navey" and quotes in the following paragraph, ending with "many Tories": Fields, 166–67.

110 "to see the Deserted lines": *Adams Family*, 1:385.

111 "Mrs. Washington is still here": *PGWRWS*, 4:173.

112 "begen to think" and "I thank god": Fields, 172.

113 "the strapping Huzze": Ibid., 170–71.

114 "mortifying, as it deprives me": Flexner, 2:197.

114 "Old Man" and "They are very happy": Richard K. Showman, ed., *The Papers of General Nathanael Green*, 12 vols. (Chapel Hill: University of North Carolina Press, 1980), 2:54.

115 "politeness and attention" and all other quotations on this page: *Proceedings of the New Jersey Historical Society* (July 1933): 152.

117 "they have been exceeding good": Fields, 174.

117 "she was the greatest favorite" and all other quotations on this page: Ibid., 174–76.

CHAPTER SEVEN: Valley Forge and Eventual Victory

118 **"Several general officers":** Stanley J. Idzerda, ed., *Lafayette in the Age of the American Revolution: Selected Letters and Papers, 1776–1790*, 5 vols. (Ithaca, N.Y.: Cornell University Press, 1977), 1:225.

119 **"motherly care":** John F. Reed, *Valley Forge: Crucible of Victory* (Monmouth Beach, N.J.: Philip Freneau Press, 1969), 34.

119 **"I hope and trust":** Fields, 177–78.

120 **"Assemblies, Concerts, Comedies":** Jared Brown, *The Theatre in America During the Revolution* (New York: Cambridge University Press, 1995), 45–47.

120 **"we are in a dreary kind of place":** John C. Fitzpatrick, ed., *The Writings of George Washington*, 39 vols. (Washington, D.C.: U.S. Government Printing Office, 1931–1944), 10:414.

121 **"The rations they have consumed":** Dennis P. Ryan, ed., *A Salute to Courage: The American Revolution as Seen Through Wartime Writings of Officers of the Continental Army and Navy* (New York: Columbia University Press, 1979), 186–87.

121 **"The Generals apartment":** Fields, 177–78.

121 **"her presence inspired fortitude":** Reed, 34.

122 **"In the midst of all our distress":** Gilbert Chinard, ed., *George Washington as the French Knew Him: A Collection of Texts* (Princeton, N.J.: Princeton University Press, 1940), 14, 16.

123 **"camp followers":** Holly A. Mayer, *Belonging to the Army: Camp Followers and Community During the American Revolution* (Columbia: University of South Carolina Press, 199).

124 **"We arriv'd at about ½ past one" and quotes on the following page:** Elaine Forman Crane, ed., *The Diary of Elizabeth Drinker* (Boston: Northeastern University Press, 1994), 74–76, 82.

125 **The Quaker prisoners:** A story based on the memoirs of a Hessian major, often circulated since, incorrectly credits Martha Washington with intervening to liberate Henry Drinker and the other prisoners, thereby earning the gratitude of the entire Quaker community. The prisoners' release was already under way, however, and Martha had no influence with the state government. Far from being grateful, Elizabeth Drinker declined to join her friends Phebe Pemberton and Molly Pleasants, her companions at Valley Forge, to call on the general's lady when she returned to Philadelphia later that year. Carl Leopold Baurmeister as quoted in Flexner 2: 285; Crane, 74–76, 82.

125–6 **"most perfect confederation"; "a profusion"; "I was never present":** Flexner, 2:290–91.

126 **"when we arose":** Crane, 77.

128 **"Ms. Bet has grown very much":** Fields, 179.

128 "my letters doe not come": Ibid., 180.

129 "Speculation, peculation": Flexner, 2:336.

129 "I have lately been several times": William Spohn Baker, *Itinerary of General Washington from June 15, 1775, to December 23, 1783* (Philadelphia: J. B. Lippincott, 1892), 149.

130 "infinitely more pain than pleasure": Flexner, 2:336.

130 "During the course of his short stay": Baker, 151.

130 "Mrs. Washington combines": James Thatcher, *Military Journal of the American Revolution* (Philadelphia: J. B. Lippincott, 1892), 160–61.

132 In an almost certainly apocryphal: James Rivington, a Tory editor, went on to claim that the thirteen stripes around the tomcat's tail suggested the flag's stripes to Congress. It is unlikely that there is any truth to the tale, but it has been quoted as fact frequently and recently. James Rivington in the *Royal Gazette*, quoted in Mary Gay Humphreys, *Catherine Schuyler* (New York: Charles Scribner's Sons, 1897), 173.

133 "some rice powder": Fields, 182. Rice powder was a common cosmetic; it was transcribed incorrectly by Fields as "nice" powder.

134 "I suffered so much last winter": Ibid., 183.

134 "the offering of the ladies": Cokie Roberts, *Founding Mothers: The Women Who Raised Our Nation* (New York: William Morrow, 2004), 128.

138 "I hope you will keep Lord Cornwallis": *Writings of George Washington*, 23:110.

138 "An elegant seat and situation": Flexner, 2:446.

138 "her great Age": Fields, 187.

138 "the General tho in constant Fatigue": Ibid.

139 "a summary return": *Writings of George Washington*, 23:253.

139 A messenger was sent: As an adult, Elizabeth Custis claimed that she accompanied her mother and grandmother to her father's bedside, but it seems unlikely that a five-year-old would have been brought into contact with a man dying of a possibly communicable disease. "Self Portrait by Eliza Custis," *Virginia Magazine of History and Biography* 53 (April 1945).

140 "I would have wrote": Flexner, 2:471–72.

140 "I shall attempt to stimulate": *Writings of George Washington*, 23:346.

141 "parties of pleasure": Ibid., 24:495.

142 "Time passed heavily": Flexner, 2:497.

142–3 "disapprobation of such disorderly proceedings"; "Gentlemen, you will": Don Higginbotham, *The War of American Independence* (New York: Macmillan, 1971), 409–11.

143 "exceedingly unwell": *Writings of George Washington*, 22:230.

143 "I was quite at home": Baker, 306–7.

144 "before the weather and roads shou'd get bad": *Writings of George Washington*, 27:188.

145 "to postpone the visit": Flexner, 2:517.

CHAPTER EIGHT: Mount Vernon and a New Family

146 "You took the advantage of Me": Fields, 178–79.
147 "My pritty little dear Boy": Ibid., 206.
147 "little family . . . prattling about me": Ibid., 193.
148 "My dear sister": Ibid., 175.
148 "her Major": *PGWCFS*, 1:250.
149 "Poor young fellow!": Ibid., 2:147.
149 "Clerk or Secretary" and "& occasionally to devote": *DGW*, 4:158.
151 "the character of a Gentleman": *DGW*, 4:338.
151 "everything that is benevolent & good": Tobias Lear to William Prescott, March 4, 1788. Manuscript, Massachusetts Historical Society; photostat, PS-636/A-I, MVLA.
151 "It's astonishing": "An Account of a Visit Made to Washington at Mount Vernon, by an English Gentleman, in 1785, from the Diary of John Hunter," *The Pennsylvania Magazine of History and Biography* 17 (1893): 76, 78, 81.
152 "simple dignity": Durand Echeverria, ed. Jacques Pierre Brissot de Warville, *New Travels in the United States of America* (Cambridge: Harvard University Press, 1964), 343.
152 "Doubtless, that lady's independency of spirit": Katherine Anthony, *First Lady of the Revolution: Mercy Otis Warren* (New York: Doubleday, 1958), 126.
153 "introducing a Lady": Fields, 196.
153 "I was, as you may well suppose": *PGWCFS*, 6:227–28.
155 "but not perfectly recovered" and "She is a child to me": Fields, 201.
155 "Civilities & attention to me": Ibid., 198–99.
156 "I do most truly sympathize": Ibid., 201.
157 "Secure as he was in his fame": Flexner, 3:110–11.
157 "Mrs. Washington is become too Domestick": *Writings of George Washington*, 29:210.
158 "God grant I may not be disappointed": *PGWCFS*, 5:321.
158 "The only stipulations": Ibid., 5:365.
159 "We have not a single article": Fields, 205.
159 "About ten o'clock": *DGW*, 5:445.
159 "grow old in solitude": Fields, 223.

CHAPTER NINE: The President's Lady

161 "I was unable to attend to any business": *PGWPS*, 2:248.
161 "on other days": Ibid., 2:247.
162 "He tosses up such a number": Ibid., 2:248.
162 "Madam Washington": Ibid., 2:248–49.
163 "to gratify him": Ibid., 2:134.

163   "The House he is in" and all quotations on this and the following page: Fields, 215–17.

165   "Cut deeper, cut deeper.": Stephen Decatur Jr., *Private Affairs of George Washington* (Boston: Houghton Mifflin, 1933), 28.

166   "being confined to a lying posture": *PGWPS*, 4:1.

166   "but that plainness": Stewart Mitchell, ed., *New Letters of Abigail Adams, 1788–1801* (Boston: Houghton Mifflin, 1947), 13.

167   "a singular example": Ibid., 15.

167   "My station is always": Ibid., 34–35.

169   "After it, I had the honour": Decatur, 123–24.

170   "first care": Fields, 215.

172   "an indecent representation": Edgar S. Maclay, ed., *Journal of William Maclay* (New York: D. Appleton, 1890), 30–31.

172   "order their Servants": Frank Monaghan and Marvin Lowenthal, *This Was New York: The Nation's Capital in 1789* (Garden City, N.Y.: Doubleday, Duran, 1943), 123.

173   "Give sweet little Maria" and all the other quotations on this page: Fields, 217.

174   "in the windings of a forest obscured": Patricia Brady, ed., *George Washington's Beautiful Nelly: The Letters of Eleanor Parke Custis Lewis to Elizabeth Bordley Gibson, 1794–1851* (Columbia: University of South Carolina Press, 1991), 19.

174   "does not Love the water": *Adams Family*, 29–30.

174   "the shrubs were trifling": *DGW*, 5:458.

174   "a most Beautifull day": *Adams Family*, 29–30.

175   "on terms of much sociability": Ibid.

175   "It would be hard": Fields, 266.

175   "I live a very dull life": Ibid., 220.

176   "I have been so long accustomed": Ibid., 230.

176   "I am persuaded": Ibid., 223.

176   "As my grand children": Ibid., 224.

177   "disorderd state of my Head": *PGWPS*, 4:407.

177   "public characters" and all other quotations on this page: *Adams Family*, 34–35.

178   "Living in small Houses": Fields, 261.

180   "agitated with a warmth & intemperance": *PGWPS*, 5:525.

181   "Every eye full of tears": Decatur, 133.

181   "From total despair": *DGW*, 6:76–77; *PGWPS*, 5:396.

181   "During the President's sickness" and "the exercise, relaxation": Fields, 225–26.

182   "a rather weak woman": R. W. G. Vail, ed., "A Dinner at Mount Vernon: From the Unpublished Journal of Joshua Brookes (1773–1859)," *The New-York Historical Society Quarterly* (April 1947): 81–82.

183   "a very agreeable Tour": *Adams Family*, 51.

184   "very fine looking Men": *Adams Family*, 56.

184   "Mrs. Washington appeared greatly affected": Decatur, 150.

185   "Hospitality indeed seems": Robert A. Lancaster Jr., *Historic Virginia Homes and Churches* (Philadelphia: J. B. Lippincott, 1915), 362.

186   "that I am much better off": Decatur, 161.

187   "Philadelphia may be considered": Echeverria, 253.

189   "Do not touch the birds.": David R. Brigham, *Public Culture in the Early Republic: Peale's Museum and its Audience* (Washington, D.C.: Smithsonian Institution Pres, 1995), 12.

191   "as yellow as a mulato": Fields, 232.

193   "a shadow of what he was": Ibid., 241.

193   "I hope you will now look forward": Ibid., 244.

194   "was extremely affected": Flexner, 3:361, 392–93.

194   "spirit of party": Ibid.

CHAPTER TEN: The Torments of the Second Term

198   "like a philosopher": Fields, 250.

198   "Bring out your dead": Larkin, 83.

199   "Mrs. Washington was unwilling": *Writings of George Washington*, 33:104.

199   "excessive alarm" and "courage of which he has the reputation": Ron Chernow, *Alexander Hamilton* (New York: Penguin Press, 2004), 449–50.

199   "to soften the sorrows": Fields, 247.

199   "They have suffered so much": Ibid., 254.

200   The Washingtons arrived there: The house had been General Howe's headquarters during the Battle of Germantown. Now called the Deshler-Morris house, the building is owned by the Independence National Historical Park and is open to the public. Roger W. Moss, *Historic Houses of Philadelphia* (Philadelphia: University of Pennsylvania Press, 1998), 136–39.

200   "so full of Ice": Ibid.

203   "I hope when Nelly": Ibid., 282.

203   "In this city everyone complains": Ibid., 281.

203   "The old gentleman": Ibid., 259.

203   "I have been so unhappy": Ibid., 270.

204   "It has fallen heavily": Ibid., 291–92.

205   "It gives me pain": Ibid., 293–94.

207   "No one believed": *George Washington's Beautiful Nelly*, 19–22.

207   "as housekeeper, Nurse": Ibid., 23–25.

209   "the ministers of France, Great Britain, and Portugal": *Writings of George Washington*, 35:99.

209   "I shall make my last journey": Ibid.

211   "May the members": Ibid., 35:397.

211   "as she never expects": Bradford Perkins, ed., "A Diplomat's Wife in Philadelphia: Letters of Henrietta Liston, 1796–1800," *The William and Mary Quarterly* (October 1954): 608.

211   "The winter has been very sevear": Fields, 297.

212   "to <u>see, & be seen</u>": *George Washington's Beautiful Nelly*, 31.

CHAPTER ELEVEN: "Under Their Vine and Under Their Fig Tree"

214   "We once more": Fields, 304.

214   "deputy housekeeper"; "The opinion of the wise": *George Washington's Beautiful Nelly*, 32.

215   "she retains strong remains": Edward C. Carter II, ed., *The Virginia Journals of Benjamin Henry Latrobe, 1795–1798,* 2 vols. (New Haven: Yale University Press, 1977), 1:168.

215   "Mrs. Washington is one": Metchie J. E. Budka, ed., Julian Ursyn Niemcewicz, *Under Their Vine and Fig Tree* (Elizabeth, N.J.: Grassman Publishing, 1965), 103.

215   "The extensive knowledge": quoted in Miriam Anne Bourne, *First Family: George Washington and His Intimate Relations* (New York: W. W. Norton, 1982), 195.

216   "Were I drowning": *George Washington's Beautiful Nelly*, 41.

219   "Is he gone?": Tobias Lear, *Letters and Recollections of George Washington* (New York: Doubleday, 1906), 135.

CHAPTER TWELVE: The Widow Washington

222   "First in war, first in peace": Henry "Light-Horse Harry" Lee, *George Washington: A Funeral Oration on His Death (December 26, 1799)* (London: J. Bateson, 1800).

223   "the most lovely and engaging little Girl": *George Washington's Beautiful Nelly*, 65.

223   Besides the little Lewis girls: Patty Peter's eldest daughter, Eleanor, died in 1800; soon afterward, Patty gave birth to a son, another of George Washington's namesakes.

224   "views with gratitude": Fields, 344.

224   "She had the painfull task": *New Letters of Abigail Adams*, 227.

224   "The body of her beloved friend": *Papers of William Thornton*, 1:527.

225   Any final decision: Many years later, Congress finally proposed building a monument and transferring the first president's remains, but Washington's great-nephew John Augustine Washington, by then the owner of Mount Vernon, refused permission for the transfer.

226   "The zest of life has departed": George Gibbs, ed., *Memoirs of the Adminis-*

trations of Washington and John Adams, Edited from the Papers of Oliver Wolcott, Secretary of the Treasury (New York: 1846), 380–81.

226   **"Mrs. Washington received us"**: "Mrs. Liston Returns to Virginia," *Virginia Cavalcade* (Summer 1965): 46.

226   **"[we] were received very friendly"**: John Pintard's Journal (1759–1844), excerpt in R. W. G. Vail, "Two Early Visitors to Mount Vernon," *The New-York Historical Society Quarterly* (October 1958): 350, 352, 353.

227   **"We were all Federalists"**: William Parker Cutler and Julia Perkins Cutler, eds., *Life, Journals and Correspondence of Rev. Manasseh Cutler, LL.D.*, 2 vols. (Cincinnati: Robert Clarke, 1888), 2:56–58.

227   **"two or more disinterested Witnesses"**: Fields, 393.

228   **"The pleasure which we had anticipated"**: Eliza Cope Harrison, ed., *Philadelphia Merchant: The Diary of Thomas P. Cope, 1800–1851* (South Bend, Ind.: Gateway Editions, 1978), 111–13.

228   **"being neglected since her sickness"**: Ibid., 279.

229   **"Fortitude & resignation"**: Ellen McAllister, "This Melancholy Scene," *Annual Report 1981* (Mount Vernon, Va.: MVLA, 1982), 15.

229   **"for the last dress."**: Ibid.

229   **"On Saturday the 22nd of May"**: *Alexandria Advertiser and Commercial Intelligencer*, May 25, 1802.

Bibliography

A Note on the Sources

Martha Washington: An American Life is based almost entirely on published manuscripts. Despite Martha Washington's attempt to keep her private life from public view, many of her letters survived. Extant letters and documents were located and published by Joseph E. Fields in *"Worthy Partner": The Papers of Martha Washington* (Westport, Conn.: Greenwood Press, 1994). Subsequently, an additional letter from Martha to George Washington was discovered and acquired by the Mount Vernon Ladies Association, and a page in Daniel Parke Custis's "Invoice Book &ca." in the Lee family papers at the Virginia Historical Society was identified by the author as the earliest-known document written by Martha Washington.

The Papers of George Washington (Charlottesville: The University Press of Virginia, 1976–), a model edition not only of all Washington's writings but of incoming correspondence, began publication with Washington's diaries in 1976 and continues today. Under the leadership of a series of outstanding editors—Donald Jackson, Dorothy Twohig, W. W. Abbott, and Philander D. Chase—fifty-one invaluable volumes have appeared to date. The project Web site, at www.virginia.edu/gwpapers, is also an immensely useful resource.

This modern edition supersedes John Fitzpatrick's *Writings of George Washington*, 39 vols. (Washington, D.C.: U.S. Government Printing Office, 1931–1944), still useful for material not yet published in the modern edition. A searchable edition at lib.virginia.edu/washington/fitzpatrick/ was edited and made available online by Frank E. Grizzard Jr., an editor of *The Papers of George Washington*.

For researchers interested in the truth about Martha Washington, a book to beware is *Martha and Mary* by Benson J. Lossing (New York: Harper & Brothers, 1886). Like Mason Locke Weems with his cherry tree and other priggish fables about George Washington, Lossing was a glorifier who didn't find his subjects sufficiently glorious. Gilding the lily was essential for his nineteenth-century worldview. Besides information from the Custis-Lee family, portions of five letters supposedly to or from Martha Washington appear in this book. The letters share several characteristics: none is extant; none of those purported to be from Martha Washington is in her style; recipients' copies would have been unavailable to Lossing; all of them incorporate ludicrous errors of fact, style, place, and/or date. From Washington's love letter to his dream of death, none is acceptable to a professional historian. I contend that Benson Lossing fabricated (not forged, for there are no physical copies) all five letters.

On the basis of family lore, many Americans, white and black, believe they are descendants of the founding fathers and mothers. Some are; many aren't. Their claims are always worth investigating because they may be true in whole or in part, but must be subjected to the same intense scrutiny as any other historical data. The honesty of the informants isn't in question, but their information is often inaccurate.

The authors of two recent books have accepted post–Civil War family mythology about events of well over a century before, without either analyzing its probability or uncovering any supporting evidence. Based solely on that lore, both assert that Martha Washington had a mixed-race half-sister, John Dandridge's daughter, who lived with her throughout her life at Chestnut Grove, White House, and Mount Vernon—even though Martha never took a slave from Chestnut Grove. In *Martha Washington: First Lady of Liberty* (New York: John Wiley, 2001), Helen Bryan first published the tale of the shadow sister who lived with Martha Washington and accompanied her everywhere, her existence obscured by a "veil of secrecy." Henry Wiencek followed up with *An Imperfect God: George Washington, His Slaves, and the Creation of America* (New York: Farrar, Straus and Giroux, 2003). Although the family story was that Ann Dandridge was raised alongside Martha Dandridge at Chestnut Grove, Wiencek transformed that woman into a small child brought up by Martha, cutting several years from her age to make her just young enough for a convoluted tale of interracial incest.

Disregarding Martha Washington's moral and religious character, both authors seriously considered the possibility that she was a murderer; both charged her with condoning incest. Ignoring the legal and financial realities of chattel slavery, both posit shifting states of freedom and slavery occurring without legal action or documentation. Neither this supposed sister nor her several children appear on the 1786 or 1799 Mount Vernon lists of slaves made by George Washington, a meticulous record keeper. Absent any documentary evidence whatsoever—contemporary eyewitness accounts, legal documents, or Mount Vernon records—the story of the secret sister bearing a child by her own nephew must be rejected. No half-sister lived with Martha Washington. The story simply isn't true.

Manuscript Collections

Colonial Williamsburg Foundation, Williamsburg, Virginia
    York County Project. Research and data collection done with assistance from the National Endowment for the Humanities under Grants RS-0033-80-1604 and RO-20869, Department of Historical Research
    Colonial Williamsburg Foundation Library Research Report Series on individual houses, John D. Rockefeller Jr. Library
Mount Vernon Ladies Association
    Lewis, Robert. "A Journey from Fredericksburg, Virginia, to New York," May 13–20, 1789
    Research notebooks
Tudor Place Historic House and Gardens Archives
    Custis family letters
Virginia Historical Society, Richmond, Virginia
    Custis family papers
    Lee family papers

Selected Sources

Abbott, W. W. *The Young George Washington and His Papers*. Charlottesville: The University Press of Virginia, 1999.

Abbott, W. W., ed. *The Papers of George Washington: Colonial Series*. 10 vols. Charlottesville: The University Press of Virginia, 1983–1995.

———. *The Papers of George Washington: Confederation Series*. 6 vols. Charlottesville: The University Press of Virginia, 1992–1997.

Abbott, W. W., et al., eds. *The Papers of George Washington: Retirement Series*. 4 vols. Charlottesville: The University Press of Virginia, 1998–1999.

Baker, William Spohn. *Itinerary of General Washington from June 15, 1775, to December 23, 1783*. Philadelphia: J. B. Lippincott, 1892.

———. *Washington After the Revolution, 1784–1799*. Philadelphia: J. B. Lippincott, 1898.

Baumgarten, Linda. *Eighteenth-Century Clothing at Williamsburg*. Williamsburg, Va.: Colonial Williamsburg Foundation, 1995.

———. *What Clothes Reveal: The Language of Clothing in Colonial and Federal America*. New Haven: Yale University Press, 2002.

Bearss, Sara B. *The Story of Virginia*. Richmond: Virginia Historical Society, 1995.

Benedict, Barbara. *Making the Modern Reader: Cultural Mediation in Early Modern Literary Anthologies*. Princeton, N.J.: Princeton University Press, 1996.

Berkin, Carol. *First Generations: Women in Colonial America*. New York: Hill and Wang, 1996.

Berkin, Carol, and Mary Beth Norton. *Women of America: A History*. Boston: Houghton Mifflin, 1979.

Berlin, Ira. *Many Thousands Gone: The First Two Centuries of Slavery in North America*. Cambridge, Mass.: Belknap Press of Harvard University, 1998.

Billias, George A., ed.. *George Washington's Generals and Opponents*. New York: Da Capo Press, 1994.

Billings, Warren M., John E. Selby, and Thad W. Tate. *Colonial Virginia*. New York: KTO Press, 1994.

Blanton, Wyndham B. *Medicine in Virginia in the Eighteenth Century*. Richmond: Garrett & Massie, 1931.

Boatner, Mark M., III. *Encyclopedia of the American Revolution*. Mechanicsburg, Pa.: Stackpole Books, 1994.

———. *Landmarks of the American Revolution*. Harrisburg, Pa.: Stackpole Books, 1973.

Bodle, Wayne. *The Valley Forge Winter: Civilians and Soldiers in War*. University Park: Pennsylvania State University Press, 2002.

Bond, Edward L. *Damned Souls in a Tobacco Colony*. Macon, Ga.: Mercer University Press, 2000.

Bourne, Miriam Anne. *First Family: George Washington and His Intimate Relations*. New York: W. W. Norton, 1982.

Brady, Patricia. *George Washington's Beautiful Nelly: The Letters of Eleanor Parke Custis Lewis to Elizabeth Bordley Gibson, 1794–1851*. Columbia: University of South Carolina Press, 1992.

Bridenbaugh, Carl. *Cities in the Wilderness: The First Century of Urban Life in America, 1625–1742*. New York: Oxford University Press, 1971.

Brinkley, M. Kent, and Gordon W. Chappell. *The Gardens of Colonial Williamsburg*. Williamsburg, Va.: Colonial Williamsburg Foundation, 1996.

Britt, Judith S. *Nothing More Agreeable: Music in George Washington's Family*. Mount Vernon: The Association, 1984.

Brock, Henry Irving. *Colonial Churches in Virginia*. Richmond: Dale Press, 1930.

Brown, Kathleen M. *Good Wives, Nasty Wenches, and Anxious Patriarchs*. Chapel Hill: University of North Carolina Press, 1996.

Budka, Metchie J. B., ed. Julian Ursyn Niemcewicz. *Under Their Vine and Fig Tree*. Elizabeth, N.J.: Grassman Publishing, 1965.

Butterfield, Lyman, et al., eds. *Adams Family Correspondence*. 7 vols. Cambridge, Mass.: Belknap Press of Harvard University, 1963–.

Callahan, North. *Henry Knox: General Washington's General*. New York: Rinehart, 1958.

Cappon, Lester J., et al., eds. *Atlas of Early American History*. Princeton, N.J.: Princeton University Press, 1976.

Carr, Lois Green, Philip D. Morgan, and Jean B. Russo. *Colonial Chesapeake Society*. Chapel Hill: University of North Carolina Press, 1988.

Carson, Barbara G. *Ambitious Appetites: Dining, Behavior, and Patterns of Consumption in Federal Washington*. Washington, D.C.: American Institute of Architects Press, 1990.

Carson, Cary, Ronald Hoffman, and Peter J. Albert. *Of Consuming Interests: The Style of Life in the Eighteenth Century*. Charlottesville: The University Press of Virginia, 1994.

Carson, Jane. *Colonial Virginia Cookery*. Williamsburg, Va.: Colonial Williamsburg Foundation, 1985.

———. *Colonial Virginians at Play*. Williamsburg, Va.: Colonial Williamsburg Foundation, 1965.

———. *Travelers in Tidewater Virginia, 1700–1800*. Charlottesville: The University Press of Virginia, 1965.

Carter, Edward C., II, ed. *The Virginia Journals of Benjamin Henry Latrobe, 1795–1798*. 2 vols. New Haven: Yale University Press, 1977.

Cary, Wilson Miles. "The Dandridges of Virginia," *William and Mary Quarterly*. Series 1:5 (July 1896): 30–39.

Chamberlayne, C. C., ed. *The Vestry Book and Register of St. Peter's Parish, New Kent and James City Counties, Virginia, 1684–1786*. Richmond: Library of Virginia, 1997.

———. *The Vestry Book of Blisland (Blissland) Parish, New Kent and James City Counties, Virginia, 1721–1786*. Richmond: Library of Virginia, 1997.

Chase, Philander D., et al., eds. *The Papers of George Washington: Revolutionary War Series*. 13 vols. Charlottesville: The University Press of Virginia, 1985– .

Chernow, Ron. *Alexander Hamilton*. New York: The Penguin Press, 2004.

Chinard, Gilbert. *George Washington as the French Knew Him: A Collection of Texts*. Princeton, N.J.: Princeton University Press, 1940.

Clark, Ellen McAllister. *Martha Washington: A Brief Biography*. Mount Vernon: The Association, 2001.

———. "This Melancholy Scene," *Annual Report*. Mount Vernon: The Association, 1981.

Clinton, Catherine. *The Plantation Mistress*. New York: Pantheon Books, 1982.

Crane, Elaine Forman, ed. *The Diary of Elizabeth Drinker*. Boston: Northeastern University Press, 1994.

Cunliffe, Marcus. *George Washington, Man and Monument*. Mount Vernon: The Association, 1998.

Cunnington, C. Willett, and Phillis Cunnington. *Handbook of English Costume in the 18th Century*. London: Faber and Faber, 1964.

———. *The History of Underclothes*. New York: Dover, 1992.

Custis, G. W. P. *Recollections and Private Memoirs of Washington*. Washington, D.C.: William H. Moore, 1859.

Cutler, William Parker, and Julia Perkins Cutler, eds. *Life, Journals, and Correspondence of Rev. Manasseh Cutler, LL.D.* 2 vols. Cincinnati: Robert Clarke, 1888.

Dalzell, Robert F., Jr., and Lee Baldwin Dalzell. *George Washington's Mount Vernon: At Home in Revolutionary America*. New York: Oxford University Press, 1998.

Darter, Oscar H. *Colonial Fredericksburg and Neighborhood in Perspective*. New York: Twayne Publishers, 1957.

Decatur, Stephen, Jr. *Private Affairs of George Washington*. Boston: Houghton Mifflin, 1933.

Detweiler, Susan Gray. *George Washington's Chinaware*. New York: Harry N. Abrams, 1982.

Downer, Alan S., ed. *The Memoir of John Durang: American Actor, 1785–1816*. Pittsburgh: University of Pittsburgh Press, 1966.

Duffy, John. *Epidemics in Colonial America*. Baton Rouge: Louisiana State University Press, 1979.

Echeverria, Durand, ed. J. P. Brissot de Warville. *New Travels in the United States of America, 1788*. Cambridge, Mass.: Belknap Press of Harvard University, 1964.

Ecker, Grace Dunlop. *A Portrait of Old George Town*. Richmond: Dietz Press, 1951.

Eisenhart, Luther, ed. *Historic Philadelphia*. Philadelphia: American Philosophical Society, 1953.

Estes, J. Worth, and Billy G. Smith, eds. *A Melancholy Scene of Devastation*. Philadelphia: College of Physicians of Philadelphia, 1997.

Farish, Hunter Dickinson, ed. *Journal & Letters of Philip Vickers Fithian, 1773–1774: A Plantation Tutor of the Old Dominion*. Williamsburg, Va.: Colonial Williamsburg, 1957.

Felder, Paula S. *Fielding Lewis and the Washington Family*. USA: American History Company, 1998.

Fitzpatrick, John C., ed. *The Last Will and Testament of George Washington*. Mount Vernon: The Association, 1992.

———. *The Writings of George Washington*. 39 vols. Washington, D.C.: U.S. Government Printing Office, 1931–1944.

Flexner, James Thomas. *George Washington*. 4 vols. Boston: Little, Brown, 1965–1972.

Forman, H. Chandlee. *Early Manor and Plantation Houses of Maryland*. Baltimore: Bodine & Associates, 1982.

Fox, Vivian C., and Martin H. Quitt. *Loving, Parenting and Dying: The Family Cycle in England and America, Past and Present*. New York: Psychohistory Press, 1980.

Fox-Genovese, Elizabeth. *Within the Plantation Household: Black and White Women of the Old South*. Chapel Hill: University of North Carolina Press, 1988.

Freeman, Douglas Southall. *George Washington: A Biography*. 7 vols. Fairfield, N.J.: Augustus M. Kelley, 1948–1957.

Furnas, J. C. *The Americans: A Social History of the United States, 1587–1914*. 3 vols. New York: Capricorn Books, 1969.

Garrett, Elizabeth Donaghy. *At Home: The American Family 1750–1870*. New York: Harry N. Abrams, 1989.

Gately, Iain. *Tobacco: The Story of How Tobacco Seduced the World*. New York: Grove Press, 2001.

Gibbs, George, ed. *Memoirs of the Administrations of Washington and John Adams*. 2 vols. New York: Printed for the subscribers, 1846.

Glanville, Philippa, and Hilary Young. *Elegant Eating: Four Hundred Years of Dining in Style*. London: V&A Publications, 2002.

Gould, Lewis L., ed. *American First Ladies*. New York: Garland, 1996.

Greenberg, Allan. *George Washington, Architect*. London: Andreas Papadakis, 1998.

Greene, Jack P. *The American Colonies in the Eighteenth Century, 1689–1763*. New York: Meredith, 1969.

———. *Pursuits of Happiness*. Chapel Hill: University of North Carolina Press, 1988.

Griswold, Mac. *Washington's Gardens at Mount Vernon: Landscape of the Inner Man*. Boston: Houghton Mifflin, 1999.

Griswold, Rufus W. *The Republican Court*. New York: D. Appleton, 1854.

Grizzard, Frank E., Jr. *George Washington: A Biographical Companion*. Santa Barbara, Ca.: ABC-CLIO, 2002.

Hall, Virginius C., Jr. *Portraits in the Collection of the Virginia Historical Society: A Catalogue*. Charlottesville: The University Press of Virginia, 1981.

Harris, C. M., ed. *Papers of William Thornton*. Charlottesville: The University Press of Virginia, 1995.

Harris, Malcolm H. *Old New Kent County*. 2 vols. West Point, Va., 1977.

Harrison, Eliza Cope, ed. *Philadelphia Merchant: The Diary of Thomas P. Cope, 1800–1851*. South Bend, Ind.: Gateway Editions, 1978.

Harvey, Sheridan, ed. *American Women*. Hanover, N.H.: University Press of New England, 2001.

Hawke, David Freeman. *Everyday Life in Early America*. New York: Perennial Library, 1989.

Hedrick, U. P. *A History of Horticulture in America to 1860*. New York: Oxford University Press, 1950.

Hendrickson, Charles Cyril, and Kate Van Winkle Keller. *Social Dances from the American Revolution*. Sandy Hook, Conn.: Hendrickson Group, 1992.

Henriques, Peter R. *The Death of George Washington: He Died as He Lived*. Mount Vernon: The Association, 2000.

Hess, Karen. *Martha Washington's Booke of Cookery*. New York: Columbia University Press, 1981.

Hiden, Martha W. *How Justice Grew: Virginia Counties, An Abstract of Their Formation*. Charlottesville: The University Press of Virginia, 1973.

Higginbotham, Don. *George Washington Reconsidered*. Charlottesville: University Press of Virginia, 2001.

———. *George Washington: Uniting a Nation*. Lanham, Md.: Rowman & Littlefield, 2002.

————. *The War of American Independence.* Boston: Northeastern University Press, 1983.

Homberger, Eric. *The Historical Atlas of New York City.* New York: Henry Holt, 1994.

Hood, Graham. *The Governor's Palace in Williamsburg: A Cultural Study.* Williamsburg, Va.: Colonial Williamsburg Foundation, 1991.

Idzerda, Stanley J., ed. *Lafayette in the Age of the American Revolution: Selected Letters and Papers, 1776–1790*, 5 vols. Ithaca, N.Y.: Cornell University Press, 1977.

Isaac, Rhys. *The Transformation of Virginia, 1740–1790.* Chapel Hill: University of North Carolina Press, 1982.

Jackson, Donald, and Dorothy Twohig, eds. *The Diaries of George Washington.* 6 vols. Charlottesville: The University Press of Virginia, 1976–1979.

Jeremy, David John, ed. *Henry Wansey and His American Journal.* Philadelphia: American Philosophical Society, 1970.

Johnson, Odai, and William J. Burling. *The Colonial American Stage, 1665–1774: A Documentary Calendar.* Madison, N.J.: Fairleigh Dickinson University Press, 2001.

Keller, Kate Van Winkle. *George Washington: Music for the First President.* Sandy Hook, Conn.: Hendrickson Group, 1999.

Keller, Kate Van Winkle, and Charles Cyril Hendrickson. *George Washington: A Biography in Social Dance.* Sandy Hook, Conn.: Hendrickson Group, 1998.

Kierner, Cynthia. *Beyond the Household.* Ithaca, N.Y.: Cornell University Press, 1998.

Kopper, Philip. *Colonial Williamsburg.* New York: Harry N. Abrams, 2001.

Lancaster, Robert A. *Historic Virginia Homes and Churches.* Philadelphia: J. B. Lippincott, 1915.

Larkin, Jack. *The Reshaping of Everyday Life, 1790–1840.* New York: Harper Perennial, 1988.

Lear, Tobias. *Letters and Recollections of George Washington.* New York: Doubleday, Page, 1906.

Leavitt, Judith Walzer. *Brought to Bed: Child-Bearing in America, 1750–1950.* New York: Oxford University Press, 1986.

Lebsock, Suzanne. *Virginia Women, 1600–1945.* Richmond: Virginia State Library, 1987.

Lewis, Charlene M. Boyer. *Ladies and Gentlemen on Display: Planter Society at the Virginia Springs, 1790–1860.* Charlottesville: The University Press of Virginia, 2001.

Lewis, Jan. *The Pursuit of Happiness: Family and Values in Thomas Jefferson's Virginia.* Cambridge, Mass.: Cambridge University Press, 1983.

Lynch, James B., Jr. *The Custis Chronicles: The Virginia Generations.* Camden, Maine: Picton Press, 1997.

Maccubbin, Robert P., ed. *Williamsburg, Virginia: A City Before the State, 1699–1999*. Williamsburg: The City, 2000.

Maclay, Edgar, ed. *Journals of William Maclay*. New York: D. Appleton, 1890.

Mayer, Holly A. *Belonging to the Army: Camp Followers and Community During the American Revolution*. Columbia: University of South Carolina Press, 1999.

Mays, David J., ed. *The Letters and Papers of Edmund Pendleton, 1734–1803*. 2 vols. Charlottesville: The University Press of Virginia, 1967.

McMillen, Sally G. *Motherhood in the Old South: Pregnancy, Childbirth, and Infant Rearing*. Baton Rouge: Louisiana State University Press, 1990.

McNeill, William H. *Keeping Together in Time: Dance and Drill in Human History*. Cambridge, Mass.: Harvard University Press, 1995.

Miles, Ellen G. *George and Martha Washington: Portraits from the Presidential Years*. Charlottesville: The University Press of Virginia, 1999.

Miller, Helen Hill. *Colonel Parke of Virginia: The Greatest Hector in the Town*. Chapel Hill, N.C.: Algonquin, 1989.

Mitchell, Beth. *Fairfax County, Virginia, in 1760. An Interpretive Historical Map*. Fairfax County, Va.: Office of Comprehensive Planning, 1987.

Mitchell, Stewart., ed. *New Letters of Abigail Adams, 1788–1801*. Boston: Houghton Mifflin, 1947.

Monaghan, Frank, and Marvin Lowenthal. *This Was New York*. Garden City, N.Y.: Doubleday, Doran, 1943.

Montgomery, Florence M. *Printed Textiles*. New York: Viking Press, 1970.

———. *Textiles in America, 1650–1870*. New York: W. W. Norton, 1984.

Moore, Charles. *The Family Life of George Washington*. Boston: Houghton Mifflin, 1926.

Morgan, Edmund S. *American Slavery, American Freedom: The Ordeal of Colonial Virginia*. New York: W. W. Norton, 1975.

———. *The Genius of George Washington*. New York: W. W. Norton, 1980.

———. *Virginians at Home: Family Life in the Eighteenth Century*. Williamsburg, Va.: Colonial Williamsburg Foundation, 1952.

Morgan, Philip D. *Slave Counterpoint*. Chapel Hill: University of North Carolina Press, 1998.

Moss, Roger W. *Historic Houses of Philadelphia*. Philadelphia: University of Pennsylvania Press, 1998.

Mott, Frank Luther. *American Journalism*. New York: Macmillan, 1950.

Munson, James D. *Col. John Carlyle, Gent., 1720–1780*. Alexandria: Northern Virginia Regional Park Authority, 1986.

Nelson, John K. *A Blessed Company*. Chapel Hill: University of North Carolina Press, 2001.

Netherton, Ross, and Nan Netherton. *Fairfax County in Virginia: A Pictorial History*. Norfolk, Va.: Donning, 1986.

Norton, Mary Beth. *Founding Mothers and Fathers*. New York: Vintage Books, 1997.

Nye, Russell Blaine. *The Cultural Life of the New Nation, 1776–1830*. New York: Harper & Row, 1963.

Parsons, Jacob Cox, ed. *Extracts from the Diary of Jacob Hiltzheimer*. Philadelphia: William F. Fell, 1893.

Peiss, Kathy. *Hope in a Jar: The Making of America's Beauty Culture*. New York: Henry Holt, 1998.

Perkins, Bradford, ed. "A Diplomat's Wife in Philadelphia: Letters of Henrietta Liston, 1796–1800," *William and Mary Quarterly*. 3rd. ser. (Oct. 1954): 592–632.

Rankin, Hugh F. *The Theater in Colonial America*. Chapel Hill: University of North Carolina Press, 1965.

Rasmussen, William M. S., and Robert S. Tilton. *George Washington: The Man Behind the Myths*. Charlottesville: The University Press of Virginia, 1999.

Rath, Richard Cullen. *How Early America Sounded*. Ithaca, N.Y.: Cornell University Press, 2003.

Reed, John F. *Valley Forge: Crucible of Victory*. Monmouth Beach, N.J.: Philip Freneau Press, 1969.

Rees, James C. *Treasures from Mount Vernon: George Washington Revealed*. Mount Vernon: The Association, 1999.

Reps, John W. *Tidewater Towns: City Planning in Colonial Virginia and Maryland*. Williamsburg, Va.: Colonial Williamsburg Foundation, 1972.

Rice, Howard C., Jr. *Travels in North America in the Years 1780, 1781 and 1782 by Marquis de Chastellux*. 2 vols. Chapel Hill: University of North Carolina Press, 1963

Roberts, Cokie. *Founding Mothers: The Women Who Raised Our Nation*. New York: William Morrow, 2004.

Ryan, Dennis P., ed. *A Salute to Courage: The American Revolution as Seen Through Wartime Writings of Officers of the Continental Army and Navy*. New York: Columbia University Press, 1979.

Sarudy, Barbara Wells. *Gardens and Gardening in the Chesapeake, 1700–1805*. Baltimore: Johns Hopkins University Press, 1998.

Savitt, Todd L. *Medicine and Slavery*. Chicago: University of Illinois Press, 1978.

Scharf, J. Thomas. *Chronicles of Baltimore*. Baltimore: Turnbull Brothers, 1874.

Scharf, J. Thomas, and Thompson Westcott. *History of Philadelphia: 1609–1884*. 3 vols. Philadelphia: L. H. Everts, 1884.

Schmit, Patricia Brady, ed. *Nelly Custis Lewis's Housekeeping Book*. New Orleans: Historic New Orleans Collection, 1982.

Schwarz, Philip J., ed. *Slavery at the Home of George Washington*. Mount Vernon: The Association, 2001.

Scott, Anne Firor. *The Southern Lady: From Pedestal to Politics, 1830–1930*. Charlottesville: The University Press of Virginia, 1995.

Scott, Anne Firor, and Suzanne Lebsock. *Virginia Women: The First Two Hundred Years*. Williamsburg, Va.: Colonial Williamsburg Foundation, 1999.

Sharpe, Cecil J., and A. P. Oppe. *The Dance: An Historical Survey of Dancing in Europe*. London: Halton & Truscott Smith, 1924.

Showman, Richard K., et al., eds. *The Papers of General Nathanael Greene*. 12 vols. Chapel Hill: University of North Carolina Press, 1980.

Silverman, Kenneth. *A Cultural History of the American Revolution*. New York: Columbia University Press, 1987.

Smith, Thomas E. V. *The City of New York*. Riverside, Conn.: Chatham Press, 1972.

Smith, William Francis, and T. Michael Miller. *A Seaport Saga: Portrait of Old Alexandria, Virginia*. Norfolk: Donning, 1989.

Sontag, Susan. *Illness as Metaphor*. New York: Vintage Books, 1979.

Sorley, Merrow Egerton. *Lewis of Warner Hall: The History of a Family*. Baltimore: Genealogical Publishing, 2000.

Spruill, Julia Cherry. *Women's Life and Work in the Southern Colonies*. Chapel Hill: University of North Carolina Press, 1938.

Steele, Valerie. *The Corset: A Cultural History*. New Haven: Yale University Press, 2001.

Stegeman, John F., and Janet Stegeman. *Caty: A Biography of Catherine Littlefield Greene*. Providence: Rhode Island Bicentennial Foundation, 1977.

Steiner, Bernard C. *The Life and Correspondence of James McHenry*. Cleveland: Burrows Brothers, 1907.

Stephenson, Richard W., and Marianne M. McKee, eds. *Virginia in Maps*. Richmond: Library of Virginia, 2000.

Sydnor, Charles S. *American Revolutionaries in the Making*. New York: The Free Press, 1965.

Tannahill, Reay. *Food in History*. New York: Three Rivers Press, 1988.

Tate, Thad W., and David L. Ammerman. *The Chesapeake in the Seventeenth Century*. New York: W. W. Norton, 1979.

———. *The Negro in Eighteenth-Century Williamsburg*. Charlottesville: The University Press of Virginia, 1972.

Thatcher, James. *Military Journal of the American Revolution*. Hartford: Hurlbut, Williams, 1862

Thompson, Mary V. " 'As If I Had Been a Very Great Somebody,' Martha Washington in the American Revolution: Becoming the Nation's First Lady." Mount Vernon Ladies Association, 2002.

———. "Different People, Different Stories: The Life Stories of Individual Slaves from Mount Vernon and Their Relationship with George and Martha Washington." Symposium: "George Washington and Slavery." Mount Vernon, 2002.

———. "Foods and Beverages Used at Mount Vernon," Mount Vernon Ladies Association, 2002.

————. " 'In the Hands of a Good Providence': The Practice of Religion at George Washington's Mount Vernon." Mount Vernon Ladies Association, 2003.

————. " 'The Lowest Ebb of Misery': Death and Mourning in the Family of George Washington." *Historic Alexandria Quarterly* (spring 2001).

————. " 'The Only Unavoidable Subject of Regret': George Washington and Slavery." Symposium: "George Washington and Alexandria, Virginia: Ties That Bind." Alexandria, Va., 1999

————. " 'Served Up in Excellent Order': Dining with the Washingtons at Mount Vernon." Mount Vernon Ladies Association, 2002.

————. " 'Testimonials' About and Descriptions of Martha Washington." Memorandum, 2001–2002. Mount Vernon Ladies Association. This memorandum was the source for finding many of the quotations cited in this book.

Tinling, Marion, ed. *The Correspondence of the Three William Byrds of Westover, Virginia, 1684–1776.* 2 vols. Charlottesville: The University Press of Virginia, 1977.

Torbert, Alice C. *Eleanor Calvert and Her Circle.* New York: William Frederick Press, 1950.

Turman, Nora Miller. *The Eastern Shore of Virginia 1603–1964.* Bowie, Md.: Heritage Books, 1988.

Turner, Jane, ed. *Encyclopedia of American Art Before 1914.* New York: Grove, 2000.

Twohig, Dorothy, et al., eds. *The Papers of George Washington: Presidential Series.* 11 vols. Charlottesville: The University Press of Virginia, 1987– .

Upton, Dell. *Holy Things and Profane: Anglican Parish Churches in Virginia.* New Haven: Yale University Press, 1997.

Vail, R. W. G. "Two Early Visitors to Mount Vernon." *New-York Historical Society Quarterly* (Oct. 1958): 349–65.

Voges, Nettie Allen. *Old Alexandria: Where America's Past is Present.* McLean, Va.: EPM Publications, 1975.

Wayland, John W. *The Washingtons and Their Homes.* Staunton, Va.: McClure, 1944.

Weigley, Russell F., ed. *Philadelphia: A 300-Year History.* New York: W. W. Norton, 1982.

Wharton, Anne Hollingsworth. *Social Life in the Early Republic.* Philadelphia: J. B. Lippincott, 1900.

Wright, Louis B. *The Cultural Life of the American Colonies, 1607–1763.* New York: Harper & Row, 1962.

————. *Life in Colonial America.* New York: Capricorn Books, 1971.

Zagarri, Rosemarie, ed. *David Humphreys' "Life of General Washington."* Athens: University of Georgia Press, 1991.

Index